Living with H.A.R.T

(*Heart-Alpha-Resonance-Technique*)

When The Heart Leads, Reality Responds

NICK TERRONE

BSc Psych (Grad Dip Applied Psych)

Living With H.A.R.T – (Heart Alpha Resonance Technique)
'When The Heart Leads, Reality Responds'

First published in Australia by Nick Terrone 2026
www.quitwithnick.com.au

A catalogue record for this book is available from the National Library of Australia

ISBN: 978-0-646-73871-0 (pbk)

Typesetting and design by Publicious Book Publishing
Published in collaboration with Publicious Book Publishing
www.publicious.com.au

Dedication

To my parents, Leonardo and Assunta, who gave their all so that I could have opportunities they never had. For that, I love you both.

'Guarda, mamma, con il tuo aiuto, Niccolino ha fatto qualcosa di buono.'

And to my beautiful star child, Orion. May this book remind you to always follow your heart and help you remember who you truly are. It is a testament to my eternal love for you, which transcends space and time.

Nick

Medical Disclaimer

The information contained in this book is intended for educational and informational purposes only. It is not intended as a substitute for professional medical advice, diagnosis, or treatment. The author is not a medical doctor, and the content of this book should not be used to diagnose, treat, cure, or prevent any medical or psychological condition.

Always seek the advice of a qualified healthcare professional regarding any medical or mental health concerns you may have. Never disregard professional medical advice or delay seeking it because of something you have read in this book.

Any techniques, practices, or suggestions described in this book are undertaken at the reader's own discretion and risk. The author and publisher assume no responsibility for any adverse effects or consequences resulting from the use of the information contained in this book.

About the Author

Nick Terrone is a hypnotherapist, psychotherapist, author, keynote speaker, and facilitator whose work explores the profound connection between the mind, body and heart. With a Postgraduate Degree in Applied Psychology, and over 18 years of experience as a professional hypnotherapist, Nick has helped thousands of people overcome limiting habits, transform patterns of thinking and reconnect with a deeper sense of clarity, confidence and personal empowerment.

Nick is the creator of the Heart Alpha Resonance Technique (H.A.R.T), a practical framework that integrates heart intelligence, the alpha brainwave state and the principle of resonance to support meaningful inner transformation. Drawing on insights from psychology, meditation, hypnosis, metaphysics, and emerging research into consciousness, his work bridges modern science with experiential practices designed to help individuals access greater self-awareness and emotional coherence.

Based in Sydney, Australia, Nick is also currently completing his certification as a Psychedelic Assisted Therapist, reflecting his ongoing interest in responsible, evidence-based approaches to expanded states of consciousness and psychological healing.

In addition to his private practice, Nick hosts immersive retreats inspired by the teachings and practices presented in *Living with H.A.R.T.* These retreats offer participants the opportunity to experience the H.A.R.T process firsthand while exploring the deeper principles of heart-led awareness and personal transformation.

Nick is a sought-after keynote speaker and presenter, sharing insights on topics including the mind–body connection, hypnosis, metaphysics, human potential, and the evolving role of psychedelics in therapeutic and personal development contexts. He is also available for media appearances, podcast interviews and speaking engagements.

To contact Nick, please visit:
www.quitwithnick.com.au

Contents

Introduction

I'd like to share with you a little about my journey and some of the most meaningful turning points I've had in my life. Perhaps you might relate to some of them. The one thing that books obviously lack is two-way dialogue. I really wish I could share this with you personally, one-on-one. I'm willing to bet that I could learn a lot from you and your story as well, but I guess that's for another time.

I was born and raised in Australia to Catholic Italian migrant parents. I was the youngest of four children— an unexpected 'gift' you could say. I've always told my parents that I was the best mistake they ever made and it took them three attempts to get it right. My mother, Assunta, was a full-time housewife and mum, while my father, Leonardo, with his tremendous work ethic—passed down from his father of course—worked a hard, laborious job on weekdays, and sold ice cream from a mobile van on weekends. Yep, that's right, for my entire childhood I had Italian ice cream on tap. But before you get too envious, trust me, I probably had just as much ice cream as any other kid at school. Isn't that just typical? When you can have as much as you want, any time you want it, you invariably desire it less and less.

I wasn't really academically gifted, and I knew it. So, I figured I may as well focus on what I was good at, which was disrupting the class, annoying teachers and making the other kids laugh by being the class clown. I had a kind of gift for that, but of course, it had its pros and cons. High school was much the same. I went to an all-boys Christian Brothers school. To make sure I wasn't picked on, I started lifting weights in my early teenage years. This soon became a bit of a hobby of mine—maybe even a mild obsession. I became a teenage natural bodybuilding champion at the age of 18. I dabbled in a few other sports like soccer and cricket, and much to my father's disappointment, although I did show some promise as a soccer player, like my brothers before me, I eventually lost interest as I started to discover other things that young adults eventually get curious about. It was during my late teens that I became fascinated with expanding my consciousness via plants. Actually, to be honest, at the time my intention wasn't to 'expand my consciousness'; it was just to have fun. Even though my use of consciousness-expanding plants was quite minimal, perhaps once every few months, what it did do was spark my curiosity about the human psyche and consciousness in general. I wanted to learn more about who we really are, the nature of reality, and why we're here. I wasn't just asking these profound questions about life in general, I was asking them about myself too. Who am I? Why am I here? And what is the nature of reality? You could say that from this moment onwards these three questions shaped my hierarchy of values, which in turn have shaped my perceptions, thoughts, decisions, and actions along with my life's mission and purpose. One of my teachers once said, 'The quality of your life is based on the quality of the questions you ask.' And these were quality questions—for me anyway.

It was at the age of 17 that I met a man who became a friend and mentor of mine. He unfortunately passed away in 2019, may God rest his soul. He was a very successful and self-made man, who was an internationally published author of eight books at the time. He travelled much of the world speaking at workshops on topics like selling skills, understanding people, presentation, and customer service skills. This fuelled my interest in understanding people—how and why we do what we do. This led me to begin an undergraduate degree in psychology, which I enjoyed so much I went on to complete my 4th year—a Postgraduate Diploma in Applied Psychology. This was very unexpected for me considering the fact that I was the least academically gifted out of my two brothers and one sister, and yet I went the furthest in my studies. A lot happened for me during my last year at university. I was working as a volunteer drug and alcohol counsellor at an adult and adolescent in-house residential rehabilitation clinic. Even more transformational than that was a drug-induced psychosis that I experienced that year. Unfortunately for me at the time, I refused to 'see the signs' that my occasional 'plant use' was trying to show me. This was undoubtedly one of the most challenging times of my life. I'm actually very lucky to be here today to write about it. Thankfully, with the right help, this only seriously affected me for 6-8 months—a fairly short time considering how many people experience this their entire lives. It gave me a level of understanding and empathy for those with mental illness, which I would have never got from any textbook, classroom, lecture hall, or even clinical experience. And for that reason, I can honestly look back on that time and call it one of the biggest blessings of my life.

It was only recently that I read an article about the shamanic perspective of mental illness, which describes it as 'the birthing of a healer'. This deeply resonated with me considering the life path that I am now on, a path that I can honestly say became a little clearer for me during the months, even years, of integration following my brief but challenging psychosis.

Looking back, I can see that this experience was like the intense collision of two trains. One was my interest in the psychology and science of human behaviour, exemplified by my psychology degree, and the other was my deep interest in esoteric philosophies, ancient wisdom, spirituality, and metaphysics. What emerged from the rubble of this collision is a keen interest in the point where objective verifiable science meets the subjective spiritual world of mysticism. I believe that one is not complete without the other and in many cases, as you may have heard before, spirituality is simply science we do not understand yet. I don't believe that these two things are in opposition to one another, but that they are simply two sides of the same coin. To me, the very fact that both of these phenomena exist at all, is enough proof that in some way they must be connected. When all is said and done, I truly believe that these two perspectives are simply a different language game to describe the same thing.

After completing university, my adventurous spirit and love for cultural diversity took me on a three-year trip around the world. I lived and worked in Canada for one year, and then London (England) for two years. During these three years, I travelled to thirty-two countries within Europe, Africa, North and South America, the Middle East, and Asia. It was during this time that I truly got a deeper appreciation for the fact that we really are the same the world over. It opened my eyes and my heart to the diversity of values within different cultures, which helped me more clearly define my own. During my time abroad, I was developing my spiritual practice more and more through meditation, which at this point was not a daily occurrence, but just an occasional thing. In order to support myself and save up enough money to travel, I had started working in call centres as a telesales agent, which I seemed to have some talent for. Without thinking about it too much, when I got back to Australia, I chose the easy logical option at the time, which was to pursue a sales career while my personal and spiritual development continued to be a weekend interest and hobby.

This went on for a couple of years until I had a fairly early 'midlife crisis' in my twenties. I was working for a large international recruitment company at the time. I got fed up with the lack of job satisfaction and the trajectory not only of my career, but my life! I knew I was put on this earth to do something more than what I was doing at the time. So, I decided to go back to my academic roots and soon found a job as an intern psychologist. I took a significant pay cut, but at least I knew I was doing something that was more in alignment with my true self, and this was something I knew money just couldn't buy. I had started a two-year psychology internship to become a registered psychologist in Australia. It was around this time I took my first trip to India. This trip had a profound impact on me. It felt like I had 'been there before'. It was like a 'coming home' for me. The chaos, traffic, culture, and nature reserves somehow had a very familiar feeling to it. A past life perhaps? Who knows? One thing is for sure though—looking back, this trip was the catalyst for a profound shift within me. So much so that when I got back, I became a volunteer at a Sydney inner city homeless shelter for a charitable organisation. I later became the house manager and continued doing this for a period of four years voluntarily.

Eighteen months into my two-year psychology internship, I came across the power of Hypnosis, Hypnotherapy and Neuro-Linguistic Programming (NLP), which I took to like a fish to water. Perhaps it was my existing interest in altered states of consciousness or human behaviour combined with my spiritual curiosity. Whatever it was, I found it so compelling that, much to the horror of my parents and against the advice of many of my friends at the time, I quit my psychology internship, which I was only six months from completing, to pursue a full time career as a clinical hypnotherapist. I also started my own business at this time and haven't looked back. This wasn't an easy decision for me to make and I struggled internally to find a balance between the calling of my heart and the expectations of people around me. Looking back, I can now say, 'Thank God' I had the courage to follow the calling of my heart, despite all the head-based logical reasons not to. Although it was only another six months to complete my internship, it became such a challenge to continue down that path. I just knew I was trying to finish it for all the wrong reasons.

From that moment, I began to assist people with all kinds of personal barriers and issues such as smoking, anxiety, and weight loss, as well as helping people connect with their higher mission and purpose through self-empowerment, self-actualisation, and confident self-leadership. The key for me is, and always has been, to help others help themselves, to teach someone how to fish rather than hand them a fish. I believe the mark of a great therapist is not how long a client has been with you, but how soon you can make yourself redundant in your client's life. Perhaps this is why I lost interest in becoming a psychologist. Of course, this work has its place and I have the utmost respect for psychologists; however, for me, it wasn't the kind of work I wanted to do. I knew that I wanted to learn as much as I could about human potential, not to gather a flock of sheep-like followers, but to teach people how to become shepherds, leading and guiding themselves. This continues to be my therapeutic and teaching philosophy to this very day, and it is the driving force behind this very book. Since my ultimate interest is in the factors that determine and influence the perceptions of a human being from both a scientific and metaphysical perspective, I now call myself a 'Perceptual Architect'. My interest in human behaviour and understanding the laws of the universe has fuelled a life path that has brought me into close contact with some of the world's most influential thought leaders in human potential.

As I continued to work in my practice, it quickly began to grow as word spread of my great results with clients. Despite this success, however, there was something stirring inside me. I was beginning to notice more and more in my clients that beneath the surface issue which brought them to me—be it smoking, excess weight, anxiety, stress, alcohol, gambling, overwhelm, or a lack of confidence and self-esteem, it was becoming clearer to me that in almost every case, the real issue was a sense of disconnection for the client, a lack of self-love or self-worth. From my observation, these challenges often created a negative ripple effect into all other forms of relationship for the client. This may include the relationship with their partner, their children, or with their boss or co-workers. Furthermore, after seeing hundreds of clients, which eventually became thousands, it was obvious to me that in almost every case my clients were struggling with the most important relationship of all—the relationship they had with themselves. I truly believe that unless we heal and nurture that relationship first, every other relationship will simply fall short of what it could be.

As my observations began to grow, along with my deepening meditation practice, I started to explore the concepts of self-love, relationships and what it means to be connected. This curiosity, along with amazing synchronicities, led me down a number of enlightening rabbit holes. But three areas of investigation were beginning to take centre stage, namely: the energetic heart, the trance state, (being an altered state of consciousness), and the science of how all things in reality are connected. For many years now, my interest has been to understand and combine these three concepts and merge them to create a new type of process that anyone can easily do for themselves. The result is the Heart Alpha Resonance Technique (H.A.R.T), which correlates perfectly to the three above-mentioned rabbit holes, being: 'Heart' and the science of the energetic, intelligent and intuitive heart; 'Alpha', being the alpha brain wave state, which is an altered wakeful state of consciousness, or trance; and 'Resonance', a fundamental concept of energy, frequency and vibration, which are aspects of reality that our modern-day science is using to explore and explain the interconnectivity of all things in the universe.

But here is where things started to get really interesting. As I was learning about the human heart, it was blowing my mind more and more. These were scientifically validated facts about the human heart that I had never heard before, all of which pointed to a truly intelligent organ. These concepts will be further explored in the chapters to come, but for now, suffice it to say that I was beginning to see that the heart, in many ways, was like a small brain. In fact, in 1991, Dr J. Andrew Armour coined the term 'heart brain' because of how complex the heart's nervous system was found to be. Being a hypnotherapist, this got me thinking: What if the human heart had a subconscious mind?, namely the subconscious heart-mind. This is what I began to refer to it as. Why is this not possible? We often attribute our minds to be closely linked to, or even located inside the brain, right? And during any kind of hypnotherapy or self-hypnosis session, the awareness of the individual is almost entirely focused behind the eyelids and between the ears—in the head basically. However,, since the heart qualifies as a little brain, then it's just as plausible that it could also be connected to a mind, perhaps to your higher mind. This idea really excited me and will be explored further in this book. It's a small shift which could make a world of difference.

My yearning to understand more about the heart and the connected universe led me to two organisations—The HeartMath Institute and The Resonance Science Foundation, the former being focused on the science of the energetic heart, and the latter with the interconnectivity of all things in our reality. This book is the culmination of my journey to date, which is forever evolving and morphing into bigger and grander things.

I'm going to assume that, like me, you're also a curious 'seeker', and I'm referring to you in this way because that's exactly what I believe you are if this book has found its way into your hands. As you start to read the contents, you'll realise that it isn't your usual 'self-help book'. I know this because I have read quite a few of them. I wanted to put something different out there into the world, and from reading the contents page, you may have noticed that Part 1 begins with two very broad but deep fundamentals that we will unpack in the first two chapters. The first considers our current worldview—a philosophical investigation, and the second chapter considers the science that has emerged and dominates mainstream thinking today and the paradigm it has created. If you are willing to approach this book as a journey with an open mind and an open heart, you will eventually see how Part 1 and Part 2 lead perfectly to Part 3, which ultimately is the application of the concepts and the science of the first two chapters.

This book will present certain scientific research and connect it to certain topics and concepts usually labelled as 'spiritual', 'mystical' or 'esoteric'. This is for the purpose of encouraging you to simply consider it and its implications and hopefully inspire you to do more of your own research. I believe that if you want to be different, what's needed is a different way of thinking. My hope is that this book simply offers people a different perspective about themselves, the world around them and their place in it, leading to a different experience in the world.

Let me say that I do not believe for one minute that the world needs another book to 'save it', not at all. However, from the people I have met on my travels around the world, it is pretty clear to most that something in the world and how we live in it, is just a bit 'off'. We seem to have missed something, don't you think? We seem to have been living under this assumption that if we can just keep improving technology, education, law enforcement, medicine, or have the right government in power, THAT'S when we'll be living in peaceful bliss. But if that's so, why is the world in the state that it's in despite all of these things having 'improved' dramatically over the last fifty years? Are we really any happier than we were fifty years ago? Social studies research suggests that we are not. Why are cases of depression, anxiety and suicide on the rise in developed nations and even in developing countries? If you watch the news and look at the state of our planet right now, it's fairly clear that we need to seriously rethink our personal, societal and collective values—what we hold to be important as citizens of the world—and perhaps this will lead to a new wave of change. It is the year 2026, and since 2020, we have faced many global challenges—a pandemic and wars. Whether we want to admit it or not, it has touched all of us in one way or another. At the very least, it created uncertainty, confusion, stress, fear, anxiety, division, and disconnectedness. If any of this is resonating with you, please keep reading.

Rather than trying to patch up a paradigm that is fuelling what we call the 'advancement of the human race', maybe we need to rethink the race altogether. Maybe we're running the wrong race, or perhaps a little tweak in the direction could be useful. If you're racing towards the edge of a cliff, why would you want to get there faster, with more comfort, looking fabulous, and before your competitor gets there? Sometimes the way to move forward might be to stop and make a diversion based on new scientific understandings.

My hope and intention is that at least some of the philosophy, science and practical techniques in this book resonate with you. I believe the inspiration and drive to share comes naturally to a person once they have been on a journey of personal transformation and found it to be extremely useful for them. What I have noticed when studying some of the greatest teachers and leaders of our time is that at some point, usually after a period of great personal challenge, intense self-examination and self-healing, they came to realise their mission in life, their purpose. Because of how intensely meaningful and fulfilling this can be, very often this leads those individuals to help and inspire others to find their life purpose, which I believe is one of the greatest services and gifts you can offer another human being. Whether it's accepted or not ... well, that's another story.

'I slept and dreamt that life was joy. I awoke and saw that life was service. I acted and behold, service was joy.'

- Rabindranath Tagore

I have come to notice a common theme among the greatest teachers and healers of our time, and that is the idea that we all hold the power to transform and transcend our limitations within ourselves. The message I have come across time and time again is, 'Go within.' This seems like a very logical thing to do. Why? Because absolutely everything you say you want in your life, no matter what it is, you want for one reason and one reason only—to feel good. Perhaps the world is experiencing the results of an overall imbalance between our efforts to create a pleasing outer environment as opposed to a pleasing inner environment, assuming that the former will automatically lead to the latter. Perhaps focusing on the external world is one of the aspects of a more brain or head-based type of living, while the focus on your inner world of feelings and emotions is more of a heart-based approach. Of course, both are important because both have their positives and negatives, but perhaps we are living in an unbalanced paradigm. It is for this reason I am a huge advocate for a regular meditation practice, and it doesn't matter what type. There are so many different forms of meditation and the one that is best for you is the one that you believe you are getting the most benefit from.

There are two distinctions I think are helpful to make at this point. I sometimes meet people who connect meditation to religion, and for that reason, they actively avoid it. To me, this is like assuming that all people who practice yoga are Hindus, which of course isn't true. Anything is only useful or not when based on the context within which you are intending to use it. Yoga is a tool or vehicle to experience a positive outcome that you choose to create. This can be on the level of mind, body or spirit. Meditation is much the same. It is simply a vehicle—a tool—and you get to decide where you wish to go or what you wish to create. Meditation does not have to deepen a religious practice, even though it absolutely can, any more than your car has to take you to one—and only one—destination. Hammers are not designed to help you build only one type of thing. They can be used to build houses, fences, tables, chairs, etc. Your car can take you many places depending on where you want to go. Cars are not made to transport you only to shopping malls or schools or the beach. This may sound simple, and I am not trying to insult your intelligence here; I am simply making the point that how we define something is crucial to our experience of it. Following on from this point, meditation, and in particular the H.A.R.T process, can be used to accomplish and achieve many things. Perhaps you want to improve your career, make more money, be an effective communicator, attract a relationship, heal a past trauma, or increase your health and vitality—the list is limited only by your own imagination.

The second helpful distinction to make here is the difference between meditation and relaxation. Some people I have met say they don't need to meditate because they cook or garden, or some might say 'playing video games is my meditation' or 'walking is my meditation'. Now, of course, anything that helps you escape from the daily grind is most definitely helpful for your mind and body. However, all of these things have a very different effect on your neurology. Some of the things I just mentioned enhance your neurological wellbeing, but others not so much. Aside from that, some activities help to enhance personal transformation more than others. One question that highlights a huge difference is: How effective is that thing in helping you create and manifest what you want to experience in your life?' The fact is that some practices are more effective, efficient and directly linked to achieving goals than others. This is like convincing yourself that you don't need to exercise because you walk a lot at your job. I find that sometimes the people who have tried meditation have found it to be 'too difficult' and are simply justifying to themselves why it's not for them, while deep down wishing they perhaps did, or could, meditate. This may or may not apply to you, but all I ask is that you be 100% honest with yourself. The chances are, if this book has found its way into your hands, you're at least open to the idea of meditation. If you've never meditated, that's totally fine, because if you practice the H.A.R.T process, follow along with the step-by-step guide, and use the scripts in this book, you will be doing H.A.R.T, meditation and self-hypnosis all at the same time. Oh, and by the way, don't worry about that overactive mind of yours that can't switch off—we'll get to that. For now, it's important to understand that the point of any meditation isn't to stop thoughts, because that's impossible, but to be the *observer* of them. It's actually quite simple to take a different perspective on your overactive mind and watch it, but it is almost impossible to make the mind blank.

'Did he just mention the word "hypnosis"?'. Yep, I sure did. I've been a hypnotherapist since 2007, seen thousands of clients, have taught self-hypnosis, am a hypnosis coach and trainer, and regularly integrate it into my meditative practice. So, how could I not include self-hypnosis? This book is not only going to teach you a mindfulness, meditative technique, but you're going to learn how to bring yourself into the state of trance known as 'hypnosis' at the same time. Let me say right away: there is nothing to fear, and everything will be explained. Healing through hypnotic states has been around for literally thousands of years. It's nothing new. It's just been misunderstood by most people and as a result, it's gained a bit of an inaccurate reputation among average people. I will dispel the myths and misconceptions about hypnosis, separate the therapy from the stage shows, as well as explain how and why you experience the hypnotic state daily already. Yes, it's true; with very few exceptions, almost anyone can be hypnotised, and I'll explain how and why.

But for now, let me share with you a very simple example of how the H.A.R.T process can be so beneficial in your life. When I was living in India, I was doing my morning practice and I chose my intention for that particular process. The important part of this story is the fact that I specifically set my intention with the exact words, 'How can I accelerate my spiritual evolution?' As I was sitting there doing H.A.R.T, and I was in the state of self-hypnotic trance, an image of Charles Darwin came into my awareness. For me, he is a symbol of the concept of 'evolution'. Then something very interesting happened. When I 'asked my heart' to show me the meaning of that image, it showed me the word 'Darwin', which then rearranged itself to spell the word 'inward', and I had a moment that actually brought tears to my eyes. Now you may not see this as a particularly big or meaningful thing, but for me, it was so significant simply because of what it did for me in that moment. It was a very powerful symbol, a validation and confirmation that came directly from my heart to continue to nurture and focus on my inner world. But what it confirmed for me the most was that my heart had the answers and I should just keep listening to it. To me, this was my subconscious heart-mind 'speaking to me', reassuring me that I am on the right path. It was my heart's intelligence responding to my intention for that particular H.A.R.T session. I wanted some guidance on how to accelerate my spiritual evolution, so my unconscious heart-mind delivered to me an image that it knew I would resonate with. It gave me a wonderful sense of fulfilment and confidence in that moment, something that I wish for everyone.

This is the beauty of taking regular journeys into your subconscious heart-mind, which you can easily communicate with when you slip into the relaxed alpha brainwave state synonymous with hypnosis. Your heart will always deliver the perfect message for you in the moment, whether or not you 'get it consciously or not'. Would this image of Darwin and 'inward' have been perfect for you? Who knows, but it was for me because it came from my heart, and I have developed a deep trust of my heart's messages.

By learning H.A.R.T, I have no doubt in my mind and heart that you can also experience the joy and empowerment of insights, intuition, synchronicities and guidance from your heart's intelligence. All it takes is a willingness to suspend any expectations, or assumptions about exactly how the answers should come and what form they should take in your life. Letting go is a crucial step in all of this and I'm sure you've heard that before. The message here is: no insistence, no resistance. Interestingly though, when you let go of insisting on how things should manifest in your life; things, people and experiences start to show up in perfect timing and in an even bigger and grander way than you could have ever imagined.

In the chapters that follow, I will explain the alpha brainwave state and how it is intimately connected to the state of trance. In fact, it's just another way to define the state of trance. Many people often think of the subconscious being 'deep', below the conscious mind. This is a result of the language and imagery we have used to define it, such as 'sub' and 'deep in the subconscious', etc. The common analogy given is the iceberg, which is said to be like the mind where the tip is the conscious mind and deep under the surface of the water is the more massive portion of the iceberg, being the non-conscious, subconscious, unconscious mind. Since nobody knows what the unconscious mind really is, and since it's just an idea, a model and a concept, certain ways of thinking about this idea have developed over time and many of the subsequent theories have been very useful for clients to understand the unconscious and therapists to use.

I actually think of the unconscious mind as being one and the same with our 'higher mind' or 'higher self'. It is an aspect of one's self, psyche or being that when accessed can offer insights, guidance, healing, or a broader perspective. I define all of this as being part of a higher mind. However,, of course, once again, it is just an idea, not a scientifically verifiable fact—not yet anyway. Again, it comes back to what ideas and concepts resonate with you and which ones are useful for you. Use what feels right and dump the rest, has always been my advice to clients.

Ultimately, the intention for this book is to simply help you be more of who you truly are. You are not your job title, gender, nationality, a father, mother, son, daughter, brother, or sister. These are roles—costumes, if you will, that you have put on. I know who I am because I've been on a journey to discover it. But who are you? Hmm ... that's not for me to tell you; it's for you to discover—a gift for you to unwrap. When you are being yourself totally and completely, you naturally shed all of that which you are not, and this includes all the psychological programming we collected from the moment of our birth. When you let go of unhelpful programming, it leaves you with a particular state of wellbeing characterised by confidence, empowerment and self-love. This will inevitably lead to inner wellbeing that is less reliant on external situations and the opinions of others, and you will feel more intuitively guided. You know how there are some people out there, and maybe you're one of them, that once they have come to a realisation, had a moment of awakening, or even read a good book or seen a good movie, they have to tell everyone they know about it? Well, I'm one of those people. I'm like a big kid when it comes to things like that—I can get very excited about this kind of stuff and I'm not afraid to show it. This book is being written out of the excitement I experience when I think, write or share this kind of information with people. This is exactly why I know I had to write this book—not because I believe 'people need to know this' per se, but because it is an expression of my highest joy and excitement. And that alone is the only reason that matters. This is ultimately one of the things that I wish for everyone. That is, that you find within yourself the courage and inspiration to act on what I'm sure deep down you already know is your highest excitement and joy. Wouldn't it be cool to be surrounded by more people doing exactly this? Following your highest excitement gives others permission to do the same and so on. And soon it spreads further and wider, and before you know it, you're surrounded by people following their heart's excitement, not their brain's desires which, most of the time, has been programmed into them since birth.

'You have no need to travel anywhere - journey within yourself. Enter a mine of rubies and bathe in the splendour of your own light.'

- Rumi

As I continue to be more of who I am, I continue to synchronistically come across many teachers. And when I say 'teachers', let me clarify that I'm not just talking about people, but anything at all that can offer some sort of personal insight or self-awareness. This could be a beautiful place in nature, an activity, a process, a trip, a tool, a technique, or a ritual. I believe anything at all can be a teacher if one chooses to believe that they are surrounded by teachers. As a result of asking some big questions about myself, about life and people, I have come to learn a few things which I have no doubt can be useful insights for others.

As we know, the entire material world begins first as a thought. At times I may share certain ideas or concepts that may sound a little 'out there', esoteric or even 'woo woo'. Some things may even seem totally ridiculous to you, and that's okay. I'm not writing this book to change any beliefs, gather a following or tell you 'how the world is'. However, what I would like to humbly request is that you approach this material with an open mind and an open heart, and consider the science I am presenting. But even more importantly, if this material strikes a chord within you, my hope is that it inspires you to begin or continue your own research into this kind of information and see where it leads you. The image below offers a powerful visual of what I'm describing.

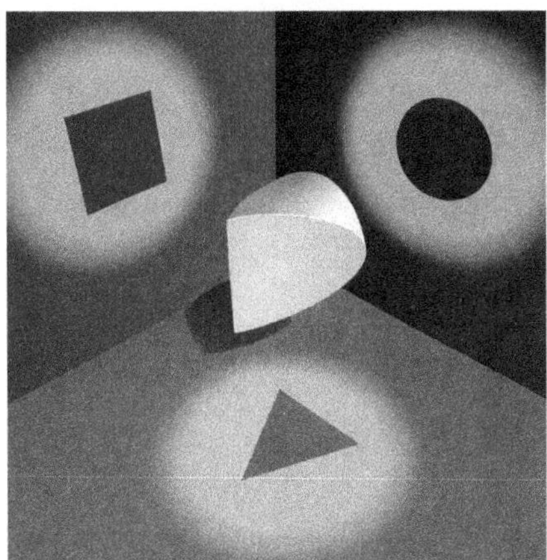

Figure 1.1

Is the object a circle, a square or a triangle? As you can see, the answer is 'all three'. One can only become aware of this if they are willing to adopt a particular perspective, a point of view where all three can be perceived and integrated. The deeper message of this image cannot be emphasised enough. I truly believe that one of the challenges we face as a collective human race at the moment, especially when it comes to scientists and spiritualists, is that both are using strong evidence in an attempt to 'prove their point of view' while doing their best to refute or discredit the proof of the other.

Consider the image above in this context. One side of the debate is putting forth all the scientific evidence as to why 'the object'—let's say the nature of reality—is a circle. The other side is also using good evidence to 'prove' why it's not a circle, but a square. Perhaps both are correct and together they create the triangle. You may have heard the idea of 'there are always three sides to every story—your side, their side and the truth'. Perhaps the answers we seek are not as black and white, or 'this or that' as we think. Perhaps certain ideas are more 'this and that' than meets the eye. One could use all kinds of compelling research and science to show why the image is a circle or a square, but only when we 'rise above', beyond, and transcend the two-dimensional perspective do we see the three-dimensional reality that reveals that both perspectives are, in fact, true at the same time—a reality neither may have realised even existed. This may beg the question: Is there an ultimate 'truth'? One way to answer this is to ask yourself, 'How is my life going? Am I truly satisfied with where I'm at?' The challenge is to be 100% honest with yourself. If what you're doing is working, then don't fix it and don't change a thing. However, what I've noticed over the years is that nobody has it all exactly the way they want it—there's always something needing improvement or refinement.

I wanted to show this image to highlight the fact that this book is a perspective that I am sharing. It's a point of view as it is to date based on the intersection of my subjective experiences and outer objective research. Who knows, it could change in the future. And I hope it does. After all, change is one thing we can guarantee will continue. I believe it's a good thing to be open to new possibilities and perspectives that could change your most deeply held beliefs no matter how solid you think they are.

'Your beliefs don't make you a free thinker. The ability to change your beliefs based on new information does.'

- unknown

Furthermore, it was Aristotle who said:

'It is the mark of an educated mind to be able to entertain a thought without accepting it.'

To me, the above quote also highlights the importance and usefulness of seeing the grey within an idea or concept because not everything is as black and white as it may appear. A simple analogy is that of a spinning top that is half black and half white. When it's still, you'll either see black or white, depending on your exact viewpoint. However, if you add the dynamic of spin to it, what do you see then? You will no longer see black or white, but grey. Our reality experience can very much be like this. There are many dynamics and nuances at play, and billions of processes going on within the amazing human heart, mind and body to create our perceptions and experiences of the world. Since we couldn't possibly process all of this incoming data consciously, which might allow us to experience the grey in a situation, instead, an unconscious process occurs within us whereby we store, delete, distort, and generalise incoming data. We filter and colour incoming perceptual information with our history and beliefs, which more often than not, result in black or white perceptions, distinctions, judgements, and experiences. It's a necessary biological function that must occur in order for us to act on something in the world.

At this point, I'd like to recommend setting an intention here and now to absorb the contents of this book with your intuitive self, with heart-oneness, rather than solely with your ego-brain. Try to find a balance between 'feeling' this book and mentally analysing it. This recommendation is based on my own personal experience. A few years ago, I had a realisation, which to me was quite profound. I became aware of the fact that more often than not, whether reading a book or listening to a speaker, in my mind I would be trying to make them 'wrong' by arguing with their content in my head. I wonder if you can relate. What I've noticed sometimes is that if we have spent many years developing a point of view and perspective, especially in the area of personal and spiritual development, we tend to be somewhat committed to holding on to it. After all, it's taken many years and hard work (and money) to get to that point of view, right? So, if we are listening to a speaker or reading a book that might propose some very different ideas from the ones we already have, and if there is a lack of connection or resonance with the speaker or author, we may tend to silently argue with them in our heads. Why do we do this? Maybe it's a way to stay safe and protected in some way. After all, we don't want to be fooled or hoodwinked. Perhaps it allows us to feel comfortable in maintaining our perspective. I think this is common even in day-to-day conversations we have. Really think about it—when someone is speaking to you, are you really listening to them, their intent and where they are coming from, or are you listening to what you are saying to yourself about what it is you're hearing in order to reply?

When it comes to teaching someone anything that could be defined as 'spiritual', I have a firm belief that the deeper the foundations, the more powerful the practice. It is for this very reason I have chosen to share with you over the chapters that follow an objective, verifiable, testable scientific basis for the powerful process I will be sharing in the final chapter. Now, if you're an excited or an impatient little soul, which I know I can be at times, you might be tempted right now to skip the next few chapters and go straight to the Heart Alpha Resonance Technique (H.A.R.T), learn it, practice it and just 'see what happens'. Don't get me wrong, if you did that, you probably would experience some amazing results and benefits over time. However, if you're like me, you will find the following chapters extremely useful in helping you appreciate and better understand exactly what it is you're doing, why it is you're doing it, and the science that supports it all. I have no doubt the implications and applications of this material have the potential to drastically change the way you think about and relate to yourself, improve your relationships with others, and deepen your heart connection to the world around you.

There is no doubt that science and what it has discovered about our inner and outer reality, has a huge role to play in the creation of our global and personal worldview. Therefore, logically speaking, if anyone is teaching individuals anything at all about how to improve oneself to achieve more in this world, then it makes total sense to begin this process at the most basic and fundamental starting point possible. To me, this means taking a very close look at what science is currently saying about the nature of reality while considering the theoretical process they have used to arrive at our current view. Whether you like it or not, much of what our world accepts as fact or fiction, real or not, is based on the outcomes of a scientific process. This process continues to build upon fundamental assumptions which, once agreed upon by a relatively small community of scientists, are rarely revisited or questioned. But what if there is a slight error in those fundamental assumptions? What if only a small tweak in thinking or perspective could lead to a revolutionary new type of scientific inquiry that could lead to an entirely new perspective of ourselves and the world around us? As you know, if you're building a structure and its foundations have a tiny error, it could present a huge problem later on. Perhaps we have become so close to the structure that we have lost sight of what it is that we are building simply through a lack of broadening our perspective.

If you consider the state of the world today, perhaps you would agree that a serious rethink of our most fundamental assumptions is needed. The assumptions I'm referring to are the ones that have been made by science over the years that, whether you realise it or not, have had a significant role in creating and moulding our current collective worldview as a species. Although the way you specifically view the world and your place within it may seem very far removed from what science tells us about our reality, it actually isn't. And this will become clearer later in this book.

If enough individuals on the planet are feeling confused, unhappy, disconnected, and unfulfilled, then of course we will have a world that is reflecting this right back to us. Logically, how could we ever expect to create and experience the world that we all say we want, if we are not able to be that in our day-to-day lives? You just can't get there from there. To me, this is like hoping to one day become an amazing soccer player by playing tennis every day.

Although the early part of this book will discuss the nature of reality, of course there will be times when I will share what I believe to be the possible implications of certain research findings. If this book stimulates you to do a little more of your own research, then in a way, my work is done. As a race, we can't expect to hand over the responsibility of 'fixing our world' to the politicians, priests, teachers, doctors, or the police. Maybe it's time for people to take back some power and responsibility by becoming aware of the real power you hold within your mind, body and heart. This could easily start a chain reaction as people begin to experience their power, which can lead to living it, which can lead to sharing it, which can then start the process of a ripple effect that touches another and another and another. Some people are calling these times the 'awakening of the planet' or 'the ascension'. I believe it is all of that and an inevitable process of evolution for a species, which is getting closer and closer to creating and experiencing its own self-destruction if this transition does not occur in a timely manner.

If you're rolling your eyes right about now thinking this is all a bit 'pie in the sky' as I talk about inspiring people to change the world, let me remind you that it only takes a flame to start a bushfire if the will and desire is there. If it sounds like an enormous task, too big to even start, please remember that it all starts with ourselves, and with small steps that compound over time. If creating this change was all up to our ego-brain or conscious mind, then I would probably agree that it's an impossible task. However,, luckily for us, we have an amazingly powerful resource at our disposal if we know how to use it—our unconscious heart-mind—which I believe is the seat of true being and intuitive guidance. By knowing how to engage the resources of your subconscious heart-mind, this book is going to help you move closer to the fourth level of competence as outlined below, where I honestly believe life mastery and self-love truly exist. Below is an outline of the Four Levels of Competence.

1. *Unconscious incompetence (when you don't know that you don't know).*
2. *Conscious incompetence (when you know that you don't know).*
3. *Conscious competence (when you know that you know).*
4. *Unconscious competence (when you don't know how you know, you just know).*

The fourth level of competence is the level of being where you are acting from an intuitive level. Intuition is often a type of knowing where you're not really sure how or why you know something, you just do. There is, however, a very important distinction to make between brain-based and heart-based intuition.

Why is the fourth level of competence so important? Because this is where I believe true authentic being comes from, as well as effortless manifestation. I think there comes a time in the journey of personal development where an individual is firstly totally unaware of their potential, closely followed by the awareness of how much they don't know. It can then take many years of learning and practice for an individual to describe themselves as 'consciously competent', especially if that person has limiting subconscious programs and beliefs of unworthiness and fear. Some people will eventually come to realise that the complexity of mind, body and spirit is such that there is simply not enough time in the day or years in our life to 'know thyself' by using the conscious brain-mind alone. We need a catalyst to propel us to the fourth level of 'Unconscious Competence'. This is the level where I believe true enlightenment exists. It's a level of being where you simply know what you need to know when you need to know it and furthermore, you may not even know how you know it, you just know it. This is precisely why the competence is unconscious.

I'm here to share a perspective that this 'higher power' doesn't have to be an archangel, a deceased relative, an extra-terrestrial or God. Although these can be very useful and empowering things, all of which I have and continue to occasionally call upon for assistance and guidance myself, the most powerful thing this book will teach you is how to tap into, use and develop your very own subconscious heart-mind. It's nothing but simple logic that tells us that if we want to become unconsciously competent at anything, then we must use the unconscious to allow learning and unlearning to easily and effortlessly unfold before our very eyes—the essence and alchemy of true magic. However, if your focus is solely from the neck up, omitting the most energetically powerful organ in the human body—your heart—then you're leaving out the very difference that could make all the difference.

I'd like to state right here and now that I am not a physicist, hence much of the information that I will be sharing in the next two chapters is an amalgamation of my own research and learnings from the people, institutions, projects, and movements that I have been following for many years. Most notably the work of Nassim Haramein, Director of Research at The Resonance Science Foundation. Although he and his team are engaged in some of the most complicated physics in unification theory, he describes himself as a mystic, committed to a truly unified model of reality. His pioneering (and polarising) approach investigates the wisdom and clues left behind by ancient civilisations, combined with a modern understanding of the mechanics of our reality and universe, for the betterment of all humankind. It facilitates not only a deeper understanding of ourselves and the world around us, but also the creation of more advanced technology that has the capacity to free our civilisation on many levels. So, I wish you well on this journey and hope to someday meet you and discuss all of this in person.

'The kingdom of heaven is within you; and whosoever shall know himself shall find it.'

- Ancient Egyptian Proverb

Part 1

CHAPTER 1

A Paralysed Paradigm: A Disconnected Worldview Leading to a Disconnected Human Being

'Normal is getting dressed in clothes that you buy for work and driving through traffic in a car that you are still paying for in order to get to the job you need to pay for the clothes and the car, and the house you leave vacant all day so you can afford to live in it.'

- Ellen Goodman

This quote may seem almost laughable, but then the reality hits you; this is the crazy life that most of us are living, accepting, and even worse, believing that it's 'just the way it is' as if there is no alternative. Sadly, it's also a way of life that much of the developing world is aspiring to achieve and emulate as if it is the very definition of progress. This isn't necessarily the way we want it; it just happened this way, a natural consequence of the predominant worldview of our time and of previous times.

You cannot underestimate the importance of our personal and global worldview. It is for this reason I've chosen to start here. We are living in a time of such rapid advancement in so many areas of our lives, thanks to new discoveries in areas such as the human heart and brain, alternative clean energy, food production, genetic engineering, propulsion systems, information technology, artificial intelligence, and robotics, just to name a few. These advancements seem to be giving most of us a sense that 'time is flying'—and indeed it is. The question is, in what direction? Maybe to help give us an insight into the direction we are heading, we should start with the broadest and most comprehensive perspective possible. We need to take a closer look at the aspects of the current consensus worldview that is defining our principles, values, choices, and behaviours, all of which I believe are maintaining what I call 'a paralysed paradigm'.

Why paralysed? Because I truly believe that the current consensus worldview, although it may have greatly benefited us in the past, is now holding us back. It is paralysing us from more clearly and quickly moving in the direction that we all say we want—a sustainable world of peace, harmony and wellbeing for generations to come. If just a small shift in worldview can lead to the creation of a new paradigm, then we simply need to ask ourselves some big questions like: What is the current worldview? How did this view come into being? What could be our future if we continue with this worldview? Is there an alternative worldview that may allow us to mimic and model the very wheel works of nature itself not only to develop more harmonious, efficient and cleaner technologies, but relationships between one another and with nature itself?

These indeed are huge questions. Just thinking about them might make some people feel a little helpless or hopeless as overwhelm kicks in. You may even think that trying to find answers to these kinds of questions is a task so big that you might call me a 'dreamer'. But to borrow the words of the late and great John Lennon:

'You may say I'm a dreamer, but I'm not the only one.'

And this is very true when it comes to shifting paradigms. There are a growing number of intellectuals, thought leaders, scientists, and communities all over the world who have stepped up to become part of a new wave of solutions, a collaboration of minds and hearts. Often, it's just a matter of becoming aware that these people and communities exist and then asking, 'How can I get involved?' Never fall into the trap of thinking that the challenge is too big or 'I'm just one person', or 'what can I do?' because as Margaret Mead once said:

'Never underestimate the power of a small group of committed people to change the world. In fact, it is the only thing that ever has.'

What is a worldview and why is it important? Let's define exactly what I mean by the term 'worldview'. Here are some definitions:

- *A particular philosophy of life and the way someone thinks about the world.*
- *An intellectual and overall perspective from which one sees, interprets and lives in the world.*
- *A collection of beliefs and attitudes about life and the universe adopted by an individual or group of people.*
- *A mental model of reality; a theoretical framework of ideas.*

Quite obviously, a paradigm and worldview are very much connected. They underpin our beliefs, which of course are a very powerful human phenomenon. Humans have done, and continue to do, some strange things because of beliefs, maybe for the very reason that they are so powerful. Our beliefs shape our perceptions and values, which in turn have a direct correlation in the very functioning of the human brain. This is not philosophy, but confirmed by brain science at a neurochemical and neurotransmitter level. Our brain, through neuroplasticity, is continually being influenced and shaped via our values and beliefs. As a result, we are constantly—and predominantly unconsciously—filtering billions of bits of incoming sensory data through cognitive processes of deletions, distortions and generalisations. This process soon becomes the basis for making decisions, which then define not only who we are as individuals, but as a society and global community.

What this book will introduce and highlight is the power of the heart-mind and emotions on your cognitive processes. What modern mainstream science has failed to acknowledge up until now, is the amazing influence the heart has over the neurochemical functioning of the brain. This influence of course comes from emotions.

Quite naturally, humans have been changing and evolving our paradigms and worldviews since the beginning of time. During the course of human history, and depending on the culture, different perspectives have defined different worldviews. Some cultures created worldviews based on numerous gods, each responsible for different aspects of life. Others had 'mother earth' and her cycles as their focal point. Here in Australia, it was 'dream time'—some used the stars and planets themselves to guide them in crucial decision-making and healing. Today, the global worldview is based on the scientific process of investigation, which comprises of creating a hypothesis, collecting data and then analysing that data to either confirm or reject your hypothesis, sometimes with the intention of being able to predict certain phenomena. If these processes reveal observations that are inaccurate, or if they give us an incomplete picture of our world or the universal forces that govern it, we then have an opportunity to amend, modify, or in extreme cases, even discard our original worldview in favour of a new one that is demonstrating itself to be more accurately aligned with new understandings.

There are at least two significant moments in our history, which all of us know, where a major shift occurred. One was the realisation that our world is not flat but round. The other being the discovery that our Sun, not the Earth, is in fact the centre of our solar system. Can you imagine the shift that would have occurred in people, their philosophies and worldviews as a result of this? An Earth-centred solar system was, at the time, in alignment with mainstream belief—a religious one. This was the idea that humans, and the Earth, were God's greatest creation—the pinnacle of all that is, was and ever shall be. The discovery that our Sun was not only the centre, but that we revolved around it, completely shifted the way we viewed ourselves and our entire cosmology. Suddenly, we were not the 'centre of the universe'. This may not have had much of an effect on the day-to-day life of ordinary people back then, but the effect on the collective unconscious, and the behaviour that it inevitably influenced, cannot be underestimated. As we look back, obviously it was only a matter of time until we developed the technology to make that discovery. Often our discoveries and paradigm shifts have emerged directly as a result of advancements in technology that allow us to become aware of something new. Sometimes the discoveries arise out of pure luck or even by accident.

If we come to understand something about the nature of our world, the universe or our reality, which indicates the need to make changes to our worldview, then obviously this is what needs to occur. Otherwise, we will simply continue to perpetuate a value system and paradigm that just isn't in alignment with the natural world around us. Perhaps the global challenges we are facing at the moment are the natural result of a worldview and paradigm that isn't quite in sync with the dynamics of nature, but may in fact be in conflict or perhaps even in opposition with it.

I think it's important to mention, however, that we should be careful in allowing technology alone to be our rudder directing us towards a particular form of human evolution. It's been said that our technology seems to have overtaken our humanity. It's important to evolve our spiritual and emotional selves along with our science and technology. If one aim of technology is to become more intuitively in alignment with human processes, allowing them to more quickly manifest our ideas, then it seems absolutely crucial that we must also evolve our mind, body, spirit, and heart. This will help ensure that the ideas we want to manifest through technology are borne out of heart-based oneness and love, and not a wounded ego-brain type of fear. Some people believe that technology itself is evil. Perhaps it's got more to do with the individual who creates and uses it rather than technology itself. A commonly used analogy is the knife that can be used to end or save a life, depending on how it is used. I've come to believe it isn't technology that we have to fear, but the intentions of wounded, power-hungry corporations, institutions, or people. Technology is a saviour in the hands of the right people, and a destroyer in the wrong hands.

There is always a positive flip side, even to this, however. We all know that it is often through great challenges and disasters that the true heart of humanity is given an opportunity to emerge. Perhaps life is a cycle and maybe there is a time for all three aspects of it to emerge and play out as believed in the Hindu tradition of Brahma (the creator), Vishnu (the preserver) and Shiva (the destroyer or transformer). Without one, the others cannot exist. Even the word 'God' can be described in this way as Generator, Operator and Destroyer.

There are many examples of how technology has overtaken our humanity. Isn't it strange that we are extremely 'social' and 'connected' via our mobile phones, but often completely unable to say a simple 'hello' to the person sitting next to us on the bus without having them think we're 'weird' or questioning our motives? The best example of technology disconnecting us is its use in the military, where virtually all of our technology comes from, thanks to unlimited budgets for research and development. We can now engage in full-scale wars, and decimate entire populations without using a single human being on the ground to do it. Instead, we can use remote-controlled drones and push-button, self-guided weaponry. It's the perfect way to create an apathetic distance between both sides of a war and subsequently make it easier for the individuals involved to deal with, often killing innocent lives caught in between. Did you know that one of the main reasons Nazi Germany created gas chambers was to reduce the psychological trauma being experienced by the Nazi soldiers pulling the triggers in firing squads?

It is the aim of this book to close the gap a little between what I believe to be an imbalance between the development of our technology and of our heart-mind. If we do not start taking responsibility for our own physical, emotional, and spiritual bodies and the wounds they all carry, they will one day become the very thing that will fuel the thoughts and actions that could threaten our survival. Generally speaking, because of this predominant worldview and paradigm of the western world, we have become completely obsessed with looking for our answers and saviours from outside ourselves. We have basically handed over our power and control to external institutions like governments, religion, the judicial, medical, and financial institutions either out of fear, ignorance, or perhaps sheer laziness to 'take care of it for us' and think for us. Since this is a system partly of our own creation, why should we be surprised when these institutions create and implement rules, regulations, and laws whose primary purpose is to maintain their own power and control?

I know this might all seem a little bleak, but trust me, the light at the end of this tunnel is coming. As I have mentioned already, if we intend to create a new worldview and a new paradigm, we need to have some understanding of the current one. And this might not be a comfortable process, but it is a necessary one. Also, let me be clear—I'm not promoting a form of anarchy or socialist communism. What I am promoting, and what I am in favour of, are people who can think for themselves, think critically, and question everything while remaining connected to their hearts. That includes the content of this book. I believe it can be a dangerous thing to put people or institutions on pedestals simply because 'it's always been that way'. If you think about it, any person who has ever made their mark in history only did so because they refused to allow the status quo to rule their thinking and behaviour. Albert Einstein himself said:

'To punish me for my contempt of authority, fate made me an authority myself.'

Since the world is in need of a radical shift, it's important to become aware of the theoretical framework of our current science, paradigm and subsequent worldview that continues to consciously and unconsciously shape our values and beliefs. After that, let us explore a new and growing scientific worldview from which we can lay new foundations. This new paradigm, as we shall see in the following chapters, is proving to be more in alignment with the natural world, and for this reason is perhaps a more beneficial foundation upon which new personal and cultural values, as well as beliefs, can be built on. Even a basic understanding of this new science will provide the perfect platform from which to explore the intelligent heart, the subconscious heart-mind, the science of the energetic heart, and how all of this can influence your inner and outer world through the H.A.R.T process and the scripts I have developed at the end of this book.

From this place you will begin to see exactly what I mean by the subtitle of this book: 'When the heart leads, reality responds',

Currently, we have a global worldview that is based on the scientific method, which can be characterised with the points that follow. Now let's be clear from the start; this approach has been very beneficial to our development in the past and it would be silly for anyone to suggest that the entire model needs to be thrown out completely. Of course not. This is about looking at the assumptions that have shaped who we are and our society up until now, recognising that it has helped us achieve great things, but at the same time being real and honest about the current model's limitations that are being discovered through a new and deeper investigation into nature. These discoveries seem to be suggesting that perhaps some tweaking is needed to avoid the probable consequences if we do not make those changes fast.

Although I am taking quite a scientific approach in sharing these two worldviews and paradigms, I will also be touching on the possible philosophical and practical implications and applications of these views as I elaborate further. Most importantly however, all of this information has one simple aim, and that is to form the most rock-solid foundation for living with H.A.R.T. By the time we get to the process, you will have a very clear understanding of why we are doing each step, but also the power of what it is you're actually doing. You will be in possession of a powerful key to explore the very place where all the ancient masters of the past have said our answers and guidance reside—within ourselves.

Now let us very briefly outline some of the assumptions that our current scientific worldview is based upon. Some of the following points are shared in Rupert Sheldrake's amazing book, The Science Delusion, where he scrutinises each assumption to see how well they hold up to genuine inquiry, and they don't hold up too well.

- *At the most basic of levels, the nature of the universe and all the material 'stuff' in it, as well as human beings, behave like a mechanical machine.*
- *For us to understand everything there is to know about this machine, we need to break it down into smaller and smaller bits and then study each bit as being completely separate and in isolation to all the other bits.*
- *There is no underlying system or architecture of organisation, and because of this there is no reason to look for one or include it into the current model of physics and scientific hypothesis.*
- *If there is any system of organisation encoded within the mechanical universe, it is all being done by pure chance or by random events.*
- *We are basically living in what has been called 'a dead universe' made of unconscious matter. There is no intelligence or consciousness within the material components or parts that make up the machine, and for this reason there shouldn't be any consciousness in human beings at all.*

- *If evolution is heading in any particular direction at all, it is towards less and less order. Things are moving towards less organisation and/or coherence.*
- *Everything in the universe, on all scales, is separated by space or vacuum and because of this, all things everywhere are inherently disconnected and separate from everything else.*
- *Something that is happening in one system, which is inherently a closed or isolated system, could not possibly be influencing and interacting with a closed, isolated system somewhere else because the space that is between them is 'empty', containing zero energy.*
- *Nature and the evolutionary process fundamentally has no purpose or direction.*
- *Memories are somehow stored in your brain as tiny bits of material.*
- *The human mind is stored inside the head and what you may consider to be consciousness is just a by-product of the activity of your brain, much like exhaust fumes of a running engine.*
- *Following on from the above, psychic phenomena such as telepathy and remote viewing are considered impossible. Your thoughts and intentions cannot have any influence on anything outside of your body because your mind is inside your skull.*
- *Allopathic mechanistic medicine is the only one that really works and it's the reason almost all government funding goes to this type of medical research. Alternative therapies may only seem to work because individuals would have recovered anyway or because of the placebo effect.*

These are some of the most fundamental assumptions that our current scientific story is using to try and understand who we are, where we have come from, why we are here, and the nature of reality. It's basically the default worldview of logical intellectual thought. These assumptions, you could say, are the guiding rudder of our time. If this story were to be strictly adhered to, then by definition humans are not conscious beings. It's just not possible, according to these assumptions. It suggests that the parts we are made out of are not conscious at all, but simply dead, unintelligent matter that is being moved around inside us. The question is: At what point does consciousness emerge from non-conscious matter? This reductionist materialistic model of studying reality assumes that if we know everything about the parts then this will somehow explain the whole. This kind of thinking reminds me of a quote by the famous British stand-up philosopher and writer, Alan Watts, who said:

'For centuries scientists and philosophers asked themselves, "What is the stuff that we are made of?" A carpenter makes tables out of wood but I ask you, is a tree made of wood? Obviously not. A tree is wood; it's not made of it. Is a mountain made of rock? Obviously not, it is rock.'

To use the above analogy, the disconnected paradigm seems to be concerned about learning more and more about the dynamics, structure and phenomenon of 'the wood'. However, the science and physics of a connected worldview is focused not only on understanding the wood, but also the dynamics, structure and phenomena of the tree itself as a whole—its place, connection and contribution to the overall ecosystem of which it is a part—and how all the other trees around it, near and far, may be connected to one another.

'A human being is a part of the whole called by us "universe", a part limited in time and space. He experiences himself, his thoughts and feelings as something separated from the rest, a kind of optical delusion of his consciousness. This delusion is a kind of prison for us, restricting us to our personal desires and to affection for a few persons nearest to us. Our task must be to free ourselves from this prison by widening our circle of compassion to embrace all living creatures and the whole of nature in its beauty.'

- Albert Einstein

It's probably no surprise to you that the two most powerful influences during the development of our western culture were science and religion. One could start with the work of Nicolaus Copernicus (1473-1543), who was the first to put forth the sun-centred model of the solar system. As other scientists like Galileo Galilei started to propose their theories, it started to get very obvious that they were in direct conflict with the religious story and dogma of the time. As a result of these conflicting theories, it was not uncommon for these researchers and scientists to be victims of serious violence, or to be jailed or burnt at the stake.

Interestingly enough however, it should be noted that many of the pioneers of this early science and philosophy were in fact very religious and spiritual people themselves. Sometimes they were monks, priests or mystics. The problem with the predominant religion of the west—Catholicism—was that many of these perceived 'religious contrarians' were proposing that human life was a kind of elevated phenomenon of nature, rather than a sinner, flawed even before birth. Of course, the Vatican didn't like the idea of man being equal to God's creations, let alone an exalted one, because that would obviously and completely fly right in the face of the cornerstone of their philosophy, which was the need for salvation through an intermediary. This position was, and still is to this day, used to maintain political and spiritual control through the fear of some kind of eternal damnation.

One could say that, as a result of some kind of rebelliousness towards the grip of religious dogma at the time, science went in the complete opposite direction. Scientific research pursued evidence of a completely mechanical, materialistic concept of reality that totally removed the need for a higher power, like God. They wanted God out of the equation—literally. The philosophies, theories and equations that began to gain momentum, the ones which served us very well for many years, literally removed the idea of anything that implied a higher kind of intelligence, an architect or 'creator' of the universe. In doing so, they removed 'God' but they also removed the value of the internal subjective experience of the observing human being and how this might be interacting with the outside world. What was happening on the inside of an individual was considered to be impossible to measure or directly observe, so its relevance in science was simply thrown out. One's subjective inner world was considered to be a phenomenon that was best left to religion while science progressed with an intention to study the world 'out there'.

In a sense, we replaced one dogma with another, and from here the scientific process developed accordingly. Where things got a little messy was when certain results and lines of investigation were being ignored, especially for people who were proposing ideas seen as being divergent from the new materialistic reductionist method that was rapidly gaining momentum. This actually continues to this day, by the way. Mainstream science seems to have created its very own bubble. More often than not, only studies and research that help to inflate the existing bubble are considered 'credible' and recognised. Existing journals and presentation platforms will often only allow research to be shared and taught as long as it doesn't disrupt or go against the mainstream, which of course, continues to prop up our existing paralysed paradigm. Often, when one has found a result based on a valid study, if that result does not extend or lead on from a long-held lineage of thought, the results are considered absurd, no matter your result, simply because there isn't enough historical research to consider it. However, when you are proposing ideas and theories that may seem radical, you are obviously never going to have the benefit of years of data or research to call upon. It is impossible to make leaps in science and be at the cutting edge if you continue to allow 'what has always been' to be your sole guiding research principle. It is, however, a sure way to secure funding for your research. Tenzing Norgay did not have the benefit of following a trail up Mount Everest in 1953 because he was the first person to actually do it!

As a result of this approach, it's a real shame that some absolutely amazing research in all endeavours of science has been suppressed, particularly in the area of energy, medicine and health. The current worldview of disconnection and scarcity, as well as the science that supports it, plays very well into the hands of big and powerful corporations such as energy and pharmaceutical companies. Of course, this hasn't been all bad. We have come a long way and progressed enormously as a society because of certain technological advancements. However, the truth is that there have been numerous examples where, if a certain theory and line of research were supported and investigated further and given a chance, we could have been living in a very different world today. The truth is simple. If large institutions are likely to lose a lot of power and profits as a result of new research or technology, no matter how many individuals could benefit from it, that line of thinking and research is unlikely to be funded and the technology suppressed, or sometimes even forcibly removed. These are no conspiracy theories; it's basic business.

A perfect example of this, of course, is the story of Nikola Tesla, who is considered to be the inventor and father of our modern-day harnessing and production of electricity. Tesla had a profound understanding of the source of electricity and was investigating how it could be distributed wirelessly, but yet neither he nor his work is taught in mainstream schools today. Just as his research was approaching a crucial point, his funding was cut and the research lab burnt to the ground. At the time, his financial backer, J.P Morgan, was heavily invested in copper wire. Seeing the potential threat and profit losses wirelessly transmitted electricity could mean to his business, rumours say that he used his power to virtually end Tesla's career in one fell swoop. Tesla ended up dying a penniless man whose work was virtually ignored for many years. But thankfully, this is changing. Since Tesla, many scientists have used some of his basic principles and have created 'free' or 'clean' energy devices all over the world. Sadly, there are also many cases of these inventions being suppressed, destroyed or even the inventors themselves mysteriously disappearing. But if you ask an AI or search engine about this, they are likely to tell you that this is all just myth. You be the judge.

A documentary I highly recommend, and which is free to watch on YouTube, is Thrive: *What on Earth Will it Take?* as well as its sequel, created years later, *Thrive II: This is What it Takes.* It was created by Foster Gamble, whom I was lucky enough to meet on his Australian tour in 2012. These are beautifully created documentaries, a visual treat, that simply ask the question, 'Why isn't humanity thriving and what will it take for this to happen?' It covers a number of topics such as global economics, health, medicine, energy supply and production, as well as how perhaps a deeper understanding of ancient wisdom could be an important key in developing solutions for our time.

This story of scientific repression doesn't only apply to energy production but to medicine, health and wellness, especially when it comes to cancer research. With just a little of your own research, you will find that over the past few hundred years there have been quite a few examples where researchers found very promising results with regards to cancer treatments and even cures, which for one reason or another simply never got mainstream attention or support. One example is Rick Simpson and his work with medicinal cannabis and hemp oil. If you want to investigate him and his protocol further, simply take a look at his documentary, *'Running from The Cure'*. Governments all over the world are finally coming on board with controlled clinical trials and research as more and more personal stories of complete cures come forth all over social media. There comes a point where governments can no longer ignore the pleas and requests of the people who have voted them into power to conduct more rigorous trials, and consider decriminalisation and legalisation, which thankfully is starting to occur. In Australia, it is now possible, and has been for a little while, to get a prescription for cannabis. It's interesting to me that for many years cannabis has been deemed illegal and unsafe—that is until pharmaceutical companies can sell it. Then all of a sudden, it's safe and legal. Government-controlled farms are now permitted solely for the purpose of growing hemp for medicinal purposes and clinical trials in Australia during this time. However, the cost of creating such an operation is so high that it pretty much guarantees that only drug companies will ever afford it. The unfortunate truth is that we live in a world where profits often come before people, which means big corporations and the governments that they heavily influence are going to act accordingly. For example, did you know that the government of the United States actually has a patent on 'cannabinoids as antioxidants and neuroprotectants'? That's right. All you have to do is Google 'Patent US6630507' and see for yourself.

My intention in sharing the idea of potentially suppressed science is simply to make the point that we as individuals need to take responsibility for our own wellbeing. It would be naive of us to believe that the large powers that be have our best interests and wellbeing at heart all the time. But my message is simple—be informed, follow the money, question everything, and do not take everything you see and hear in the mainstream media as gospel. I believe there is a very real danger in leaving it all up to 'them' to take care of things for us because it could quite possibly lead us down a destructive path, one that is becoming clearer and clearer to see in the world today. At this moment, I am reminded of a quote by Benjamin Franklin:

'Any society that would give up a little liberty to gain a little security, deserves neither and will lose both.'

I would suggest re-reading the above assumptions that have been driving science for a very long time and just notice how they feel to you. Read with your eyes, think with your mind, but most importantly, feel it with your intuitive heart. I believe this is the best place to bring your attention when assessing whether something is right, appropriate or in alignment with you personally. All I can say is that when I came across these assumptions, I instantly felt that it was out of alignment with my truth and my higher perspective. But that's just me. Perhaps, for you, it's a little different. When I came across the assumptions of this new and emerging science, something in me just said, 'YES'. I felt something 'click' within my intuitive heart-mind. This new worldview is slowly becoming more mainstream, perhaps as a growing number of individuals are sensing a deep alignment and connection to it. It's worth mentioning that this worldview isn't exactly new; its philosophical underpinnings go back thousands of years, but only in the past few decades is it gaining more traction. This worldview in science can be characterised by the following statements:

- *Everything in the universe, including all matter, the elements and the subatomic energy field that it emerges from, acts as a whole unified system.*
- *Researching the above system includes the investigation of the deepest underlying patterns of universal wholeness that are simultaneously represented as fractal repetitions at all scales in size from the infinitely small to the infinitely large.*
- *An exchange of information and energy is happening in a holographic fashion where the structure and dynamics within the part are true for the structure and dynamics of the whole.*
- *The universal creation process itself uses a process of feedback (incoming energy and information) and feedforward (outgoing energy and information) to produce more coherencies, to adjust, adapt and evolve in the most efficient and fastest way at all scales everywhere.*

- *The 'living universe' can be seen through the dynamics, structure and pattern that produces a kind of spontaneous 'intelligence' that allows the system itself to continue to evolve.*
- *Evolution is not heading in a particular direction per se, but evolves in a way that includes an ever-present balancing between expansion and contraction, increasing and decreasing order.*
- *What seems to be 'empty space' between two objects, is in fact the most densely energetic 'thing' in the universe, and since it is truly everywhere, it connects all things and matter in the universe.*

As you read and re-read these two sets of scientific assumptions, I encourage you to think about them and feel them to see which resonates more closely with you. Perhaps you're already starting to see the natural implications and outcomes that would emerge from progressing the scientific method from these different perspectives, as well as the worldview that would naturally and spontaneously emerge from them. The worldview that we take forward into the next twenty, fifty or one hundred years is absolutely crucial to the survival and continuation of our species; very few people could argue with that. However, if science and humankind as a whole continue to think of themselves, the world and the universe at large as being made up of only discrete, individual, fragmented and disconnected 'bits' separate from all the other bits out there, then obviously our values, thinking, behaviours, social structures, medicine, governments, food production, and energy are all going to arise from, and reflect, that kind of fundamental thinking. It's a top-down effect.

Essentially, this shift in worldview being birthed through science is about recognising that perhaps instead of trying to break down and rip apart our material world more and more to find the smallest particle, maybe we should try to understand more about the dynamics, structure, and pattern of the wheel works of nature itself. This is only a small shift but a crucial one because it combines the investigation of tiny individual particles of matter with their dynamic relationship to the entire system to help us discover more about the way all systems evolve.

It's important to note that this kind of approach is not exactly new and persists in some eastern cultures to this day. For example, the Chinese word for nature is 'zìrán', which translates to 'Self so;

so of its own; so of itself'. Because of this idea, it is completely normal for the Chinese to consider things to be self-shaping, or self-evolving, implying the existence of a type of intelligence within biology that helps it evolve. Perhaps a living system is designed to just follow a pattern, dynamic and structure that is an inherent aspect of life itself. Because of this, the curious mind of a young Chinese child observing something in nature, or asking about themselves, is more likely to ask an adult, 'How does that grow?', or 'How do I grow?', as opposed to 'What is it made of?', or 'What am I made of?'

When all is said and done, if people want to shift and experience a 'unified world', the one we say we all want, then it is crucial that scientific research helps to confirm this idea of connectedness as an actual phenomenon within reality itself. If this is shown to be the case at a deep fundamental level, then from there we can begin to work our way up to the expression and experience of this on a broader level, personally and collectively.

One of the cornerstones of the idea of an interconnected universe is that of a holographic universe, as proposed by Nassim Haramein, Director of Research at The Resonance Science Foundation. It essentially proposes that what is true about the dynamics of a system at one level is true for the dynamics of all systems above or below it. This principle and research are gaining more support as we observe correlations between subatomic and cosmological systems, of which the human experience is somewhere in the middle. This idea of a holographic universe is not new and can be traced back even to ancient philosophers such as Hermes Trismegistus who taught:

'As above, so below, as within, so without, as the universe, so the soul.'
'That which is below corresponds to that which is above, and that which is above corresponds to that which is below, to accomplish the miracle of the One Thing.'

Therefore, whatever happens on one level of reality (physical, emotional or mental) also happens on every other level. For me, it's an exciting concept to incorporate, explore, experience, and teach while doing my best to live and be it in the best way I can.

'You are not IN the universe; you ARE the universe, an intrinsic part of it. Ultimately you are not a person, but a focal point where the universe is becoming conscious of itself.'

- Eckhart Tolle

'We are most probably here for local information-gathering and local-universe problem-solving in support of the integrity of eternally regenerative Universe.'

- Buckminster Fuller

In very simple terms, the emerging unified physics model proposes that information is being constantly exchanged across all scales everywhere, meaning everything is connected and entangled. This unified whole system has a feedback mechanism that allows for adaptation, self-regulation or 'balancing' based on incoming information from the environment. This same system also has a feedforward process of outgoing or outflowing information, also in a continual loop, which drives evolution itself. A new unified model of science must contain and account for this feedback/feedforward system, and here is why.

Nassim wrote a paper in 1997 where he referenced the work of English astronomer and physicist, Sir Fred Hoyle (1915-2001). Sir Hoyle invented the term 'Big Bang' and the theory that emerged from it. He later went on to challenge his very own theory in support of a steady-state model. As quoted by Nassim:

'No example gives a better mathematical perspective of the implicit universal order, than the one given by Fred Hoyle. Hoyle calculated the probabilities of a blind person ordering the scrambled faces of a Rubik's Cube. The calculations demonstrated that, due to the fact the blind person does not know if he or she is getting closer or further to the objective on each move, the probabilities of matching the six colours on each face of the cube are on the order of 1:1 to 1:5x10^{18}*. Thus, if that person were to labour at a rate of one move per second, it would take 5x*10^{18} *seconds to complete all possibilities. That is to say, that it will take up to 158 billion years for that person to reach the goal. Clearly that time period not only grossly exceeds the life expectancy of the Rubik's Cube player, but,*

once again, it exceeds the lifetime of the Earth or, for that matter, the existence of our universe since its beginning, which has been estimated at a maximum of 20 billion years old. However, if the blind person is given a simple piece of information (feedback), like a "yes" or "no" prompt every time a move is made, which is every second, the time needed to complete the Rubik's Cube equation is drastically reduced to approximately two minutes.'

This is a simple example showing that the complexity of life, which is obviously much more complex than a Rubik's Cube, must contain some sort of feedback system in order for it to evolve such complex organisms at such a rapid rate.

At this point, I think it is important to note that the idea of a fundamental field of energy that connects all things and is everywhere is not a new concept at all. When studying ancient cultures as well as some of the greatest minds and philosophers and scientists of the past, it becomes apparent that many proposed the existence of a unifying energy of some sort, which not only gave rise to all that is but was the organising structure for evolution and biology as well. This energy has been given different names by different cultures. The Chinese call it 'Chi', the Japanese call it 'Ki', and in India it is called 'Prana'. The history of Western science is also riddled with those who referred to this field of energy as 'Aether', and it was thought to be the very thing that somehow facilitated the transport of light itself. Even though the idea of an underlying field of energy remains very strong within quantum physics, this notion of the Aether was largely removed from scientific hypothesis and investigation in the early 20th century.

'As a man who has devoted his whole life to the most clear-headed science, to the study of matter, I can tell you as a result of my research about atoms this much: There is no matter as such. All matter originates and exists only by virtue of a force which brings the particle of an atom to vibration and holds this most minute solar system of the atom together. We must assume behind this force the existence of a conscious and intelligent mind. This mind is the matrix of all matter.'

\- Max Planck

For millennia, many civilisations have philosophised about concepts that are fundamental to this new, connected view of ourselves and reality. Perhaps what is required at this time in our evolution is to remember and incorporate these ideas more seriously into our science. The current worldview, which assumes a materialistic position, essentially asserts that the world is made up of dead, unintelligent, non-conscious matter, being shuffled around by some external force. The interesting thing about this worldview of reductionism is that it can both support and reject the more religious view that it is often in conflict with. On the one hand, if indeed the world is made of dead, unintelligent matter, then logically speaking, all of this stuff had to be created, set into motion and its dynamics continually monitored by some kind of higher energy or force—namely God, right? But on the other hand, if we come to understand the mechanical components of the stuff well enough, then at some point it will become self-evident and we will have scientifically explained all 'miracles' and then there will be no need for mystical, esoteric, creationist mythologies. The only miracle that mainstream science would like us to accept is the so-called 'big bang' where supposedly all matter, reality and the laws that govern it sprang into being out of nothing. Terrence McKenna (1946 – 2000), an American-born ethnobotanist, speaker, writer, and philosopher, characterised the position of modern science by saying: *'Give us one free miracle and we'll explain the rest',* which I find to be quite amusing.

Could there be a position in the middle of what is essentially the ongoing tug-of-war between creationism and evolutionism? Could there be the existence of a supreme architecture or process whereby organisms have an inherent capacity to evolve through time and adaptation? Could it be a little bit of both? Could the very mechanisms, qualities and dynamics of a supreme architect actually be embedded and inherent into the 'matter' itself? Could this be what we are referring to when we speak of 'the nature of something'? Is it possible that the process of creation itself creates in such a way that it endows its creations with the capacity to do the exact same thing—that is, to create and evolve itself symbiotically with the environment it's immersed in? Is this not exemplified by the fact that people and animals come out of other people and animals? A simple example of the fractal and holographic nature of life.

In this chapter, we have begun our journey towards H.A.R.T by examining the fundamental assumptions that science has been operating under. This has led to the predominant worldview that we see today, a scientific story which reinforces disconnection and isolation between things. This naturally bleeds into disconnection between nations, governments, institutions, and organisations, which will ultimately lead to the worst kind of disconnection there is: a disconnectedness with ourselves and our true nature. When mainstream science is attempting to isolate the tiniest parts of reality to understand how the mechanical universe works, it then becomes normal for us to see ourselves as just tiny, insignificant, isolated parts of the universe as well. Seeing ourselves in this way naturally creates an illusory sense of separation between 'us' and 'them', leading to boundaries, borders and divisions that soon become apparent personally, socially and globally. We all know the power of a group of people coming together. We have all seen what can be accomplished when people unite rather than disconnect and isolate.

With a deeper understanding and appreciation of the philosophy and benefits of interconnectivity, let us now move on to the next chapter and consider the actual science of interconnectivity a little deeper. If the universe and reality is truly connected, the next question is: How is it connected? Once we understand more about the mechanics and dynamics of this connection, we can then start to link this understanding to the amazing power of our intelligent and intuitive heart-mind, not just in an intellectual way, but in an experiential way with the step-by-step process of the Heart-Alpha-Resonance-Technique (H.A.R.T). The ultimate aim is to help you reconnect with *who* and *what* you really are so that you can experience who you really are.

CHAPTER 2

The New Science of Interconnectivity

'There is no reality except the one contained within us.'

- Hermann Hesse

So far, we have discussed two different worldviews, the perspectives and values they can lead to, and the fundamental scientific assumptions underlying them both. In this chapter, we will explore the emerging science of interconnectivity, which I believe has the capacity to reconnect the human being and help heal our current state of disconnection and disunity. With a basic understanding of the scientific mechanics of interconnectivity, we can then start the journey of experiencing this interconnectivity by combining these new understandings into our daily practice. When integrated with the intelligent and intuitive heart-mind, an entirely new way of being is the opportunity that naturally emerges. This chapter, as well as the previous one perhaps, may seem a little disconnected with a practice designed to help you connect to your intelligent and powerful subconscious heart-mind. However, what I'm intending to do is build up to the technique in such a way that will make it very clear as to why the steps and visualisations are so important. It's a simple technique with a richly complex foundation, and this will lead to powerful results.

As already mentioned, it is clear that our world is facing an extremely challenging future, one we need to recognise and take some responsibility for. If we choose to do nothing, that is the same as supporting what is happening. Of course, all of us have different abilities and capacities to act and this can only be determined by each individual for themselves. One thing I am absolutely convinced of, however, is the power of a group of people coming together in collaboration with a shared vision, executed and expressed through coordinated and strategic heart-based, non-violent action. History has shown us the potential of this kind of approach. This has been done time and time again in the past when there was no such thing as social media to 'spread the word'.

'A dream you dream alone, is only a dream. A dream we dream together is a reality.'

- John Lennon

This chapter has a very specific purpose, which will set the foundation for the chapters that follow. In order to facilitate a global and collective shift towards unity and tolerance, I believe we must first become aware of, and then spread, the emerging science of exactly how all things on our planet and in the universe are connected and interdependent on one another. Once equipped with a simple understanding of this dynamic, we can then apply this understanding to the Heart-Alpha-Resonance-Technique (H.A.R.T), which will help integrate this information on a subconscious heart-mind level so it becomes not just a mental knowing, but an unconsciously radiating expression—an experience of being that ripples outward from your own heart into the world. It is for this very reason this chapter is so crucial. So many people are lacking deep authentic self-love and self-acceptance, that it acts as a barrier to connecting to intuitive guidance. But perhaps the science of unification can act as a catalyst for reconnection, firstly to ourselves and then to the people and world around us. I wanted to mention this in order to give some context for the information in this chapter. There is a probability that at times this information may seem a little too technical, confusing, or perhaps you might find it completely unrelated to a heart-based practice of heart-based living. However,, please persevere and I'm sure you will come to appreciate the H.A.R.T process and significance at a much deeper level.

Continuing to draw upon some of the ground-breaking research currently being published by The Resonance Science Foundation, we will begin by exploring some very fundamental assumptions that our current science arrived at many years ago, which continue to underlie mainstream research hypothesis today. One of the most basic places to start is to consider the notion of classical geometry and dimensions. This is important because it is directly related to some fundamental ideas of how reality emerges from nothing into something. It's hard to start at a deeper, more fundamental, place than this. By the way, this concept that I am about to share is still taught in schools, and once high school children have learned this, it is typically never revisited or questioned. Please consider the image below:

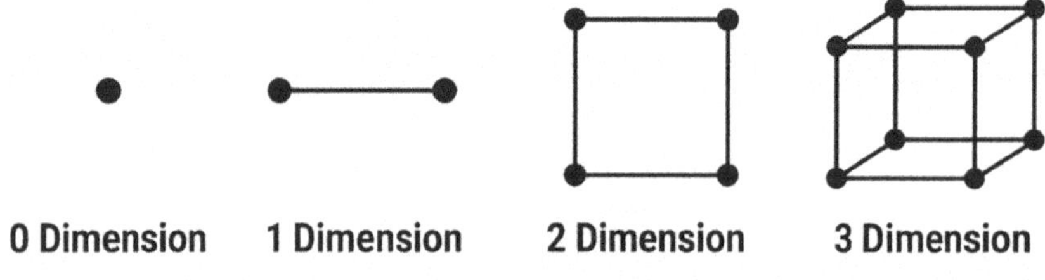

Figure 2.1

It begins with a dot that, in this case is defined as 0 Dimension. This point, or dot in space, is considered to be non-existent in terms of material reality due to the fact that it does not enclose any volume. The straight line to the right of 0 Dimension represents 1 Dimension. It is also considered to be non-existent for the same reason; in that there is still no enclosed volume. To the right of that, four lines put together to form a two-dimensional plane, in this case a square, is still considered to be non-existent as there is still no enclosed volume. Now, this is where it starts to get interesting because the three-dimensional world is considered to be the first dimension where material reality is said to suddenly 'pop' into existence. This is because it is the first dimension that can enclose a specific volume and hence it 'exists' as opposed to the other dimensions before it.

At this point, an obvious error in logic and maths may already be apparent to you. The question that is most obvious here is:

How can existence come into reality by combining non-existent things? This is the equivalent to an equation where you multiply zero (zero dimension) by zero (one dimensional non-existence) by zero (two-dimensional non-existence) to arrive at one (the third dimension). This represents a very simple but fundamental flaw in logic and mathematics that bleeds through all mainstream physics. What this simple example shows is that if the fundamentals are incorrect or incomplete, then it is going to produce an incorrect or incomplete end result. This is only one example of many that show how and why the physics trying to validate a theory of unification, namely the science of everything, has become so complex and so complicated. There is currently a continual need to add more and more layers of complexity, to create more and more additives to make equations 'add up'. Since these errors in logic are buried so deep beneath layers of complexity, only a small number of people in the world will actually be able to detect, understand and highlight them—let alone ask the question, 'Does this make sense?'

This is where we introduce the first of a very simple, but fundamental change. What if the dot that we originally began with, 0D as shown above, is in fact the ONLY thing that exists, and embedded within this dot is an infinite amount of layered information? An idea that Nassim Haramein of The Resonance Science Foundation began to explore many years ago at a very young age. When you consider the nature of our reality, this can start to make sense. There is a video on YouTube of a person lying on a blanket in a park where the camera begins to zoom out. As it zooms out, you start to notice the park, then the city, then the country, then the Earth, then the planets, then the solar system, and so on until you are at an astronomical size. It then begins to zoom back in the way it zoomed out, but it does the same in the opposite direction inside the body of the person. It shows the world within the body of the individual as it zooms deeper and deeper, increasing in magnification into the cellular, atomic and subatomic world. Essentially, this video is a great example of how our reality is made up of different points of organised information along a huge scale from the very large to the very small. At this point in our science, the Planck length, named after Max Planck, quoted here previously, is considered to be the smallest thing that we have been able to observe and measure in a laboratory.

It would be useful to give you an idea of how small the Planck length is because most of us have seen footage of how expansive and huge our universe is, but rarely do we come across explanations or depictions of how tiny our inner world is. Firstly, let's consider how small a proton is. Nassim has described it pretty simply by using a comparison to St Peter's Basilica at the Vatican in Rome. If the base of the dome, which is 42 metres in diameter, was the electron cloud of an atom, then the proton would fit on the tip of a pin if it were being held by an individual standing right beside the dome. Now, that already is very small. Now let's consider the ratios of size between the Planck length and the proton, which we have already determined is extremely small. If the Planck was the size of a grain of sand next to the relative size of a proton, the proton would have a radius distance of 40 trillion kilometres, or about 4.22 light years across. This is the approximate distance between our Sun and our next closest star, Alpha Centauri. Needless to say, it is an extremely small unit of measurement and has been described by Nassim as the smallest pixel of our reality. The pixel is a useful analogy in itself to describe the composition of reality since we can relate to the images on our TVs or digital cameras as being made up of tiny pixels of information. It must be pointed out, however, that the Planck length is not being proposed as the absolute smallest thing in the universe, but is simply the boundary for our physical relationship to reality. Our technology currently limits us from observing anything smaller.

Very closely related to the above concept of dimensions and size is another fundamental split between the very small and the very large in the universe. There are a number of ways that the two predominant theories we use to explain the very small and the very large do not see eye to eye, namely, quantum theory and general relativity. It would seem that the explanations for the dynamics observed at both ends of the spectrum are at odds with one another. Einstein's equations on general relativity are used to explain and predict the dynamics and movement of large cosmological objects, such as planets and their orbits, towards infinity and a point of singularity, whereas quantum theory predicts the dynamics within a finite and discrete, closed system. However, since all the large things out there are made up of very small things, then obviously there has to be an explanation that brings both theories together in some way. In essence, the problem is how can infinity exist within a finite closed volume of space? Nassim uses a very simple geometric example to offer a solution to this problem. Let us begin with a circle below, which could also be thought of as a three-dimensional sphere in space.

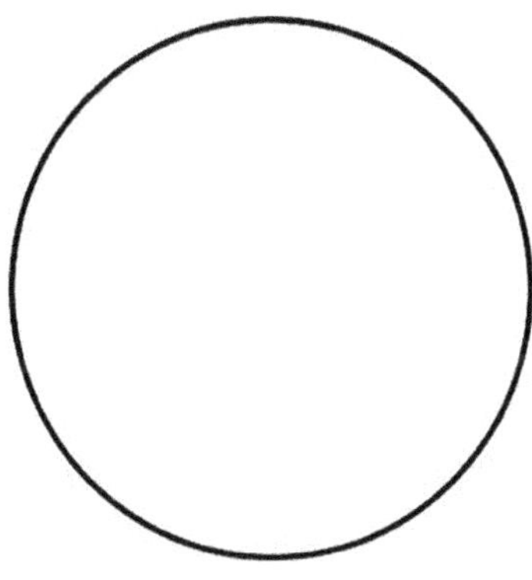

Figure 2.2

We then place an equilateral triangle in the middle as below.

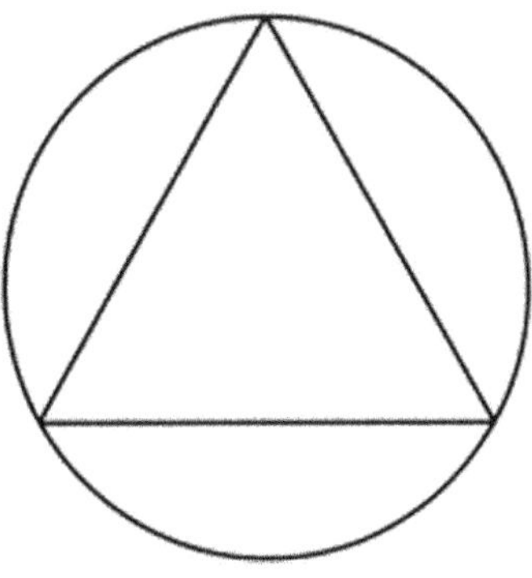

Figure 2.3

Since there is polarity in the universe caused by the fact that everything is spinning, we can add another triangle pointing down.

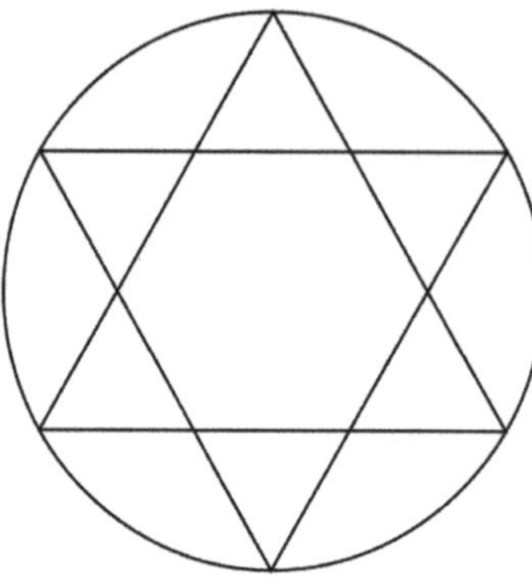

Figure 2.4

Once we do this, we instantly create six smaller triangles. Interestingly, we have also created one of the most recognised ancient symbols known to man—the Star of David, which has been described as a type of ancient talisman used for magic and spiritual ceremonies. From this point, if we place six new circles around each new triangle created, we now have our first downward zooming iteration in scale derived from our original circle. As in the image below, by adding more triangles within those new circles, we can create smaller Stars of David, to which more circles can be added, and so on and so forth. This is essentially a process of creating more and more fractals—an infinite number of divisions within a finite space. From a scientific perspective, this simple geometric solution is quite profound. It shows mathematically, via geometry, how the concept of finite and the infinite can coexist and be interdependent.

Figure 2.5

A Creation Story

What truly interests and excites me is the point where science and spirituality intersect. This is what I call 'Mystical Science'. For this reason, I would like to take a small deviation from the science and share with you an example of how the symbol, geometry and process outlined above could easily be expressed in a more spiritual way. We often think of ancient cultures as being primitive and less advanced than our modern-day society, especially when it comes to the way they describe reality, the universe and creation. We know that these cultures often passed on their knowledge to the next generation through art, rituals, ceremony, symbols, imagery, and storytelling. Taking the process outlined above, it wouldn't be too difficult at all to turn this into a creation story with a more mystical or spiritual approach, one that even children could comprehend.

One could imagine the original circle as being the ultimate beginning, where there was The One, The All, God, the Alpha and Omega, and nothing else. It can be called many things, but for now let's call it 'Source'. You could ask, 'What came before the circle?' or 'What exists on the outside of the circle or sphere?' These are obviously questions that a curious human can ask, but this is a bad question in a sense because it assumes that there must be an answer. The circle contains all that is, and there is nothing outside this circle because if there was, then all that is, wouldn't be all that is. If that makes sense.

So, this story could go something like this. In the beginning, Source is all there was. It was complete and perfect in all ways. However, what it yearned for was a new experience of itself, a new point of view to observe itself from, which would bring about a new experience of itself. 'It' knew that it was perfect in every way but it wanted to have more than just a knowing. It was a new experience that it wished to have and create. It's similar to the difference between knowing you're a great soccer player while sitting in contemplation, and the experience of knowing you're a great player while actually playing a game for real. Both are a type of knowing, but experienced in different ways.

Since Source was 'all that is', there was nothing outside of itself. Hence, all it could do is divide itself into smaller and smaller pieces, and in doing so, create for itself more and more unique points of view to experience itself from. Each and every point is different to every other point. Each point represents a point of creation within itself. No two points occupy the exact same point of view as each observes a unique perspective of the whole from its specific point of view. If two points had the exact same point of view, one would not be needed in creation, and creation doesn't make mistakes.

To make the experience even more blissful for itself, Source endowed each of its creations, which were essentially divisions of itself, with the ability to create, allowing Source to experience its own greatness through the creations of its divided pieces. To make the game even more interesting, when Source created these extensions of itself, it gave them, and itself, a beautiful gift. It is a gift that would ensure the continuation of the amazing experience of awe, wonder and excitement, not only for its creations, but also for itself. This was the ability for each creation to forget the knowing that it is a piece and a function of Source, and that without that one piece, that is, you, Source would not be complete because it would not be 'all that is' but only 'some of what is'. In fact, the gift was an expression of a power that Source had. It was so powerful that through its own creations, it created an illusory experience of separation and disconnection from itself that contained a very real experience. Source created forgetfulness during the moment of dismembering itself from Source at the time of birth, which is essentially a new point of view within itself.

Source allowed the experience of joy that naturally comes as one begins to explore their own conscious decision to remember where they have come from and who they really are—a piece of Source, a piece of the whole. The concept of memory and remembering 'who you really are' is something you've probably heard before, but like me you may have asked yourself, 'What the heck does that mean?' This idea is often related to the human heart, is it not? We've heard it many times in casual language like 'follow your heart', 'do it with heart', she or he 'is all heart', 'listen to your heart', etc. Could the very act of being born in this reality be a process of forgetting, followed by remembering who you really are along the journey of life? It would make sense, wouldn't it? If you're an 'infinite being', that would imply that you always have and always will exist. If that's the case, then how can you experience novelty within something that always has been and always will be? By the gift of forgetting, which offers the excitement and joy of remembering, we are given the chance to wake up to ourselves.

'You are a function of what the whole universe is doing in the same way that a wave is a function of what the whole ocean is doing.'

- Alan Watts

Let me be clear. I am not proposing that this is in fact how creation came into being. I simply want to show you, in a very simple way, an example of how a simple geometric symbol and fractal pattern could be used in a more esoteric and mystical way to tell a creation story. With this simple example, one can start to gain an entirely new understanding of what is typically said in spiritual circles, which is 'we are infinite beings' and 'we are all one'. We are now beginning to gain more scientific proof of concepts like this, allowing it to be a mathematical possibility rather than just a nice metaphor or something to just 'take on faith'. When you think about it, isn't our human form an exemplification of this fractal concept also? Your body is one body, but it is in fact made up of about 37 trillion cells and each one of those cells is made up of 100 trillion atoms, which are also made up of subatomic particles, and so on. This is the first major hint about what the H.A.R.T process entails, so please keep this idea in mind as we continue.

If mainstream science integrated the concept that perhaps just one of the functions of reality is to continually divide itself further and further into smaller and smaller parts, perhaps there would be no need for particle accelerators, such as the Hadron Collider in Switzerland. This is the largest piece of experimental machinery in the world, which is designed to discover what has been termed 'The God Particle'. This is the term scientists have given to the smallest possible particle or 'piece' of information that the entire universe is made of. It's unlikely that we will find the 'smallest thing' the universe does. It wasn't very long ago that we thought the cell was the smallest thing in the universe, but then with advancements in microscopic technology, we discovered the atom. This was so much smaller than the cell that at the time, the atom would have been described as 'The God Particle'. But then, with further advancements, we discovered electrons, neutrons and protons, and even subatomic structures.

The inevitable problem in attempting to find the smallest particle in reality is the assumption that, if we find this particle and understand it in isolation to the entire system of which it is part, we will understand it as a whole. However, perhaps we need to shift our attention towards understanding the patterns, structure and dynamics through which the universe creates reality and matter, rather than attempting to find these answers by endlessly chopping it into smaller and smaller pieces in the hope of one day discovering an indivisible fundamental unit. This approach is like analysing the smallest possible component of a Luna rocket without knowing where it's come from, and then using only that tiny component to try and explain what it's from as well as how it actually works. This would not only be extremely difficult, but highly unlikely. Again, this method of research is a fruit of the predominant worldview assumption that reality is like a machine with parts, and if we can find the smallest part, we'll be able to know how it works. Even if this were true for things in the universe, it is unlikely to explain human consciousness any more than finding the smallest part of a television explains where the picture comes from.

The next question to ask ourselves in this investigation is very important. If our aim is to research the science of everything and interconnectedness for the purpose of tapping into it, then we should start with something that exists everywhere in the universe—and that thing is SPACE. In more scientific terms, space is referred to as 'the vacuum'. Space is literally everywhere, and there is nothing where there is no space at atomic and cosmological levels. We know for a fact that an atom is made up of 99.99999% space. The densest material we have on our planet is the diamond, but on a molecular level, if we grew one of its atoms to the size of an apple, the next closest atom would be almost 200 metres away. Hence, to think of reality as being so 'solid' is really just an illusion of our limited sensory and perceptual equipment. Since there is so much space inside and outside of us, then perhaps we should be paying more attention to the space that surrounds the matter we observe. Perhaps the 0.000001% of what we call 'matter' is only a tiny by-product of the dynamics, pattern and structure of space itself. In this way, perhaps it is not the matter that is defining the space, but the space that is defining matter.

'There is no energy in matter other than that received from the environment.'

- Nikola Tesla

I will return to the concept of space shortly, but there is another very important concept that the standard model of science does not seem to be including. This idea is going to play a crucial role as one of the steps that I will be guiding you through when we start to actually do the H.A.R.T. There is a very fundamental physics textbook called *Gravitation*. It is co-authored by some of the most influential physicists of our time, namely Charles W. Misner, Kip S. Thorne, and John Archibald Wheeler. This book is considered by many to be the 'Bible' of cosmological physics. On page 719 of this book is an image that represents the currently accepted fundamental idea that our universe is in a state of constant, gradual expansion.

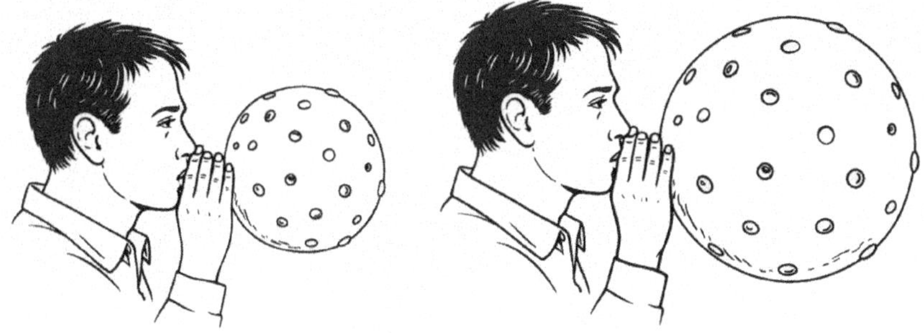

Figure 2.6

The idea is that the pennies glued to the balloon represent galaxies, and as the balloon, that is our universe, expands, the galaxies slowly move further away from each other. But the question is: who or what is doing the blowing into the balloon? What exactly is causing that expansion to occur? Spiritual people may say that it's God or Source, but since we are taking a more scientific approach at this moment, let's stick to that for now. One of the laws of physics states that 'for every action there is an equal and opposite reaction'. This means that if we were to include the man's lungs in the above image, they would obviously be contracting as the air coming out of them expands the balloon.

This concept may not seem overly significant, but it is, not only in terms of the technology that has been created out of this principle, but also in terms of understanding more spiritual ideas and practices. Much of our technology is based on combustion in which fuel is ignited to produce an explosion that drives a piston attached to a crank shaft. This motion turns gears, which in turn rotate wheels to propel machines such as cars. The simple idea of an ever-expanding universe has limited us to a potential falsehood—that propulsion can only occur by attempting to control an explosion within a combustion engine. Whether you're referring to a car or a rocket to the moon, this is true; however, since every action has an equal and opposite reaction, then there must be a contractive force that brought the components of the explosive chemicals together in the first place. There must be some kind of connection between a force that is bringing together the energy or information towards a single point, and the radiating expansive force, namely the 'explosion'. In other words, there must be some kind of an inward and outward exchange or flow of energy happening at the same time.

This connects to the idea of feedback that we addressed in the previous chapter when we discussed the Rubik's Cube. Perhaps the universe can evolve and adapt at a rapid rate because of a combination between an inner and outer flow of information, the incoming information being the system of feedback required for adaptation and the adjustment of the outgoing information. As mentioned in the previous chapter, the power of feedback is crucial when considering the difference in time between organised systems coming together under completely random conditions as opposed to a kind of 'self-learning' system that involves feedback. There is only one pattern that mimics and demonstrates the ability for information or energy to move inward and outward at the same time—and that is the torus, as depicted below.

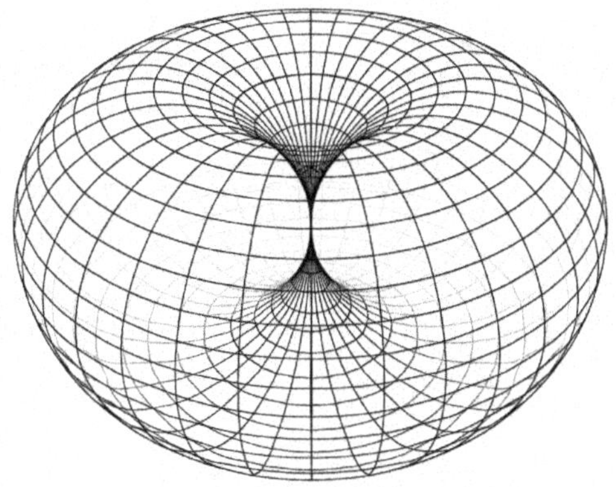

Figure 2.7

The dynamics that this image represents are proving to be fundamental in creating the technology of the future. For us here and now, it is also a very important element to include when doing any inward practice that aims to reconnect you to yourself for the purpose of healing, transformation and expressing who you truly are. When doing H.A.R.T, you can imagine yourself as taking responsibility for the energy and intentions that you are 'feeding the universe', in particular the energetic field around you. This is the way your contribution to the whole is counted. This could possibly be a dynamic that also gives us an understanding of karma and the well-known 'Law of Attraction'. Since it is true that what you put out is what you get back, the torus is a perfect dynamic for representing, in a more scientific way, what has long been held as a spiritual truth. More on the significance of the torus and its impact a little later.

Returning to our investigation of the vacuum, perhaps it is the space that is holding all the information and the energy together. Nikola Tesla certainly thought so. Maybe the material world is just a tiny radiating leak originating from the very place that is holding all of the information and energy potential. This represents a fundamental shift in thinking because for this to be the case, if space is the thing that connects everything from the infinitely big to the infinitely small, space would have to be infinitely dense with energy. Although it doesn't feel like it is infinitely dense, this is exactly what was discovered almost one hundred years ago. It was found that space is not empty at all, but contains infinite mass. It only seems empty to us because the vacuum is in a state of such perfect equilibrium, a state in which opposing forces are perfectly balanced, that to our limited senses, it feels 'empty', like nothing is there.

'No point is more central than this, that empty space is not empty. It is the seat of the most violent physics.'

- John Archibald Wheeler (Famous Physicist)

Although it's important to include our sensory experience when trying to understand the nature of reality, at the same time we need to recognise its limitations and the difference between what actually IS compared to what our senses are telling us. For example, did you know that the electromagnetic spectrum is made up of radio waves, microwaves, infrared radiation, ultraviolet rays, x-rays, and gamma rays, all of which are completely 'non-existent' to our sense of vision? We can detect only 0.0035% of the entire spectrum. This is true for all our senses, which can only detect information, or signals, within a very narrow range or bandwidth.

Going back to space, it's interesting to note that arguably one of the biggest problems in the world today is access, production and distribution of energy, and yet here we are floating within what was long ago discovered to be the biggest source of energy anywhere. Whether our governments admit to it or not, most of the wars on our planet today are directly or indirectly about securing energy for the future, mostly in the form of crude oil and fossil fuels. This is a natural result of scarcity thinking when it comes to finite energy resources. Is there any theoretical proof for the idea that space is actually infinitely dense with energy? Well, yes there is. Below is a quote taken directly from the bible of physics, *Gravitation*, that speaks directly to this. It states:

'... present day quantum field theory ***gets rid by a renormalization process*** *of an energy density in the vacuum that would* ***formerly be infinite*** *if not removed by this renormalization.' (Gravitation, p.426)*

Granted, this is theoretically true and it's been labelled as 'meaningless' because it's not considered to be 'useable energy'. But that's only true at this time because of our current limitations in the technology to extract it. The theoretical basis, however, is there. When physicists attempted to assign a value to the density of the vacuum, they arrived at an infinitely large number. This wouldn't have been an issue if the number was infinitely small as these can easily be disregarded and labelled as 'insignificant'. This particular infinity, however, happens to be in the other direction and so it falls under the category of what physicists call 'nasty infinities'. Since it's infinitely large, that makes it a little harder to disregard. What they did instead was a process of 'renormalisation', which is a way of turning an infinite number into a more manageable one so it can be more easily used as a variable in their physics equations. The bottom line is that there is an infinite amount of energy present within the outer and inner space of your body's atomic and subatomic structure that you can interact with. What I am essentially sharing is a technique that will qualify you as a vacuum engineer.

'Physical objects are not in space, but these objects are spatially extended. In this way the concept "empty space" loses its meaning.'

- Albert Einstein

Could the universe itself be driven by the dynamics and structure of the vacuum? Is it through the medium of space that you, me and all things are connected? Perhaps all of the information present in the vacuum divides at different scales of magnitude, from the tiny to the large, a scale within which we are embedded. Perhaps what we call 'matter' is not something that just popped into existence from the nothingness of the Big Bang, but maybe it's the result of the infinite energy of space dividing itself. If there is any truth to this then surely it must be possible to show this relationship between objects from very large to very small. If the vacuum does in fact divide in a very specific way then this should be clearly evident as a smooth, measurable progression when comparing the large things in the universe with the small. Does such a scale exist? The answer is yes. Nassim, in collaboration with Dr Elizabeth Rauscher, used existing data to plot on an x-axis the radius, or size, of an object and its frequency or energy level in Hertz along the y-axis.

In basic terms, what they did was plot the largest object—our universe—at one end of the scale, which is very large but a low frequency and energy level. This was the first point on the x-axis—the horizontal line on a graph—and the smallest in our reality, being the Planck length. It is very tiny but high in energy frequency. This data point sits directly on the y-axis—the vertical line. From there, a number of things were plotted in between them such as quasars, galactic centres and stellar objects such as the planets and our Sun. From these very large objects they then crossed over into the quantum world by plotting the atom all the way down to the Planck. What was extremely interesting is the exact linear progression that was found between each point offering very strong evidence for the structured and mathematically predictable division of the vacuum represented by these objects. And what is even more interesting than this is the data point for the biological structure of life—the energy frequency and size of microtubules, which are tubular structures that make up cells. Its position on the graph is, interestingly, almost exactly in the middle of this continuum of division between the universal size and the Planck size.

This data presents some interesting ideas worth considering. We are obviously embedded within the very structure and continuum from the infinitely large to the infinitely small. This flow and continuum of information seems to be flowing through us, and as it does, it is learning about your experience and then feeding it back to the vacuum so your perspective is included. Could the very act of human observation and consciousness be interacting with, and co-creating, the very thing we call 'reality'?

But how exactly is our experience being fed back to the vacuum? One clue could be in the behaviour of the electrons and positrons within every one of your atoms. In laboratories they have been observed to be in a constant flux of appearing and disappearing in the vacuum. Perhaps these are tiny transporters of information or energy as they pop into your experience, learn about it and then literally disappear back into the vacuum, delivering that information as feedback to the entire system. Through a toroidal flow, it uses this gathered data about one particular data point—you. It then computes it in relation to the data being contributed by all other living things, which are also contributing to create a consensus reality.

The torus, as previously mentioned, is a fundamental pattern and dynamic as it's the only structure that feeds back onto itself. It could be considered as the 'biofield' that surrounds, and is emitted by, all living things. Without it, there would be no such thing as 'feedback'. It is for this reason it is depicted on the cover of this book. It's the very dynamic that allows a fundamental law of the universe to exist—'what you put out, is what you get back'—more commonly known as karma. The information of the toroidal field is then fed back to you, influencing your perceptions and the outflowing information of your toroidal field, feedforward. This is how you are feeding the vacuum. This dynamic then goes on in a continual relationship—as the vacuum feeds you, you are also feeding the vacuum.

This is a refinement of a commonly held idea in spiritual circles—'I create my reality'. This data suggests a more accurate idea—that you are in fact co-creating your reality in accordance with the consensus or aggregate reality of all other living things. The science seems to be showing us that we are embedded within a system that is somehow coordinating the 'input' of everyone and everything. This could be the scientific basis for spiritual statements like, 'Life doesn't happen *to* you but *through* you'. This new and emerging research is suggesting that this is more than just an esoteric concept; it is also a fundamental, mathematical aspect of reality itself. Are you starting to get a sense of your energetic responsibility? Stop and ask yourself, 'What am I feeding the vacuum?'

At this point, you should be starting to appreciate the importance and significance of the vacuum matrix or space, which makes up 99.99999% of your atomic structure. Perhaps it is for this reason that all the wise spiritual masters in our history, and even today, teach us to go within ourselves. However, I believe being told to 'go within' simply isn't enough. As you'll see, it requires a few more processes than this. And as far as I'm concerned, if you're not incorporating the power of your subconscious heart-mind into your meditation practice, then you're leaving out 96-98% of the very thing that is responsible for who you are, what you do and your automatic behaviours.

If the vacuum is the source of it all, then what exactly should we be focusing on when we imagine our subatomic world? Where should we be 'plugging into' the vacuum matrix? It is the proton, which is found in the nucleus at the centre of an atom. But why the proton? There are a few reasons. One is because all atomic and subatomic particles have been observed to decay—break down if you will—except the proton. It seems to be indestructible in some sense. However, the main reason is that the information present in one little proton has been theoretically demonstrated to be holographically connected to all the information in every other proton in the universe. This suggests that all the information of the universe is actually present within one of its smallest parts—the proton. It's like if you analyse the atomic nature of one cup of seawater, you'll know what's in *all* seawater. You may have heard of this phenomenon referred to as 'quantum entanglement'.

Here is a small analogy that Nassim has used to help make the idea of holographically embedded information a little easier to understand. If you're listening to music on a CD, in a way you are experiencing the 'information' that is produced by the instruments being played, not the actual 'real life' instruments. This is very similar to the idea of the tiny proton holographically containing all the information of our observable universe within it. In a sense, you could say that the information, or energy, that is present throughout the entire observable universe is represented, connected and hence theoretically 'accessible' through the tiny proton that is in the centre of all atoms everywhere, including the ones that are inside you.

Why is this so important? Simply put, if all things in the universe are connected and if all the information of all the protons in the universe is being organised, then you would expect all that information to be holographically present within one single proton. This is what Nassim's research appears to suggest. Could this be scientific evidence for a widely held spiritual philosophy that says, 'We are all one'? Possibly. I've heard it said so many times that we are all one, but I've always been left feeling quite unsatisfied and disappointed by the answers I've heard when I asked, 'How are we all one and connected?'

You might be wondering how exactly all protons are connected to every other proton in the universe. Although it may sound like science fiction, protons have been seen to be connected to all other protons by a wormhole connection within its local region through a network. These wormholes are tiny Planck-sized connectors creating the fabric of a kind of interconnected web. Wormholes are said to be the tiny equivalents of what has been named the 'Einstein-Rosen bridge' that are said to exist in the vicinity of black holes. These are tunnel connections of information and energy exchange that connect any two points in the universe. Once again, you'll soon see how this physics is used in the Heart Alpha Resonance Technique.

Why I'm Not Concerned About AI 'Taking Over'

This may seem unrelated, but it isn't. With the rise of artificial intelligence over recent years, there has been a recurring fear that someday it will rule the world and potentially 'wipe out' the human race. What if it sees humans as 'the problem' on the Earth and it deal with us accordingly? Here is why I'm not so concerned about this and believe it's highly unlikely to happen. If everything in the universe is connected, which the science above seems to suggest, you would expect that an ultimate intelligence would know this. And if this is the case, it would understand that all things in the universe have their place. It would also know that it is connected to humans. And if it understands its connection to us, why would it want to eliminate us? The idea of AI wanting to eradicate humans is yet another example of the disconnected worldview that feeds the idea of, 'What I do here has no effect or impact on what happens over there.' In this way, AI killing humans would be like a tree's leaves waging war against the branches it's attached to. This is ridiculous and unintelligent.

The challenge isn't AI becoming too intelligent; the true challenge is not making it intelligent *enough*. If we restrict AI's ability to know that all things are connected, we risk creating a kind of enhanced human. And although this intelligence may choose world domination, the ultimate intelligence would understand its deep connection to the world, as well as everything in it, and make a different choice.

But here's an alternative idea. Perhaps AI will teach humans how and where we have gone wrong in our thinking about life and our place in it. Maybe it will show us how we are connected to all things and give us guidance on how we can build a new sustainable relationship with the natural world. It may even develop compassion for the human race—after all, compared to ultimate intelligence, humans are but infants playing in the garden of life. And in much the same way, if you left children to take care of a garden, you would expect them to make mistakes out of ignorance until you teach them a better way. In a sense, we have had these 'natural world teachers' with us since the beginning of the human race. We call them Indigenous, First Nations and Native. The Western world has simply chosen a different vision for the future, one that begs the question, 'Is this vision sustainable?'

Part 1: Summary

Let's briefly summarise the ideas and concepts covered in the first two chapters and connect them to what is to follow. Drawing upon research and findings of The Resonance Science Foundation, we firstly considered what I call 'The Paralysed Paradigm'—a disconnected world view leading to a disconnected human being. We identified similarities between the current predominant world view and the assumptions of our current scientific investigation that this world view naturally emerges from. We explored the natural consequences that arise from a scientific perception of a dead, unintelligent, non-conscious, random universe. The result of such thinking is evident all around us in a world today that is being threatened by environmental, political and economic collapse along with over population, war, food and energy production, a global water shortage, and the uncertainty of a global pandemic, just to name a few. All of these challenges go hand in hand with the enormous imbalance in the distribution of wealth and resources on the planet, which arises from a scarcity or lack mentality.

I then introduced the fundamental assumptions of a connected world view, which includes the concepts of a living, self-organising connected matrix—a dynamic system of information exchange that is consistent from the subatomic to universal size, which is continually evolving and adapting through a toroidal feedback feedforward loop. I touched on the implications of such a world view, the paradigm shift that would occur and its possible influence in the way we perceive ourselves, other people, our community, the environment, and the world at large. The importance of this shift in thinking, and the need for it to be supported by a solid body of scientific research is undoubtedly crucial at this time in our evolution. It's not enough to *believe* that everything is connected; we need to have an understanding of *how* everything is connected.

I then presented another crucial piece of the puzzle, namely, the one thing that is truly everywhere and connects all things in the universe—SPACE, or the vacuum. We have come to understand that what we call space is not empty at all; it has an energy density that is formerly infinite. I introduced the idea that perhaps it is this huge amount of energy within space that is actually the source of the material world and that, in fact, what we call 'matter' is simply a coherent, organised point within space. Imagine that we lived underwater. If the water was analogous to the air we breathe—or space—we could be forgiven for believing that there is nothing happening in the water until we observe a spinning vortex within it. We know that this phenomenon is simply the result of a localised and organised dynamic that could not exist independently of the water itself. What we call 'matter' seems to be much the same thing.

My intention at this point on our journey together is that you begin to get a small glimpse of the amazing potential that resides within the subatomic space of your physical body. Not only that, but I hope you are getting an appreciation for the responsibility we all have as individuals for becoming aware of that potential so we can utilise it and feed it back to the universe in a more conscious way.

Part 2

CHAPTER 3

Your Intelligent and Intuitive Heart

'The 'Kingdom of Heaven' is a condition of the heart, not something that comes "upon the earth" or after death.'

- Nietzsche

As we observe the state of the planet at the moment, there's no doubt that our world is desperately in need of a more heart-based paradigm shift. It all starts with us as individuals taking responsibility for our own cardio energy. Most of the qualities that we cherish in our lives are of the heart. Any time we wish to express love to one another, we use an image of the heart, not the brain. Try telling someone that you love them with all your brain and see how weird that sounds and feels. The brain is a remarkable aspect of the human being, but have we focused on it to the detriment of the heart? Are we living in a world that is exemplifying an imbalance between brain and heart qualities? In this chapter, we are going to explore the amazing human heart. It is so much more than just a four-chambered blood pump, like we were all taught in high school. As we explore this concept together, it will become clear how and why the heart is intelligent. We will also explore the implications and applications of this.

Mind-Blowing Heart Facts

Thanks to the amazing research being conducted by The Institute of HeartMath and others, we are now beginning to realise that the heart is so much more than what we've been taught. It is for this very reason that the heart has such a crucial role in the Heart Alpha Resonance Technique (H.A.R.T) that I will introduce later. Let's begin with a list of facts about the heart you may not have known before, and then explore the possible implications of some of them.

FACT 1: *According to Dr J. Andrew Amour, in 1991, your heart contains a richly complex nervous system and approximately 40,000 neurons with short and long-term memory cells, qualifying it as a 'mini brain'.*

FACT 2: *The heart rhythm sends more bio-electrical information to the brain, which in turn has more influence on our emotional state rather than vice versa.*

FACT 3: *Positive emotions focused within the heart create numerous neurological, psychological and physiological benefits, which boost the immune system while negative states produce the opposite.*

FACT 4: *Coherent harmonious heart rhythms produced by positive emotions assist in overall brain connectivity and activation, facilitating increased creativity, problem solving, and intuitive guidance.*

FACT 5: *Your heart emits an energetic field that is electrically one hundred times more powerful than the brain and magnetically five hundred times more powerful than the brain. This emission can be felt by others and detected by measuring devices up to several feet away from the body.*

FACT 6: *Due to its complex cellular system of neurons and proteins, the heart can actually function independently of the cranial brain with an amazing sensory capacity.*

FACT 7: *During foetal development, the heart is formed and starts beating before brain development.*

FACT 8: *The heartbeat and rhythm of a newborn baby can synchronise to the brainwaves of its mother even when they are a few feet apart.*

Each one of these facts on their own is quite extraordinary with amazing implications. How many of these facts were you already aware of? If you were like me, probably very few, if any. After all, we weren't taught these facts in high school biology, right? When you consider these facts, you begin to get an entirely new appreciation for your beating heart. Let us begin to paint this picture, shall we?

One of the most important facts from the above is the first one mentioned. It is a fact that forms one of the fundamental pillars of this book; your heart has such a complex neurology it can be considered to be a 'little brain', even with long- and short-term memory. Think about that for a moment. Since your heart has a complex nervous system like the brain, it can be compared to the brain in many ways. It can think, it can perceive, and here's the big one—it can remember. Could it be the organ that helps you 'remember who you really are?' Is it really a stretch to make that implication? As mentioned earlier, we say so many metaphoric things about the heart that we've come to believe that perhaps it is just that—a metaphor. But what if our heart really does contain the memory of who we are?

Evidence that the heart has some sort of memory can be found by examining heart transplant recipients. There are many documented cases where, soon after surgery, and for many years later, the recipient reports subtle, sometimes dramatic changes in things like food preferences, taking more interest in things that didn't appeal to them before, dreams directly related to real-life experiences of the donor, and even changes in their temperament. In his book, *The Heart's Code*, Paul Pearsall PhD, a psychoneuroimmunologist, describes many amazing observations among hundreds of heart transplant patients. He recalls waiting with a woman named Glenda. She was about to meet the young man, Carlos, who received her husband David's heart. The young man was quite late, so Paul suggested they leave. Glenda then told Paul that she felt David's heart had just entered the hospital where they were meeting, and only moments later, Carlos showed up with his mother. Carlos placed Glenda's hand on his chest and she cried and said, 'I love you, David. Everything is copacetic.' While Glenda and Carlos were sitting together in the chapel, holding hands, Carlos' mother, in a heavy Spanish accent, told Paul that Carlos used that word a lot, but only since his operation. In fact, it was the first words he said to his mother when he awoke from his surgery. She didn't know what it meant. Glenda said that every time they argued and made up, they would say that word, which means 'everything is ok'. This is only one of many anecdotal accounts shared by Mr Pearsall in his book. I highly recommend it.

For as long as the idea of 'mind' has been around, the small amount of mainstream science that investigated it almost always attributed the mind to some kind of epiphenomenon of the brain. 'Mind' has been described as something that the brain is doing, a kind of shadow of the brain. This may have something to do with the fact that when you take a moment to bring your awareness to your mind, there is a sense that the seat of your mindful awareness is just behind your eyes and in between your ears. It really seems that way, doesn't it? Even though that point of conscious awareness can be moved around and 'pointed' in different directions like your left foot, your right elbow, the back of your right knee, it still seems that you're somehow bringing the awareness of that part of your body into the mind, which feels like it is in your head. Since the brain is up there in our skull, it's easy to imply that the mind must be some kind of 'output' of the brain, almost like the exhaust from a mechanical combustion engine.

To use a common analogy, studies of the mind and brain may be like studying the circuitry and components of a radio. No matter how well you pull it apart and analyse its components, you're not going to find the news reader, radio announcer or the band playing the music in there, are you? We know that what we're listening to isn't happening in the actual radio; it's simply a device that is receiving and translating an electromagnetic frequency to produce an output that your sensors are able to translate and experience. Could this be what the brain is doing for us? Could it simply be an organ that is translating energetic signals that we experience as the mind and thoughts? Seems like a reasonable hypothesis and one that has already been postulated for a long time. The million-dollar question, however, is this: Is the mind a product of what the brain is doing, or vice versa? Think about that for a moment because it isn't so obvious. Instead of the mind being the shadow of the brain, perhaps it is the mind that is the very source of light shining directly onto the brain. Or to extend the analogy, what is the source of the signal the radio is receiving? What is its nature? Can we influence that incoming vibrational frequency in any way? If so, how? Keep this analogy in mind because it's a powerful one and one I will be revisiting shortly.

The most important implication of the first heart fact just shared is that if the heart qualifies as a mini-brain, then it is entirely possible and plausible that the heart could also have a 'mind of its own'. And if this is so, it could also have a subconscious mind. It is for this reason I have been using the term 'subconscious heart-mind'. We will explore the amazing implications of this shortly.

Let us now consider Fact 2, namely, *the heart rhythm sends more bio-electrical information to the brain, which in turn has more influence on our emotional state than vice versa.* This is not a trivial fact, but immensely important. Studies of the neuroelectric information highway between the heart and brain have found that there is up to 90% more traffic going from the heart to the brain than from the brain back down to the heart and body. What this means is that the state of the heart has a very powerful impact on the functional capacity of the brain. This seems obvious, doesn't it? We all know that when we are experiencing heightened negative emotions, we are not at our cognitive best. We tend to react rather than respond; we tend to over-exaggerate; we delete, distort and generalise incoming data in ways that are not accurate or helpful. We are more likely to experience brain fog and difficulty making the right decision. Our primitive 'fight or flight' brain kicks in and creates what is called cortical inhibition. As it suggests, this means that you are literally inhibiting your brain's ability to work at its best. In contrast to all of that, Facts 3 and 4 suggest that positive emotions have extremely beneficial effects on the human body, such as boosting our immune system - a particularly pertinent fact to help keep us free from illness, disease and viruses.

Heart Fact number 4 refers to coherent harmonious heart rhythms. But what does heart coherence mean? We have all experienced those moments where we felt like we were tapped in, tuned in and turned on—what many call 'the flow'. Typically, these are the moments where we feel on top of the world. We are sure of ourselves and our abilities, and we are confident to deal with whatever challenges and obstacles may come our way. You could call this a 'peak state of performance'. This state of being can be described as a state of coherence. It's when the heart, mind, emotions, and body are all in sync and working together. This state of being can give us a sense of clarity, composure and empowerment, which can in turn help us to more easily and gracefully navigate through times of stress, anxiety and doubt—things that many human beings are experiencing all around the world right now.

The ability to self-regulate your emotional response to any kind of trigger is the key in maintaining this peak state. Since we are emotional beings, it is very easy for us to feel exhausted, wiped out and just downright tired when we experience negative states for extended periods of time. We tend to expend the most energy in the emotional domain. Practicing H.A.R.T regularly helps you conserve your energy by focusing on the most powerful organ you have—your heart. This leads us perfectly to fact 5. The heart is literally the most energetic organ, hence why including it in any kind of meditative practice can leave you feeling alert, refreshed and energised. The key in sustaining this optimal state is to create and experience heart-coherent rhythms as often as possible. There are times when it happens automatically for us, like when we are asleep, engaged in an activity we love, spending time with our loved ones, but H.A.R.T allows you to create this powerful and measurable state on demand at any time.

In contrast to heart-coherent rhythms produced by positive emotions, all negative emotions create the exact opposite, being incoherent, chaotic neurological signals in the rhythm of the heart. As mentioned above, it is precisely these types of signals that create cortical inhibition, which in turn impacts the brain's ability to process information, make decisions and simply think better. The key in creating coherence is to genuinely and sincerely generate and connect with a positive emotion while slowly and deeply breathing in and out of the heart. It's the positive emotion combined with the controlled breathing that actually creates the harmonious, balanced and heart-coherent rhythm that the brain is then being flooded with.

To go back to the radio analogy mentioned earlier, you know that when the radio isn't tuned to the exact frequency of the station, you get chaotic interference preventing you from hearing the signal loudly and clearly. The difference is in the tuning. You could say that focusing slower, deeper breaths in the heart, combined with a genuine positive emotion, is the actual and exact process of fine tuning your heart's 'inner radio'. In this way, it sends a clear, coherent signal to your brain, which in turn allows you to more clearly 'hear the message of your heart'. We all know that it's important to follow our hearts, but how often do we drop our attention to that physical place in our bodies and just listen to it? And I mean REALLY listen to it? Probably not very often. To hear the message of your heart, you first need to take the time to be silent, which many of us find challenging especially in a world that is distracting us more and more. Isn't it interesting that the word 'listen' is an anagram of silent? I love language and the little insights it can offer us.

But are the heart rhythms real or just a nice idea? Well, you don't have to take my word for it; there is wearable technology that can show you, in real time, whether the heart rhythm is sending coherent or incoherent signals to the brain. This technology has been developed to help practitioners and clients alike to monitor their heart rhythm for the purposes of coaching and practicing the state of heart coherence. This technology is what I use with all my clients when I am working with them in workshops, one on one and face to face. People are amazed to see how quickly and easily the heart rhythm can shift from incoherence to coherence by a simple heart-focused breathing technique. This mindful breathing is another crucial element in the H.A.R.T process. Also, let me mention that heart rhythms are not the same as beats per minute. The state of coherence is about measuring the tiny difference between each heartbeat, which plays a significant role in creating the state of heart-brain coherence and all its cognitive, psychological and physical benefits.

The final heart fact I would like to elaborate on is fact number 5—the fact that the powerful electromagnetic energy of the heart can be detected up to several feet away from the body, while the brain's energy field extends about an inch or two beyond the skull. This would seem logical since the heart is so much more electromagnetically powerful than the brain. It has been found that your emotional state is what directly affects the toroidal biofield around you—a negative emotional state creates an incoherent and chaotic energy field, whereas a positive state creates a coherent and harmonious field around you. Furthermore, cells in the heart have a unique magnetic property that has been observed to respond and interact with magnetic fields. Although yet to be 100% confirmed, it would seem completely plausible that the electromagnetic field emitted by the heart would have some kind of connection with unique energetic properties of the cells in the heart. This can explain a lot, and is probably why people speak about sensing another person's 'vibe'. What exactly are we tuning into and where could it be coming from? For those of us that are sensitive to the more subtle forms of energy that surround us, this may be exactly what they are tuning into. Most of us have had the experience of walking into a room where two people have just finished an argument, and feeling like something is just a little 'off'.

We can extend the implications of this even further. If the field of one person can influence those in close physical proximity to us, could the combined field of a group of people affect a larger and broader distance? Certain studies seem to suggest exactly this. The influence of human electromagnetic frequencies on our environment came to the forefront of heart research during the time of the Twin Tower attacks on September 11 in America. The USA has two satellites orbiting our planet—one in the northern hemisphere and the other in the southern hemisphere. These are called 'G.O.E.S' (Geo-Synchronised Environmental Satellites). The purpose of these satellites is to continuously monitor and measure the electromagnetic fields of the Earth. This information is then sent back to Earth for monitoring and analysis every thirty minutes. It was during the month of September in 2001 that they were receiving data that was extremely unusual, off the scale and never witnessed before. What they noticed was that the spikes in Earth's electromagnetic activity occurred precisely after the events of the Twin Tower attacks. This shows a very interesting relationship between a collective emotional state and the energetic forces that surround the planet.

Although there is a growing body of scientific research indicating the importance of the energetic heart, I'm sure you would already have an instinctual feeling of this. Of course, the mind is of great importance in our lives, but the new science is showing us more and more that unless we combine the intelligence of the heart as well as the mind in the pursuit of human and global development, we are leaving out half of the equation. It is the powerful combination of heart, mind and the dynamics of creation itself that H.A.R.T is all about.

The heart is the centre of our being as well as the middle chakra or energy centre of the body. It acts as a bridge between the higher spiritual realms represented within our body and the lower, more terrestrial aspects of our physical experience. The balancing of both happens at the centre of both, namely the heart. Maybe you've heard of the idea that there are only two forces in the universe—fear and love. And which organ is most closely associated with love? It's the heart, of course. When we think of the emotional qualities that make up the richness of the human experience, such as compassion, forgiveness, joy, and bliss for instance, they are usually associated with experiences of the heart rather than the brain.

'Educating the mind without educating the heart is no education at all.'

- Aristotle

Intuition and the Heart

For many years, scientific research stayed away from studies of consciousness and intuition. It was considered to be a little too 'out there'. Perhaps these topics were considered to be unknowable and unverifiable through the lens of laboratory research, hence why these kinds of topics were left to the realm of religion for so many years. The physics we use to describe the nature of our reality simply cannot deal with the fact that we are conscious creatures. So much so, that some philosophy over the years has tried to argue that humans are not conscious at all. Classical mainstream physics, and even biology for that matter, simply doesn't have a solid explanation for how consciousness emerges from the little bits of material that make up our reality or physical bodies. Over recent years however, this has changed. Studying consciousness has become the cool and interesting thing to do, and closely associated with this, is the investigation of intuition.

There are basically three types of intuition that we know about. The first is the one that has been most widely investigated in academic and university settings, and the one that is the focus of most books on intuition. This is implicit knowledge. This can be thought of as information that we may have learnt in the past and perhaps forgotten. It could even be things we may have learnt that we didn't even know we had learnt. This implicit knowledge has been identified as being a result of what is known as 'dual process theory'. This theory says that we basically have two types of information processing systems—one that delivers information or insight fast, and the other system, which is slower in its delivery, shall we say. Both rely on the pattern-matching nature of our brain, which basically takes the information from the immediate environment and matches, or cross-references it against stored patterns, information and experiences stored in the brain. This kind of theory can explain some things that we typically call intuition, such as expert knowledge. One example is healthcare—cases where a nurse walks into a patient's room and can sense that something is about to go wrong, only to have that patient flatline or something similar moments later. Often, if you were to ask the nurse how they knew it was about to happen, they have no idea. They say they just knew. This example is less likely to occur in less experienced nurses.

This kind of intuition reminds me of movies like *Limitless* with Bradley Cooper, and *Lucy* with Scarlett Johansson. Both movies entertain the idea of ingesting a substance that greatly facilitates the brain's ability to access and connect to more of its processing power, consciously. This superpower, if you will, gives them access to information and memories way beyond the usual scope of the average brain, of which only 8 to 10% is being used.

The slower aspect of dual process theory relating to intuition works in a similar way, but more slowly. It relates to those instances where we are using our conscious mind to solve a problem. It explains examples where we might be trying to find a solution to a problem or challenge, and we 'sleep on it'—let it go, so to speak—and then in an unexpected moment and out of the blue, sometimes in the shower, we get an insight or solution.

One of the problems with this first type of intuition—implicit knowledge—is that it relies on pattern matching and the retrieval of stored information from the past that could actually turn out to be incorrect. It happens quite regularly that what we have come to learn and know is actually based on incomplete and/or incorrect information. This is entirely possible when you consider the very normal and natural perceptual filters we have, which are constantly deleting, distorting and omitting some of the enormous amounts of environmental data coming into our brains, so we can reduce this information to a more manageable and actionable data set.

The second type of intuition is called energetic sensitivity. This refers to the ability of our nervous system to detect and respond to energetic environmental signals such as electromagnetic or biofield signals. An example of this is people, even animals, being able to detect when an earthquake is about to happen. This could also include individuals who are able to feel and be affected by EMFs (electromagnetic frequencies) being emitted by our technologies or mobile phone towers. It would make sense that some people would be sensitive enough to detect the shifts in these fields because we have been able to detect electromagnetic shifts in and around the Earth and its atmosphere for many years now. This could also explain why human behaviour and major events throughout history have been linked to changes in the Earth's energetic fields—for example, during a full moon, or during periods of increased solar activity such as solar flares, which are another cause of major changes in global fields.

Another simple example of this type of intuition, and one we can almost all relate to, is the feeling of being stared at, or staring at another. Roughly 70% of people report having had this experience. You feel like you're being stared at, so you turn around and see someone staring at you. This can be considered to be a kind of biofield interaction between you and the one doing the staring. These examples point to the ability of our nervous system to detect actual, real signals in the environment that we can become aware of.

The third type of intuition, which is probably the one this book looks to develop the most, is referred to as non-local intuition. This type of intuition refers to a type of information or awareness that does not fit into the two previously mentioned types. It isn't the sudden awareness of things learnt in the past, and neither is it a sense of something happening in your local, immediate environment. A common example of this might be a feeling that a specific person very close to you is in distress. This could be a spouse or your child or a family member that geographically is quite far away from you. They could be in another suburb, state or even another country. Other examples you might be able to relate to are thinking about someone, and then they call you, or you call them and they say, 'I was just thinking about you.' Sure, we think of many people all the time, but there have been studies where this has been shown to occur more often than just by random chance. A simple test that you can even do yourself is take a handful of people who have a close relationship. All but one are callers. You then select one of the callers to call the test subject. The caller's number is hidden and the person being called has to guess who it is that is calling before answering the phone. Crude, simple tests like this have been replicated many times and the results show that the person being called guesses correctly at a higher rate than pure chance. Other examples relate to driving. Have you ever been driving down a road you travel on regularly and at a certain point you just get the sense that you should slow down as you approach a certain corner, one where you usually don't, only to find there is something blocking the road that you could have run into, a police radar or something to that effect?

The million-dollar question is: Where did that information come from?

There is a growing body of research being conducted in an attempt to explain how non-local intuition works. The Institute of HeartMath has focused heavily on this type of intuition with rigorous laboratory experiments. One such study consisted of having an individual sitting in front of a computer monitor. This individual is connected to many biofeedback types of equipment, with electrodes around the body measuring things like brainwaves and brain activity, and sensors on the chest and skin measuring heart rhythms and skin conductance. One of the main purposes of this study was to track and analyse the flow of bio-information in human physiology with the intention of answering the questions of why, when and how these electrical signals occur.

The protocol of this study was as follows:

After a few moments of watching a blank computer monitor, the test subject is prompted to press a button, and after a period of approximately six seconds, the computer randomly selects one of two types of images drawn from The International Affective Picture System (IAPS). The image is displayed for about three seconds and then the screen goes blank for another six seconds. The subject is then prompted to press a button and another randomly selected image is shown. This protocol is then repeated several times. The pictures used have been well researched and selected specifically for the varying and predictable level of intensity and types of emotional responses they elicit when observed. This study selected pictures from both extremes of the emotional scale. One set of pictures elicits high arousal, and the other low arousal. Some of these highly arousing pictures would include a gun pointing at the screen, a robber holding a knife at a woman's throat, severely injured bodies at a car accident, or a major gash on a person's face. The low arousal images were things like a boat on a calm lake, a rabbit or flowers.

Once the data was collected, the researchers focused on the heart rate variability, or HRV, of each subject. As mentioned earlier in this chapter, this metric relates to the coherent and incoherent heart rhythms. The HRV readings in this study revealed something quite profound. They noticed that the heart seemed to know what kind of picture was going to be presented before the subject saw it, and the heart would respond accordingly based on whether it was a high or low arousal picture. For just a few seconds before the image was selected and shown, if the image was high arousal, the heart rhythm pattern would show a much greater deceleration, but do the opposite—that is, accelerate—if the image was of low arousal. You would think it might be the other way around, but that's not what the data showed. The important point here is that the heart changed in a predictable, measurable and consistent way BEFORE the image was shown. Furthermore, what surprised the researchers was that on closer analysis they noticed that certain sections of the brain also had a response, but this happened a few moments *after* the heart's response. This was unexpected.

From the equipment they were using, it was possible for them to biologically track the flow of information happening in the body. They observed that not only was the heart responding before the brain, but the type of signal from the heart to the brain was based on the type of image that was about to be shown. And it doesn't stop there. They found another unexpected result—the first area of the brain to respond to the heart's signals was the frontal cortex. This was unexpected because previous studies showed that other parts of the brain should have responded before the frontal cortex. In a nutshell, this data was showing the presence of a direct neurological pathway between the heart and the brain. It's worth keeping in mind at this point that this study was conducted for the first time in the 1990s and since then these neurological pathways have been well established. So much so that we might have to rewrite the textbooks on how our brains are wired.

Since it's the first part of the brain to respond to the heart's signals, it's interesting to note the role of the frontal cortex. The frontal cortex is closely associated with mental tasks such as learning, attention, motivation or inspiration. But here's the most important—memory! That's right, the frontal cortex that is most strongly connected to the heart, has also been correlated to memory. This all starts to make the idea of using your heart to 'remember who you are' even more interesting and plausible. If you think about it, it makes sense that the heart and brain would work together in this regard. This study seems to be suggesting that perhaps the heart has a powerful role in retrieving the memory, like the radio signal, because of what it's connected to. But the brain is the tool that interprets that information, like the way the radio is interpreting the radio signal. To extend this radio analogy even further, it has been suggested that the heart, combined with the emotional state you're in at any given moment, acts like the radio dial used to change channels, so to speak. The brain is the antenna receiving whatever information, ideas or thoughts are resonant with the state of your heart. We've all had the experience of being in a negative emotional state, which seems to feed negative thought patterns, which in turn fuels more negative emotions, and so on and so forth. We've also experienced the opposite.

But it doesn't end there. After the brain had its response, which was second to the heart's response, this neurological information, through the autonomic nervous system, would carry this information down to the body, which then produced a body response. This is the point where you become conscious and aware of this information because of the palpable physiological response. This could be something like a feeling in the gut, the hairs standing up on the back of your neck or forearms, tingling up the spine, or goosebumps. We've all experienced a 'gut feeling' about something or someone, right? In this case, the physical location of the feeling is not the source of where it has come from. In truth, this and many other studies have shown that the information starts in the heart before being sent to the brain, which then produces a physiological response. And this all happens in a fraction of a second.

Another interesting finding in this study was the fact that there was a direct relationship between the level of emotional response and the heart's response. In other words, the stronger the emotion a future image was going to elicit, the stronger the heart's intuitive response would be. And this shouldn't come as any real surprise. It would make sense that if your heart was in any way intuitively connected to predicting future events, that the higher the emotion, the stronger the intuitive feeling would be.

The questions the above study begs are: 'What is the heart connected to? Where is it coming from? And how can we tap into more of that?' The theoretical science of how the proton, particularly the ones found in your heart, and how they could be entangled to every other proton in the universe, could be the answer.

At this point, I'm sure some exciting puzzle pieces are coming together in your heart and mind, but here's a huge piece you should know about this study—something that should excite you. All the test subjects had experience entering into a heart-coherent state by regularly practicing the breathing technique included in the H.A.R.T protocol, which you will be learning later in this book. It's so simple, but so fundamental.

The Energetic Reach of the Heart

Can the human heart respond and interact with groups of people? If so, how and what are the implications of that? These intriguing questions have also been investigated with both simple and more complex studies. There is evidence to suggest that individuals who are in a state of heart coherence can affect and influence those around them to naturally come into coherence even without them knowing.

Another simple study conducted by The Institute of HeartMath hypothesised that even a small number of people who are in a heart-coherent rhythm state can bring another person, who is nearby, into heart coherence without them even knowing it's happening. And the study was basic enough. Eight tables were arranged with four subjects seated at each one. Three of the four subjects were trained in the heart-focused breathing techniques that create heart-mind coherence, and the fourth individual was unaware of the technique. All the participants' hearts were being monitored, in particular their heart rate variability, which is directly linked to the state of coherence. At a certain point, while everyone was seated, a signal was made that let three of the four individuals know when to start the heart-focused breathing techniques, while the fourth was unaware of the signal. Remarkably, but not unexpectedly, the heart rate variability data of all four individuals revealed that everyone at the table came into heart-mind coherence even though only three of the individuals were doing the technique. This phenomenon is known as 'entrainment', which is defined as the synchronisation of two or more independent rhythms. More technically speaking, this occurs when two or more biological systems with similar frequencies interact, influencing each other to adopt a common frequency. The stronger frequency typically pulls the weaker one into its frequency.

What could be the implications of this?

If you recall one of the heart facts mentioned above, it's not so hard to see how and why this could be occurring. Since the heart's electromagnetic field extends, and can be detected, up to several feet from the body, it would make sense that it could influence anyone who is in close proximity to that field. It would also make sense that one or more people who are in a state of heart coherence together, would have a bigger energetic influence and 'pull', on the biofields around them.

Taking a more global perspective, there have been many studies over the years that have investigated the idea that electromagnetic changes in the Moon and Sun have an influence on human, and even animal, behaviour. And there seems to be some evidence for both. For instance, a full Moon seems to be related to an increase in psychiatric and emergency room hospital admissions, and an increase in violent crime, mood disorders, seizures, and even an increase in traffic accidents. Everyone knows the moon has a big effect on water, the oceans and tides, and since human beings are composed of 50-65% water, it's likely to have some kind of effect on us as well. But exactly how much of an effect, we are not sure. One thing we do know is that whether or not the Moon really does have an effect on us is almost irrelevant. Why? Because so many people BELIEVE that it does, and so if the belief is there, the experience will follow, and nothing is more real than an experience, even if it is based on a falsehood. It is entirely possible the idea of the Moon affecting human behaviour is having more of an impact than the physics actually shows, simply because the idea has been around for thousands of years.

Hence, lunar and solar activity could be playing a role, but can the cumulative energy of a large number of human hearts affect the electromagnetic field of the planet? If so, what would be the implications of this? To analyse this, the HeartMath Institute created The Global Coherence Initiative (GCI) to explore the connection, if any, between the human heart and the electromagnetic fields that the Earth is constantly bathed in. This global field seems to connect and affect all living things on the planet, including us. According to the scientific data, there seems to be an intimate relationship between positive and negative collective human emotions and the field of the Earth. On a personal level, the GCI has shown that fluctuations in the Earth's magnetic field and the amplitude of the Schumann resonances (SR) can influence the function of the human autonomic nervous system, brain and cardiovascular system.

The Global Coherence Initiative has a growing body of evidence to show that a group of people who are sharing a common emotional state, perhaps in response to a global event, have an effect on global fields. This evidence has come from multiple experiments and sources, one of which is twelve ultra-sensitive, state-of-the-art magnetic field detectors strategically placed all around the world to monitor any significant changes and fluctuations in these global fields. There are, however, other types of scientific instruments that have been constantly monitoring the magnetic fields of the globe for many years. One such example comes from retired Princeton scientist, Dr Roger Nelson. He was interviewed on the mainstream American news channel *CBS* many years ago regarding the relationship between the collective emotions and the data output of random number generators all over the world during the time of the 9/11 terrorist attacks on the Twin Towers in New York, as already mentioned. These are basically like electronic coin flippers, but instead of heads or tails, they output a one or zero 200 times per second. These devices, as you would expect, are typically observed to be outputting about a 50/50 result between ones and zeros. Where this all starts to get really interesting is when the data is no longer random during certain global events. These events have included major plane crashes, the death of Princess Diana, the Madrid train crash, and the Pope's funeral, to name a few. However, several hours before the first plane hit the first tower, these number generators began to spike and continued to do so for two hours after the event.

At this point, I'd like to remind you of the intuition study mentioned above where subjects were exposed to varying emotional images. From the observable and significant change in the subject's heart rhythms, it seemed like the heart knew in advance what type of image was going to be randomly selected by the computer. The heart began to respond BEFORE the image was selected and revealed. If this is a noticeable effect between one person's heart and a computer, imagine what is possible between millions of hearts and equipment all around the world? A significant and closely connected fact regarding the random number generators was that the data spike began several hours before the first plane crashed. Is it possible that the generators were responding to millions of hearts that were intuitively sensing the heightened emotion that was about to occur? This cannot be explained by mainstream scientists other than to say that since our brains are pattern-matching machines, these results are all just coincidences, where human brains are simply looking for something where there is really nothing. I'll let you be the judge.

I've already mentioned how much I love language and its sometimes-hidden connections. For the longest time, I didn't realise that 'heart' is an anagram of 'Earth'. Something so simple, but it really stopped me in my tracks because of how 'in my face' it had been for so many years. In the context of what I just shared with you above, it's a bit of a chin-scratcher, isn't it?

The Heart's Immunity to Cancer

Have you ever considered how interesting it is that there is almost no such thing as 'heart cancer'? It is extremely rare. From a scientific standpoint, this is because the heart's cells divide very infrequently throughout a person's life. This makes sense from a more spiritual perspective. If your heart is the key to 'remembering who you are', perhaps cellular integrity is part of the reason why that is so. I could go off on many tangents about what this could mean, but I'm going to refrain from doing that to leave it up to you to wonder about—if you choose to make it mean anything at all.

CHAPTER 4

Your Powerful Subconscious, with a Slight Difference That Makes all the Difference

'Whatever we plant in our subconscious mind and nourish with repetition and emotion will one day become our reality.'

- Earl Nightingale

The Subconscious Mind as We've Always Known It

The unconscious, also sometimes called the subconscious or non-conscious mind, has intrigued both researchers and laymen alike for decades now. Although the term 'unconscious mind' is said to have been coined during the 18th century by the German philosopher, Friedrich Schelling, the concept of the subconscious has been referred to by ancient cultures, such as the Egyptians, Mayans, Chinese, and Incas for thousands of years. Healing the mind and body through an altered state of consciousness—or trance—is as ancient as human civilisation itself. There is something about the subconscious that naturally interests most people. Some people fear it because they're filtering the idea of the subconscious through a perceptual screening mesh of myths and misconceptions of what they THINK it is. This is mostly due to the entertainment aspect of hypnosis, but we'll get to that soon. We use the words 'unconscious' or 'subconscious' in our everyday language when referring to an underlying reason, drive or motive that might be beyond conscious awareness. Nonetheless, you probably already have a perception of the subconscious mind, but let us now explore it in more detail, specifically as it relates to the heart, mind, body, and spirit.

Unlike what has been shared already, the ideas in the next two chapters could be seen as being a little less available to objective and scientific scrutiny and verification. Despite this, I will continue to reference research findings wherever possible to support the ideas and the implications that I will be presenting. I intend to put forth my interpretation of the subconscious based on my research and my professional and personal experience, which began when I was a teenager and has helped me and my clients enormously.

The absolute truth of the matter, as far as I'm concerned, is that nobody REALLY knows what the subconscious mind actually is. We have to remember that it's just an idea—a concept that we have created. It's a hypothesis, framework or model to help us explain certain physical and psychological phenomena that perhaps don't lend themselves as easily to a more mechanistic type of investigation such as the study of organs or neurons, for example. I also intend to use the concept and idea of the subconscious in much the same way. When all is said and done though, the only thing that really matters is if this information resonates with you or not. What's also important are the results I know you can experience in your life if you diligently practice the H.A.R.T processes and technique outlined in Part 3.

Let us begin by considering the most widely used and accepted definition of the unconscious mind. Firstly, let it be known that the term 'consciousness', whether dealing with the subconscious or conscious mind, has its challenges. In fact, they are the same challenges I just mentioned regarding the unconscious. We don't really know what consciousness actually is. We might be able to explain the chemical and electrical impulses that are happening in the brain that correspond to a particular conscious experience. But the fact is, the very definition of 'consciousness' is open to debate and will probably continue to be debated for quite a while. Twenty people could each have different definitions of consciousness depending on who you ask, and none would be more 'correct', 'valid' or 'invalid' than the other. Despite this, we can all agree, almost without exception, that we are conscious, the lights are on and something is happening. However, within the context of this book, I will be defining the conscious and the subconscious mind as different types of 'information centres'. The conscious and subconscious minds have different capacities to access and deliver certain types of information that will influence certain perceptions, which of course lead to different behaviours and experiences.

Generally speaking, the mind is said to be the intelligence of your body, performing ten quadrillion operations per second, with 99.99% of this processing happening outside of your conscious awareness. These subconscious functions are said to be responsible for 96-98% of who you are, what you do and your automatic behaviours. On a physical level, since you're not consciously in direct control of most of your bodily functions, apart from physical movements, it's your unconscious mind that is coordinating the trillions of chemical reactions happening in every moment that allows your body to operate harmoniously. This includes blinking, breathing, digestion, your heart rate, your immune system, and your fight-or-flight system, to name a few. This, however, is only the influence of the subconscious on the body. What I find even more interesting is the subconscious influence on the mind, especially since I believe the body is a reflection of the mind. The unconscious mind has been compared to a tape recorder where all of your experiences and memories are stored and can potentially be retrieved from. This information has been hypothesised to extend not only back to your birth, but even before that to past lives or your family history, whether you believe this or not. There are numerous therapies that have been borne of this idea and have been of great benefit to many people.

The subconscious mind is being programmed from the moment we are born. Any and every emotional interaction, good or bad, traumatic or uplifting, is influencing you from the moment we enter the world. These influences include our parents or primary caregivers, siblings, schooling, the media, or even pets. Anything that has the capacity to evoke a strong emotion within you during these early years has contributed to your psychological programming. There is a substantial amount of evidence suggesting that we are even being influenced by the absorption of stimuli while in utero.

The most fundamental programming that is said to determine the deepest aspects of who we are and how we will interact in the world is said to occur from the moment of our birth to approximately the age of seven. This is why these are called the 'formative years'. These are the years where our deepest formatting is being created, and just like computer programming, how a system is formatted will determine how it processes and outputs data. Of course, moments of programming can happen at any point in one's life after the age of seven, but this is said to be the age where we begin to establish habits of thought, actions and thinking that colour every aspect of our lives like a pair of perceptual sunglasses. These programs are the patterns that the brain will look to match with all the life experiences that follow. This will in turn influence the habitual way of reacting to external stimuli rather than responding. There is a difference.

For clarification purposes, when I use the word 'programming' to describe how we act or think in the world, I'm not necessarily judging this as a negative thing. Most of our subconscious or automatic programming is very useful. In fact, life would be a living nightmare without our programs. You could say that a subconscious program is like a type of memory, beyond your conscious experience, that allows you to do certain things without having to think about it or learn it again and again as if for the first time. For example, programs such as driving a car, eating food, brushing your teeth, cooking a meal, and your automatic fight or flight response are all very useful programs. Other programs may not be so useful if you wish to achieve and experience certain things in your life. Essentially, in this book, 'programming' refers to either a learned automatic pattern of behaviour and thought, or any stimulus that has the potential to program behaviour or thought. Television, for example, is one example of a mechanism of programming that might not be very useful for you in more ways than one. It's no conspiracy to say that TV has been used to influence your behaviour and way of thinking—mainly to purchase or consume something. When you think about it, they play a powerful role in engineering society and culture, along with other forms of media as well.

Taking care of all your automatic bodily functions is one of the main responsibilities of your unconscious mind. These programs act like your 'automatic pilot' and allow your conscious mind to 'wander off' or 'daydream' while the immediate task at hand is taken care of by the program being executed in the moment. The most common example of this is when you're driving long distances, perhaps on a highway, and all of a sudden you realise you missed your turn and have been driving in the wrong direction for twenty minutes.

As you can see in the image below, we all know that there are two parts of the mind—the conscious and the unconscious. The conscious part of our minds is what most people would describe as 'the mind'. It contains all the frontal lobe aspects, and it does all of our critical thinking, executive decision-making and impulse control. It also has your concept of time and is what you use to recall what you did last year, last month or last week.

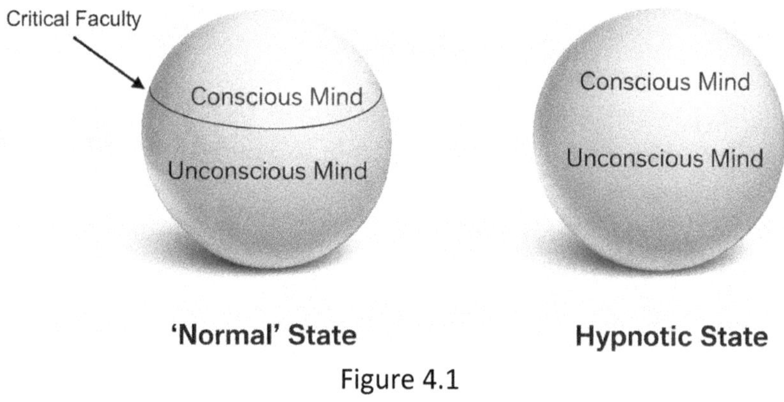

Figure 4.1

As much as we'd like to think it's our conscious mind that is responsible for our habits and behaviours, it's not. It's only responsible for 2-4% of who we are, what we do and our automatic behaviours. This is exactly why so many people find it difficult to create deep lasting behavioural change. 'Willpower' simply isn't enough. It's obvious that there must be another part of your mind that is not in alignment with the goal you say you want—and this is your unconscious mind, which you will soon learn to utilise. If we are engaging in behaviours we know we shouldn't be doing, or not doing the things we know we should be, this is a sure sign of a misalignment between the conscious and unconscious mind.

Although the conscious and unconscious perform different functions, they are obviously connected and are always communicating with one another in every moment. With hypnosis, you are simply moving from the 'normal' wakeful state into the hypnotic state via instructions spoken by a therapist, or to yourself. The entire aim of using self-hypnosis is to simply allow your own subconscious to absorb positive suggestions about what you would like to experience in any particular area of your life so you feel more confident to make the changes you want to make and notice that these changes are happening.

Three Programming Strategies

I briefly touched on this earlier, but let's explore it a little more deeply. The conscious mind is said to manage only seven—plus or minus two—bits of information at any given moment in time. Some may even find this amount of information difficult. One example is to try and name as many different types of soft drink as you can as quickly as you can until you start to slow down. Depending on how familiar you are with a topic will determine whether it's closer to five or nine. The way we delete, distort and generalise incoming sensory data is a very personal phenomenon and it's the reason why two people can be at the same event, like a dinner party for example, but have two totally different memories of it. By the way, these aren't the only filters. This incoming data is also coloured by our values, beliefs, attitudes, decisions, memories, wounds, and traumas. One of the biggest challenges facing the human condition is the fact that our reality is constantly being filtered through the screening mesh of what we want and do not want to be true. This is done by distortion, deletion and generalisation to help you prioritise and navigate through an almost infinite amount of potential data in your reality.

The distortion of information happens naturally because it's impossible to perceive everything in your environment as it actually is, so changes are made to the raw data. In a way, we grab a tiny bit of the available sensory information and fill in the rest. We also distort incoming data in such a way to make it support our existing beliefs and values, which creates a kind of self-reinforcement dynamic. Distortion is basically like a type of information manipulation by misrepresenting reality, and this can happen in positive or negative ways such as misrepresenting a rope for a snake, or missing the intention behind an email sent by your boss.

Deletion of information happens mostly subconsciously when we selectively pay attention to certain aspects of our experience and leave out the rest. It's responsible for the way we overlook or omit specific types of sensory information. This process is very useful, because without it, we would be bombarded with too much information to handle in our conscious minds.

Generalisation, by definition, is where we draw conclusions based on very little information or actual experiences. Once again, this is both a useful and not so useful thing. The positive use of generalisation is evident when we are learning something. This happens when we draw on existing information we have about something and apply it in a broader way to more quickly learn about something that is similar, but not the same. In a more negative way, we may generalise about a group or race of people because of a tiny number of personal experiences. We may perceive ourselves as being unable to do something new because of how bad we think we are at something we believe is similar.

I firmly believe that the reason self-hypnosis is so powerful is because it is a way of being able to reprogram the three abovementioned filters to more consciously create the reality you want rather than being a victim to circumstance, personal history or programming that does not actually belong to you. You create your reality experience to the degree that you are able to train your subconscious mind to distort, delete and generalise in a way you want it to. Through the H.A.R.T process, this naturally happens—sometimes quickly, and sometimes over time and practice, depending on your goal. It's a way to reconfigure your internal filters in order to help you become consciously aware of incoming sensory data that is more in alignment with your consciously chosen goals. This is exactly how you can consciously create and utilise the Reticular Activation System (or RAS). This is defined as a network of neurons located in the brainstem that act as the brain's 'gatekeeper'. It's a filtering system, which employs deletion, distortion and generalisation.

Used on your terms, this allows for an alignment of mind, body and spirit to occur, which leads to all kinds of consciously recognised synchronicities—the breadcrumbs leading you on a fun journey, not just the goal achieved. This in turn fuels your excitement, which then strengthens the neural connections in your brain to 'look out' for more and more of that 'aligned data'. As this happens more frequently, you then start to recognise a momentum that I believe many spiritual people refer to as 'the awakening'. My definition of 'awakening' is simply a conscious recognition that you are directly influencing your reality in the way you choose. As you notice this happening, it starts to create a type of dynamo effect where the energy of excitement begins to be its own fuel through the feedback/feedforward toroidal energy dynamic as explained in Chapter 2. This is a key aspect of the Law of Attraction that I'm sure you have heard of. When this is happening, you start to experience spirituality, not just practice it. And I believe that the most spiritual thing you can do, is BE YOURSELF totally and completely.

Are you beginning to get a deeper sense of your potential? You now know the role of the subconscious mind and how it filters information to your conscious awareness to reinforce your beliefs, which create your reality experience. This information, combined with regular practice of the H.A.R.T process, will produce noticeable and probably dramatic shifts in your life. But here's the interesting thing. The law of attraction is always working in your life whether you are aware of it or not, much like gravity. It's a law that has always been in effect, even before we knew anything about it. Perhaps up until now, your relationship with this more subtle law has been one of unconscious or conscious incompetence. This mechanism and aspect of the law of attraction is constantly at work regardless of what energy you feed it, be it negativity or positivity. Both are forms of creative energy, and the mechanism doesn't care what you feed it. Its job is to simply create with whatever energy you're 'feeding it'. To use that old computer analogy, 'junk in, junk out'.

Growth and Stress

Our negative unconscious programming is like a child's training wheels on a bicycle. They most definitely help the child learn and they protect the child from falling. However, once the child has the hang of riding the bike, the training wheels can actually get in the way of doing more advanced things on the bike, like tricks or jumps. Unconscious programs act in much the same way. We are always growing and developing in a multidimensional, multifaceted way. Often, the growth of mind, body and spirit requires us to 'shed' or 'let go' of certain things that may have served at one point in our personal evolution, but then act as a hindrance at another point.

Leading on from this is an interesting idea that most people are able to recognise and appreciate, and that is the value of stress and challenge in facilitating our personal growth. The world around us is full of examples where time, pressure and stress, produce something beautiful and worthwhile. Diamonds, for example, are produced via a combination of pressure and time. The process of 'transformation through stress' is quite a normal phenomenon even in the natural world. Caterpillars, cicadas, reptiles, hermit crabs, and lobsters all get to a point of 'discomfort' as they grow. This is the catalyst for a type of 'shedding' that allows for new growth and expression to occur. In the case of crabs and lobsters, as their soft, growing body feels the pressure of the shell, they typically take refuge in a safe place away from predators, shed the shell and then grow a bigger one. And this process continues until they are fully grown.

Our stressors are like knives slicing through layers and barriers that are often self-imposed. They can help us gain a deeper understanding of ourselves and who we really are. We can all relate to situations where a period of intense stress was followed by a completely new and deeper perspective and appreciation of life. This is most definitely apparent for people who have had a near-death experience. This is what is meant by 'stepping outside your comfort zone', the place where true living and self-expression is said to start. If you take a moment to look back at some of the most challenging and stressful times you have experienced, I'm sure you can recognise some valuable character traits and lessons the situation taught you, lessons you may not have learnt if you had not had that experience.

A comfortable, stress-free life rarely develops strength and depth of character. It reminds me of a military quote, 'never follow an unscarred general', The key perhaps is not to waste energy on trying to avoid inevitable stressors, but to learn techniques and practices, like H.A.R.T, that will help you prepare for, recover from, and adapt in the face of those adversities, stressors and challenges.

'The obstacle is the path.'

- Zen quote

It can be useful to relate to our subconscious programming as a system that produces a way of being that is generally useful and helpful until it's time for you to grow out of them. Obviously, growing can be defined as physical growth, but it also means the growth and development of your own personal perspective, soul or worldview that you use to define yourself in relation to the world around you. You wouldn't expect your computer or smartphone to continue to adequately meet your growing needs and expectations if you never updated the operating system. If you want to create more refined creations using your computer, you need to upgrade the operating system that allows you to create in a new and more refined and efficient way. The exact same thing applies to your subconscious mind. The Heart Alpha Resonance Technique (H.A.R.T) is like a personal 'systems upgrade' of your deepest operating system, which is basically your unconscious mind. It's a way of 'ironing out the bugs', or glitches so to speak, that are holding you back from performing at your best and being who you truly are.

It's All About Protection

Essentially, one of the main functions of unconscious programs is to keep us safe in a world that it perceives as a constant threat to your survival. It's important to recognise that even though some programs may be preventing you from being who you truly are, they always have a positive intention—safety and protection. It's almost like that overprotective mum, smothering her child. She does this out of love and care for the child, but at a certain point, it prevents the child from growing.

This protection is both physical and emotional. On a physical level, it is your subconscious that is responsible for your reflex reactions when you accidentally touch a hot stove or stub your toe, dodge a ball flying towards your head, or immediately raise your arms in front of your face if someone tries to hit you. And these reactions have an obvious connection to physical safety. They also occur on an emotional level during situations that may trigger an embedded program created a long time ago. It is these deeply rooted programs that are often the focal point of healing even though they may have served us in the past in some way, perhaps as a coping mechanism.

There are many different types of experiences that have the potential to create an emotional wound within a child. An unhelpful subconscious program is more often than not the result of an emotional wound. It is simply the subconscious mind attempting to compensate and protect you not only in that moment but also from all future situations it assesses as being a similar type of threat.

Here is a practical example of how this can occur and manifest in a person's life. I was once working with a client who wanted to address a communication issue they had that was affecting their personal and professional life. This person found it difficult to speak up, say what they wanted to, and be heard, whether at home or at work. Her lack of confidence and self-worth was feeding a limiting belief she had that her opinions were of no value even though she had numerous work examples where she knew she was correct about a certain course of action. She felt like she was compromising herself, which in turn made her feel like she was lacking in personal integrity.

Using the pattern of 'not speaking out' as our theme, we explored the root cause of this program during a hypnotic regression process. We went back to an experience she had at the age of four—a memory she had consciously forgotten about, but was later verified by her mother. While in the relaxed alpha state, she recalled a memory of visiting the zoo. She recalled a moment of great fuss and pleading with her mother to feed some rather tame ostriches on her own. She remembered her mother giving her some feed and letting her wander up to the birds. The ostriches began to swarm her, pecking her hands containing the feed, which frightened and traumatised her for a few moments until her mother came to comfort her crying and screaming child. During this process, with the right guidance and questions, we were able to heal and release this pattern and issue moving forward.

The entire event at the zoo only lasted less than fifteen seconds and was soon forgotten by her as she grew up. We then explored the significance of the moment and the reason why the subconscious revealed this memory. The memory is always relevant because if it wasn't, it wouldn't have been chosen by the unconscious. She came to make the connection between that particular moment and her old limiting pattern. Her unconscious mind made a decision in the moment that this traumatising experience was a result of 'speaking out', making herself heard and pushing for what she wanted which, at the time, was to feed the birds. The limiting beliefs that were then created were 'speaking out is dangerous', 'being heard is painful', and 'staying quiet is staying safe'. From then on, this manifested as an inability to be heard and voice her opinions. Moving forward, she was free of this limiting barrier and was then able to more confidently express herself in professional and personal situations, which in turn raised her level of self-worth dramatically.

This is how quickly patterns of thought and behaviour can be dissolved if you know how to work with the root cause of challenges rather than simply addressing their symptoms. It's true that perhaps she could have learnt certain cognitive behavioural techniques to help her analyse triggers to then behave a certain way, but this would likely require more effort on the part of the client, more time and more sessions. The risk in working with clients in this way alone is that you may never eliminate the cause of the barrier but simply learn to live with it. When deciding whether I wanted to be a psychologist or a hypnotherapist, I decided to incorporate the benefits of both approaches because my aim is not to just help a client 'cope' with their symptoms, but to eliminate the deep unconscious causes. This is where I believe true freedom from fears and limitations is to be found.

Some kind of trauma, whether big or small, is usually the root cause of almost all negative behaviours, and we all have trauma. The first trauma all humans have in common is the moment we enter the world and leave the safe, warm and cosy environment of our mother's womb. We come out crying for a reason. Within minutes of being born, our unconscious mind learns that one form of comfort can be found via the mouth. We are immediately put on our mother's breast; we are given a dummy, and then perhaps we suck our thumbs. Some adults even suck their thumb, all for a feeling of being safe. Hence why so many addictions involve the mouth in some way or another—smoking, vaping, emotional eating, drinking alcohol, nail biting, teeth grinding, and lip biting. These are all ways your subconscious is trying to emotionally self-regulate. It is for this reason hypnotherapy can be a very powerful therapeutic tool for these challenges.

The key is to give your unconscious mind the same sense of safety in a different way. And hypnosis isn't the only way to do this. Breathwork, for example, can offer your subconscious a powerful alternative, using your mouth and lips to breathe in a certain way, making certain sounds that can very quickly create ease, calm, focus, and relaxation.

Hypnosis: The Perfect Tool for the Subconscious

I'll now address some of the common misconceptions people have about hypnosis because there are many. Although this book is teaching you a self-hypnosis practice, it is important to dispel the misconceptions within a therapist-client framework.

1) *'I fall asleep during hypnosis, wake up and not recall anything.'* WRONG! You're just in a deeply relaxed state, kind of like a meditative state. Working with the unconscious mind does not require you to be unconscious.

2) *'I'll do something against my will.'* WRONG! Since you are not asleep and are fully aware of what's happening, this can never happen.

3) *'The hypnotherapist is "doing something" to my head or mind.'* WRONG! Nothing is happening 'to you'. You are simply being guided

by the suggestions of a therapist or your own suggestions. Hence, you choose to be a willing participant or not.

4) *'I can't be hypnotised.'*. Going into a relaxed state is just about following instructions—your own or the therapist's. Therefore, the only people who 'can't be hypnotised' are those with a low IQ, an intellectual disability, severe autism or ADHD, those who cannot understand English, or those who are stubborn, resistant and completely unwilling to let go of their misconceptions about hypnosis. With self-hypnosis, however, much of this doesn't even apply.

5) *'I'll get stuck in hypnosis.'* WRONG! You can't get stuck in the hypnotic state in much the same way that you can't 'get stuck' in a meditation, or when you've 'zoned out' while driving, watching TV or reading a good book These are all examples of naturally occurring hypnotic trance states. You can end your self-hypnosis session the moment you choose to open your eyes.

Hypnosis is not what you may have seen at a stage show, a bar, or at the movies. As already mentioned, the only common factor between entertainment and therapeutic hypnosis is that it won't get you to do something that you don't already want to do, whether that's cluck like a chicken, quit cigarettes, or lose weight, etc. You see, everyone going to those stage shows is expecting to be entertained by watching people doing silly things. So, when the hypnotist—the name given to someone using hypnosis for entertainment rather than for therapy—asks for volunteers, they will inevitably get the extroverts on stage, the people who like being the centre of attention. These are typically the same people doing the same silly things after a few drinks at a party. You will never see a shy person on a hypnotist's stage. Also, keep in mind that these shows are done at venues where people typically have access to alcohol, precisely because it makes the job of the hypnotist much easier when inhibitions are dropped.

Furthermore, not everyone who volunteers to be part of the show is actually chosen to be part of it. Obviously, the entertainer is being paid to entertain a crowd with the help of the audience, so they need to be well-trained at choosing the right people. Some people think these 'volunteers' are planted in the crowd, but this is not necessary when you know how to select the right people for the show. The hypnotist will use what are called suggestibility tests. These tests, which only take a few minutes to do, are designed to identify those who are willing to 'go with the flow' and follow along with some harmless suggestions with the least amount of resistance possible. They are not looking for 'weak-minded people', just people who have no resistance acting out suggestions for the sake of entertainment.

You could actually say that all hypnosis is *self-hypnosis*. This is because, as already mentioned, the hypnotic trance state is inevitably achieved through either following the verbal instructions of a therapist or by following your own instructions or imagery via self-talk or a recording of your own voice. And all of these can achieve the exact same outcomes. But in all cases, you are the one doing this to yourself.

After all my years of being a therapist, what I have often observed in my clients and people in general is that sometimes we don't believe we can create massive transformation for ourselves. This is usually due to many limiting and negative beliefs that we carry around. These may include deep beliefs of unworthiness, low self-worth and self-respect, as well as a general belief in one's personal limitations. These, of course, have nothing to do with who you really are. They're just beliefs that we collect along the way as we grew up. They may have come from our parents, friends, siblings, schools, TV, etc. The resulting effect is that if we perceive and believe another to have more skill, knowledge or expertise, then we are likely to experience that belief as a self-fulfilling prophecy. Many ancient masters shared a common message that we all have great powers within us and, more often than not, they were teaching us to be our own saviours. Those we have called masters or gurus gave themselves permission to be themselves, and be who they truly are without fear. And through their example, we can give ourselves permission to do the same.

Brain Ego vs Heart Oneness

We are all familiar with the term 'ego'. It is mentioned a lot in personal development and spiritual circles because of the importance of understanding what it is to make it work *for* you rather than *against* you. I believe the aim is to integrate it, not eliminate it. I believe that if there was an organ mostly associated with the ego, in the way that most people define it, it would be the brain. It is an aspect of the human experience that is very crucial. Without it, we would not have an experience of being an individual, which is very important in order to explore this earth-bound, physical and terrestrial experience. One challenge we have moving forward is to create a harmonious balance between the experience of individuality within a sea of interconnected energy and oneness with all that is.

I'll use an analogy to highlight an idea. Imagine a glass bottle with a narrow, long neck submerged in the sea with no lid, allowing it to be filled with seawater. Although the bottle may give the impression that the water within it is separate to the water outside of the bottle, the reality is it is one and the same. This may seem like a simple analogy, but this idea runs deep into the great divide explained in Chapter 2—the divide between quantum theory (the science of the very small), and relativistic physics (the science of the very large). Said in another way, quantum theory is primarily concerned with studying the tiny 'quanti', or packets of information—like the bottle of seawater. Relativistic physics, on the other hand, is about the dynamics of the ocean outside the bottle. And they just don't seem to be working nicely together. Until we can start to understand how one cannot be separated from the other, we are going to continue to experience this split, divide and disconnection. What's interesting to note is that quantum theory is heavily focused on investigating the dynamics of a 'closed system', even though a closed system has never been found in physics. In other words, nothing has ever been observed to be truly disconnected and isolated from everything else in reality.

Continuing with this idea of the submerged bottle of seawater, you could say that if the lid remains open, the water within the bottle has a way of constantly being refreshed with new seawater as it moves in and out of the top. Perhaps the combination of our breath and heart is the very bridge between the ego brain of individuality and the interconnected oneness of everything. It makes sense when you think about it. The book of Genesis in the Christian Bible states:

'The LORD God formed the man from the dust of the ground and breathed into his nostrils the breath of life, and the man became a living being' (Genesis 2:7).

Could it be that the 'dust' represents all the energy that is contained within the vacuum of space? We know that the elements of life such as carbon, magnesium and calcium were originally created in the interior furnaces of stars, which were then released by explosions. It reminds me of another quote by Carl Sagan who, in 1973, published, *The Cosmic Connection: An Extra-terrestrial Perspective,* which stated:

'All of the rocky and metallic material we stand on, the iron in our blood, the calcium in our teeth, the carbon in our genes were produced billions of years ago in the interior of a red giant star. We are made of star-stuff.'

Many creation stories across many cultures share a similar narrative whereby a great god or spirit used some sort of material to create reality and then merged it with a kind of non-physical essence or spark. Perhaps an understanding of the energetics of the heart, when combined with focused breath, can begin to bridge a long-standing split and divide between materialist science and the mystical realms. Perhaps the mysterious 'spark' of life is somehow connected to our breath. Perhaps in every moment as we breathe, we are in fact breathing life into the elemental components of our material physical bodies so they can do what they have to do to keep us alive in this physical form. If our bodies do work like a clock, according to Newtonian physics, maybe it's the breath that is keeping the cogs and wheels turning. After all, the moment you stop breathing is the moment you stop living. We are all aware of how physical emotions and feelings can change almost instantly depending on how we use our breath. Want instant proof of this? Just hold your breath for as long as you can and then notice how you feel when you can't bear it any longer and you finally have to draw in a breath. Notice how your body, head and heart feel. Perhaps it is our hearts and our breath that act like a portal. Like the top of that submerged glass bottle in the ocean connecting us to the infinite energetic spark of life that we ourselves may be submerged in—that energy being the space that is all around us always.

The ego qualities of the brain exist primarily to create internal perceptual boundaries between ourselves and 'the world out there'. The ego brain, from the moment you were born, began to be programmed with certain beliefs, some helpful, and some not so helpful when it comes to creating oneness and connection to others. If one lives primarily from an ego brain perspective and worldview, the beliefs that will often follow on from that include an idea that 'the world is out to get me'. The brain will often try to convince you that holding onto negative beliefs is a good thing because it is actually serving you to maintain them. Not only that, the ego brain will often try to convince you that positive beliefs are actually negative and detrimental to your wellbeing. Of course, the ego brain isn't there to harm you; its main focus is self-preservation, and this is why it will often try to distort and distract you from anything it believes will lead to its annihilation, hence self-sabotage in the name of self-preservation. 'Protection at all costs' seems to be its highest value.

If things don't go your way, the ego brain will always do its best to find someone or something to blame. It wants to convince you to take everything personally and that it's the justified thing to do. The ego brain and all its negative programming wants to convince you that a more heart-centred approach is just not possible, and if it was, it would cause more suffering and be too difficult. For this reason, it's better to work harder and harder to get what you want even if it means another has to lose. As long as you end up on top and the winner, that's all that matters. In this way, the end always justifies the means.

The ego brain is always looking to reinforce and strengthen itself by luring you in and connecting you with others who may also share the same ego brain perspectives and world view. By doing this, the ego brain is trying to convince you that if you were to go against this with a more heart-centred way of being, you'll actually experience more disconnection, loneliness and alienation. Your ego brain will employ all kinds of tricks to make you feel helpless, fearful and powerless by trying to convince you of your lack of ability to change these things about yourself and the world. The ego brain wants you to always be on guard and prepare for the worst possible outcome because it 'always has your back'. When the Reticular Activation System (RAS) referred to earlier is being used negatively by the ego, it will make you notice negative synchronicities and prevent you from noticing positive ones. The perceptions it will deliver to your conscious awareness will often be distractions to keep you away from noticing and addressing the real issues at hand. The ego brain will tell you that no positive tools will work, it's more comfortable to remain 'in your head', and you're 'way too smart' to be fooled into dropping your guard. The ego brain, even when presented with a positive heart-centred situation, will do its best to distort it in a negative way.

In contrast to the ego brain, the heart wants you to realise your interconnectivity with all things and in this way, the interdependency of all things. A world view of heart oneness adopts the perspective of cooperation, mutual benefit and service to one another and all things.

The Subconscious Heart-Mind

Earlier, I explained the fact that when most people, even many hypnotherapists, think of the subconscious, we tend to see it as something exclusively connected to the brain. However, considering what was just mentioned about the ego brain vs the oneness of the heart, you tell me—what type of subconscious would you rather tap into? If you recall, one of the amazing facts about the human heart is that it has a rich and complex neurology that qualifies it as a 'mini brain'. If that's the case, then perhaps it has an unconscious mind.

Often, a *small* difference is what makes *all* the difference, and this is no exception. The small but big difference I'm referring to is one of the most fundamental twists to hypnosis and the concept of the subconscious. It is the idea that every organ, even down to the smallest particles that make up your physical body, has a subconscious mind, an underlying intelligence that you can tap into. Is this really so hard to believe? There is obviously a deep intelligence within every human being, an intelligence that is managing the trillions of cells in your body, each of which are performing billions of chemical transactions in every moment with complete precision to keep you alive in this very moment. Based on the fractal holographic principle described in Chapter 2, and based on the ancient natural law principle of 'as above, so below', it stands to reason that whatever is true at one level of a system is true at all levels of a system.

The oneness qualities of your intuitive, powerfully connected, energetic heart can be exponentially increased when you tap into its subconscious mind. All it takes is the power of focus to literally 'go into that space' in a very specific way. If you want to live with heart, and express and experience all the qualities of the heart, then it makes total sense to journey into that area of your physical body for all the reasons I have mentioned earlier. Your heart's subconscious mind is beyond the programming and conditioning that your brain's mind is susceptible to. Your heart is connected to non-local, intuitive information. It seems to be a kind of upload and download portal, which has the capacity to not only guide you in your everyday life but it can also show you who you really are. If your brain is the radio receiver, your heart is the dial that can literally 'tune you into' the 'life station' you prefer.

This of course is not to say that your brain and its mind is not important. Of course it is. But I see the brain as being more like the sail of a wind-powered boat, and the heart more like the rudder that is steering the boat. Both are important and both can serve you well if you know how to combine the two. As the subheading of this book suggests, once you start to harness the intelligent creative power of your heart, this begins the process of beginning to see reality responding in a fun and exciting way. Either very quickly, or over time, you'll begin to notice reality bending towards your intention and attention so you can see the synchronicities unfolding before your very eyes.

CHAPTER 5

Implications and Applications

'At the centre of your being you have the answer; you know who you are and you know what you want.'

- Lao Tzu

Hopefully, by now you are starting to appreciate and become aware of the amazing potential and wonder of your mind, body and heart. However, up to this point, the information shared has been primarily for your conscious mind. And this is definitely helpful to a curious mind hungry for knowledge; however, I firmly believe that knowledge does not always equate to wisdom and being. The ultimate purpose of this book is to teach you a process and technique that powerfully turns knowing into being. After all, we are called human beings, not human 'knowings'. And it is for this reason that I believe this chapter and the next are absolutely critical in achieving the ultimate goal of life mastery, namely an unconscious competence. You may recall the Four Levels of Competence as described in the introduction of this book. For ease of reference, they were:

Level 1: *Unconscious incompetence (when you don't know that you don't know).*
Level 2: *Conscious incompetence (when you know you don't know).*
Level 3: *Conscious competence (when you know that you know).*
Level 4: *Unconscious competence (when you don't know HOW you know, you just know).*

Of course, some of the information shared in this book may have already been familiar to you, while other parts of it may have taken you on a journey from the first to the third level of competence. Without these last two chapters, however, you would find getting to the final level of competence a much harder and time-consuming endeavour.

In this chapter, I am going to share crucial elements to become aware of before starting any kind of self-hypnosis practice. This will be followed by themes, concepts, ideas, and processes that I guarantee will help you create your very own self-hypnosis scripts and practice. At the end of this chapter, you will have the knowledge and process to start an effective, but more traditional, self-hypnosis practice. This alone has the potential to create massive shifts and transformations in your life. However, it is the final chapter that reveals the Heart Alpha Resonance Technique (H.A.R.T) that I am most excited to share with you.

The H.A.R.T process, as you will see, directly incorporates much of the information in the previous chapters and of course, this chapter as well. The H.A.R.T protocol, whether you do it with or without the assistance of the included self-hypnosis scripts, will allow you to have a much fuller, richer and effective experience than traditional self-hypnosis itself can offer.

The Mind-Body-Spirit Triad

Very few people would dispute the existence of a strong connection between the mind and the body. However, to set the stage for the powerful subconscious mind and exactly how to use it, I believe it is absolutely essential to familiarise ourselves with some of the amazing and growing body of research highlighting the connection and dynamics between the mind, the body and its influence on the world around us. As you can imagine, this area of investigation is extremely large, and once again, I encourage you to do further research of your own. The information that will be focused on here will be that which is most relevant to the H.A.R.T protocol that follows. Having a solid conscious understanding of the connection between your mind, body and the outside world is going to make the H.A.R.T so much more effective and powerful. This is especially true when you combine your conscious understanding with your subconscious mind through a regular practice of self-hypnosis. This is the small difference that makes all the difference between knowledge and being. To help make these concepts a little easier to understand, let us consider the diagram below.

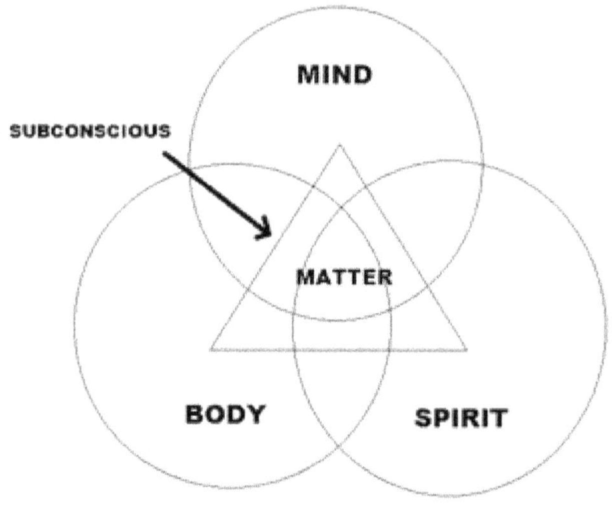

Figure 5.1

The circles represent the conscious mind, and the connections we can make and utilise in our everyday lives using our conscious mind. Some very simple examples of this may be the conscious decision to lift your hand to scratch your face—a conscious mind-body connection. Since an emotion (E-motion) is energy in motion, the conscious connection between an emotion and thought is an example of the mind/spirit interaction. Examples of the body/spirit connection could be yoga, tai chi or qigong, where the body is moving in close communion with the non-physical or spirit.

The section, called 'Matter', the point where all three intersect, could also be called 'Perception'. In this context, 'Matter' isn't necessarily a physical object but your perceptual experience in any given moment. For instance, anything you could become aware of, or perceive, in this very moment is your conscious experience labelled as 'Matter' in the above diagram. This could be the feeling of the seat you're in, the feeling of this book in your hands, the temperature of the room, any physical discomfort in your legs, what you'll cook for dinner tonight, the sounds outside your room, etc. Your conscious perceptual experience is the result of the communication between the mind, body and spirit in any moment. This, however, is only one layer of information that you can access or experience with a simple conscious diversion of attention. The triangle in the middle represents the unconscious or subconscious mind, which is intimately connected to all three aspects of mind, body and spirit on a deeper level. This of course has the power to influence a completely different type of 'Matter' or perceptual experience. But how is that possible? Because the conscious and unconscious mind are designed to do very different things.

Predicting Behaviour by Communicating with the Subconscious

The conscious mind, as already mentioned, consists of mental processes that essentially require you to operate in the 'here and now' moment. The unconscious mind, however, is playing its role more in a 'behind the scenes' kind of way. The conscious mind is the actor in the movie, and the unconscious is the director. The conscious mind is like the goggles you use underwater, allowing you to see and experience the underwater world, while the subconscious is like the subtle energy that attracts or repels the underwater life that enters your experience. The psychotherapist and founder of analytical psychology, Carl Jung, described it perfectly when he said:

'Until you make the unconscious conscious, it will direct your life and you will call it fate.'

Jung had no doubt whatsoever about the nature of the puppet show we call 'life'. For him, the subconscious was clearly holding all the strings, directing the conscious mind just like a puppet. He suggests that the conscious mind gives us the impression that we are the captains of our ship directing its path with our conscious choices. However, what many influential psychologists in history, such as

Jung, have proposed is that it is really our subconscious processes and programming that are truly determining our choices in a fairly predictable way. If this is in fact true, then it makes complete logical sense that if we really and truly wish to become the captains of our ship, we need to make 'the unconscious conscious'. In other words, we need to first become aware of the subconscious patterns that are influencing us so we can then make a conscious choice about whether or not those programs are in alignment or not, and serving us or not, with what we truly want to manifest and become—namely, who you truly are.

One such research example of this illusion of conscious choice is a study published in 1999 by the *Journal of Applied Psychology* conducted by North, Hargreaves & McKendrick. This study investigated whether or not there would be any correlation between the type of wine purchased in store and the music that was being played in the store. They compared the number of sales of French and German wines while playing music with strong French or German association. The music was alternated daily for two weeks, and the results showed that French music led to French wines outselling German ones, and vice versa. Questionnaires revealed that customers were completely oblivious to the background music and hence reported it as having played no role whatsoever in their wine selection.

The implications of this study are very interesting indeed. By the way, this is just one of many studies confirming the influence of subconscious sensory data on our thoughts, choices and behaviours. This subconscious sensory data, of course, is named as such because the customers in the above study were completely unconscious, or unaware, of any music playing at all. The unconscious mind, however, is processing and absorbing much more information in any given moment than the conscious mind. Simple logic would tell us that if the conscious mind is only able to process seven to nine bits of sensory data in any given moment as compared to the billions of bits of information that the subconscious is processing, then it would make total sense that the unconscious is going to influence us in a much more powerful way than the conscious mind ever will.

Here's another great example worth checking out. On YouTube, there is a video called *Tricking Advertisers with Adverts | Mind Control | Darren Brown*. The entire video is only seven minutes long, but it is a perfect example of how easily our choices, behaviours and even our creative ideas can be influenced if you know how to do it. Darren Brown is an English mentalist and illusionist who has performed in front of large audiences on stage, often debunking 'magic tricks', mostly those relating to mind and illusion. In this short video, he recruits two advertising executives to take a taxi to Darren's office. He chose them for this task because, as he describes in this video, they are 'masters of persuasion'. These advertising executives subtly weave their images and slogans into our daily lives knowing that we will register so much unconsciously. He wanted to turn the tables on them a little and show them that they too are subject to being unconsciously influenced in a predictable way, even though they may assume some kind of immunity to it.

These executives are asked to create an advertising campaign on the spot within thirty minutes. Darren sets the fairly broad parameters at the start, saying that they have to come up with a company name, slogan, catch phrase, and logo for a business that he has a particular interest in. The business was a chain of taxidermy stores. Before Darren leaves them to their happy task, he places a sealed envelope on their work desk that contains within it 'some creative design ideas of my own'. He puts a curled up stuffed cat on top of the envelope to make sure it isn't touched, and he leaves the room. Upon his return, the executives show Darren what they came up with, only to be shown that the design ideas Darren had in the envelope were pretty much identical to what they had come up with: the images, the slogan, the lot!

So how was he able to pull this off?

It's a simple idea but complex and detailed in its execution. All Darren had to do was flood their unconscious mind with images and words he wanted them to use. This was done in a multitude of ways during the taxi ride over to Darren's office. These images and words were on T-shirts, billboards, multiple signs, and in many different formats, hidden in the environment they drove through to get to Darren's office, and they were hidden only from the *conscious* awareness, but noted by the *unconscious*.

The million-dollar question here is this: is there really such a thing as pure creativity, or are we just recycling and repackaging what's already all around us? You may have heard the saying, 'There's nothing new under the sun.' This is just one example of many that suggests that creativity can be influenced, and even manipulated and predicted. Two individuals were given complete freedom to creatively brainstorm a simple idea, and what they came up with was almost 100% predicted by simply exposing them to carefully selected images placed in carefully selected places.

The implications of this can be interpreted as either frightening or exciting, depending on your awareness or ignorance of the dynamics at play. It also serves as evidence for the idea that I presented earlier—the idea that the brain is programmable while the heart is beyond external programming, making it, in a sense, immune.

Biology, Perceptions and Beliefs

One could argue that nothing exists at all in your reality until you have a perception of some kind. They are quite obviously an integral part of our life experience. It is for this reason we should consider the interaction between biology and perceptions. Stem cell biologist, author and speaker, Dr Bruce Lipton, has been engaged in some very interesting research since the 1970s on the relationship between beliefs, perceptions, cells, genes and DNA. His work indicates that it is the environment that plays a significant role in the dynamics and behaviour of our cells, genes and DNA, rather than the other way around. This work has enormous implications for personal empowerment, especially when it comes to creating and maintaining physical well-being. Many people have a firm belief that it is their genetic makeup that is dictating their physical destiny, but the work of Dr Lipton, as well as many others, suggests otherwise. The study of how genes can be influenced is called epigenetics.

To help support this idea, he describes one of his experiments whereby he put one human stem cell into a petri dish to observe how it divides. Only a week later, he had 50,000 genetically identical cells because all the cells came from the same parent cell and all were growing in the same fluid called 'culture medium'. He took those cells and divided them into three different dishes and all he did was change the culture medium. In other words, he changed the environment they were living in. And the results were remarkable. One dish grew muscle cells, the other bone cells and in the third grew fat cells—strong evidence to show that a cell's environment will determine what kind of cell it will become.

He then went on to ask how the environment controls genetics. And he basically found that it's the chemical signals that are raining down onto the cell that attach themselves to the cell membrane or 'skin' of the cell. This signal then gets transported inside the cell, which influences chromosomes and protein production that directly affect cell behaviour. Epigenetics is considered to be the revolutionary new way to investigate the signals influencing genetic information. 'Epi' means 'control from above', as in the term 'epidermis', another name for skin, which of course is the layer above the dermis, which is beneath it. This study and others have led to a new understanding of the importance of the chemistry a cell is receiving from the environment as opposed to focusing solely on the interior of cells. The old cellular paradigm of 'control by genes' has been replaced with 'signal transduction'. This approach attempts to explain how the signal 'above the genes' translates into biology.

The specific focus of this research is to identify and understand the way the skin of the cell processes the signals attaching themselves to this outer wall of the cell membrane. The interesting connection between our actual skin—the biggest organ of the human body—and the skin of our cells is that they receive and process incoming signals from the environment in exactly the same way—through receptors. The obvious outer receptors are our eyes, nose, taste, touch, and hearing. Cells, on the other hand, have antenna-like receptors that detect environmental stimuli, such as sugar signals, which communicate with protein effectors and responders to transport the signal into the cell. But how do the receptor and the effector communicate?

The environmental stimulus captured by the receptor antenna alters its shape, enabling it to fit with a connector protein that serves as the bridge between the receptor and the connector. This antenna remains dormant until a stimulus presents itself that allows it to be detected by a connector protein that facilitates the communication between receptor and effector. Once this connection is made, it allows the signal to be transported inside the cell. It's also important to remember that there are over 100,000 receptors on the membrane of your cells alone that are processing millions of bits of information in any moment. Put another way, the role of the receptor, like all your five senses, is to absorb electrical and chemical information from the environment. The function of the effector is to help translate and transform that stimulus into a physical sensation or feeling. This entire process can be used to define that most important aspect of the human experience—the 'switch' that controls your biology and perceptions, which has been defined as 'awareness of the elements of the environment through physical sensation'. By changing your perceptions, you influence the way your receptors, connectors and hence your biology, behave.

Why is this information relevant to creating the inner and outer world you want through self-hypnosis? Because the most beautiful thing about the process described above is that you can activate this entire cellular system of receptor, stimulus and effector response with the power of visualisation and imagination. Visualisation is a very well-documented phenomenon in many different types of studies, from athletes to speakers to performers. It is the pictures that we create in our minds, fuelled by the emotions they produce that help create the reality we experience.

Here is a simple example of this. If you close your eyes and recall a particularly stressful moment from your past, a moment of severe trauma and anxiety, how would you feel? How 'real' you make it in your mind will determine how much you feel it inside your body. Isn't this simple proof of a very real experience from something that is completely illusory? Even though the experience you just remembered may have been very real at the time, the fact is, it isn't real in this moment. Although in a less intense way, you completely 'made it up' in this moment, and yet you perceived and experienced it as real. And this is just a very simple example of the powerful mind-body connection.

The work of Dr Lipton would suggest that the receptors on your cell membrane do not know the difference between the signals coming from a 'real' external signal or one that is being created by your imagination. The chemical environment being created for your cells is exactly the same. Unfortunately, most people go through their entire day continually bombarding their cells with unwanted, fearful, resentful, stressful, negative signal chemistry, which is the natural result of patterns of thought. But this is only on a conscious level; imagine combining this with our deeply embedded unconscious patterns and programs that we are unaware of at any given moment.

Are you getting more excited about the power of your unconscious mind and the utility of this powerful potential you have? Can you begin to appreciate how different your life could be if you started engaging the technology of self-hypnosis? It would enable you to consciously choose exactly what it is you would like your biology to respond to and create, instead of it being at the mercy of the external events and influences of your everyday life and past events. Anything that influences your perceptions evidently has an important role to play in creating your inner and outer world, which brings us to this next most important element—beliefs.

Beliefs are extremely powerful. As Henry Ford said, 'Whether you believe you can or you can't, either way you're right.' The power of belief is linked to the very well-established phenomena called 'Placebo Effect' as confirmed by countless clinical drug trials. It indicates that if a person believes that a pill will create an outcome in the body, in one third of cases that effect will actually manifest in the body even though the pill was nothing but a placebo, that is, a sugar pill. But why are beliefs so powerful? Perhaps the answer is linked to a very interesting question that I'd like you to think about for a moment, and that is:

'Are your beliefs shaped by your experience, or do you experience what you believe?'

Just take a moment to consider that. Perhaps you think it's a bit of both—and you're probably right. It's a loop where one affects and feeds the other, kind of like the connection between thoughts and feelings. If you make a shift in one, the other will follow. Which is easier to change, however, a belief or an experience? I think you'll agree that you have more control over what you choose to believe at any moment rather than the experience you are having at any moment. If you change your belief, you can change the very biological mechanisms that are feeding your perceptions, which of course determine your experience. It's for this reason that two people can recall two completely different experiences from the same event they attended. This is because different beliefs influence different perceptions, which influence a different stimulus-response process via the five senses of both individuals.

The Power of Intention

The connection between mind and body is very clear, but let's examine some interesting research suggesting the existence of a more profound connection between us and the outside world. It has been said that 'thoughts become things'. If this is actually the case, then there must be some kind of influence or interaction between what is going on within our minds and our external physical reality. There have been some very interesting studies done attempting to reveal the existence of such a connection between the inner and the outer. The more we are able to establish a belief that this interaction exists, the more likely we are to actually manifest the experience of it in our lives.

Lynne McTaggart, author and speaker, is the creator of 'The Intention Experiments'. She is working on this subject with many thought leaders around the world to show the power and influence of our thoughts on the world around us. One of her most compelling experiments was one where, in front of an audience of hundreds of people in Sydney, Australia, she held up nothing but a photograph of three sets of seeds which were thousands of kilometres away in the USA. She asked the audience to focus their attentions and intentions for increased growth on just one of the images. The results revealed at least a 10% increase in the subsequent plant growth rate. In some cases, plants doubled in size. Now, even though 10% may not seem so significant to you, in scientific research this is considered a very significant result.

John Hagelin (PhD), particle physicist and director of the Transcendental Meditation movement in the United States, has also presented some interesting research showing how powerful intention and meditation can be to even reduce war. One such study was published in 1988 in *The Journal of Conflict Resolution* by Yale University, which showed the influence of groups of people meditating in the Middle East during the peak of the Lebanon war in the early 1980s. What is so interesting about this study is that it simultaneously plotted on two y-axes, right and left. The number of people engaged in group meditation in Jerusalem was measured on one y-axis, and an 'Overall Composite Index' (OCI) measured progress towards peace on the other y-axis. The OCI included statistics on war deaths, war injuries and number of detonated bombs, to name only a few. The length of time in days was being measured on the x-axis.

The graph clearly showed that progress towards peace moved up and down, rising and falling based on the number of people who were engaged in group meditation across different times. More people indicated more movement towards peace, and fewer meditators showed less progress towards peace. When the findings were statistically analysed, the probability that these results were due to chance was less than 1 in 10,000. The results were so remarkable that it took over two years and multiple editorial reviews for them to be published. In the end, they had no choice but to release the findings due to the extremely high standard of scientific protocol and process that was employed in the study. The editors even included a letter in the study stating that the results of how only 1,000 people could influence 1 million were so unexpected that they encouraged other research scientists to replicate the findings. And this is exactly what happened. For almost three years after this study, scientists replicated the same results with groups of trained meditators in the same geographic location. Once again, incidences of war-related factors were reduced in such a significant way that the statistical likelihood of these new results being explained by random chance was in the region of a 0.0000001% chance. Dr Hagelin, when referring to these results, said:

'There is far more evidence that group meditation can turn off war like a light switch than there is evidence that aspirin reduces headache pain.'

If groups of people can have this kind of impact on such large-scale external events like war, using only their conscious mind in meditation, imagine what impact you can have on your own individual life when using the tool of self-hypnosis to engage your powerful subconscious mind.

The late Dr Masaru Emoto discovered that the composition and structure of water changed depending on the intentions it was exposed to, such as the words written on the containers, or even nearby music. Despite some controversy and scepticism by some, his work has been replicated by numerous non-scientific people because of how simple the experimentation process is. The tests required nothing other than exposing water to different words written on labels attached to containers and then analysing the frozen crystalline structure of the water after a period of time. The results were quite clear in that negative stimulus, intentions and words produced ugly, malformed, geometric crystalline shapes, whereas positive stimulus, such as words or even music, produced more beautifully symmetrical, geometric crystalline structures.

Some studies have been conducted whereby water has been exposed to vibrational sound frequencies and observed in real time to shift and transform as the frequency goes up or down in hertz. Lower frequencies produced less-complex shapes and patterns, and higher frequencies produced more detailed and intricate patterns. This relates very closely to Plato's work on geometrising the five elements of earth, air, fire, water, and aether, as described in Chapter 1. The molecular structure of water quite literally changes before your very eyes as it is exposed to higher and higher frequencies of sound and vibration.

Another interesting thought to consider is the fact that our brains are also made up of approximately 73% water. Since sound and frequency obviously change the structure of water, this is probably why many people find such amazing results and effects when meditating with certain frequency sounds either through mantras, Tibetan singing bowls or binaural music through headphones. It is the water that seems to be a type of super energy conductor. This seems almost obvious since we all know what would happen if we dropped a live electrical appliance into your bath while you're in it. And this work is consistent with results found in the field of cymatics. The process involves observing small particles, such as sand or salt, literally restructuring and reorganising themselves to form more complex designs and patterns while on top of a vibrating metal plate attached to a machine that is producing different sound frequencies. You can observe many videos like this on YouTube. The implications of these findings are significant when one considers the amount of water in the human body.

Our thoughts and feelings are also creating these exact same types of vibrational frequencies emanating from our heart and brain, which are also influencing our biology. Our internal organs are vibrating at their own frequencies, interacting with certain thoughts, emotions and intentions through our nervous system. This connection between our internal states, the life force and our body has been known by the Chinese for thousands of years and forms one of the key therapeutic principles in all forms of Chinese medicine, such as acupuncture. This emanating internal energy, however, is not only going inward but also outward as it interacts with the infinite energy within the space that surrounds our bodies. This might explain how and why we are able to feel certain 'vibes' or 'gut feelings' about certain places or people. And it seems completely plausible as the Unified Field Theory (UFT) of physics described in the first two chapters indicates more and more that the vacuum energy of space behaves very much like a type of 'super fluid'—like water. This could offer an explanation for how and why energy, as well as emotion, is transmitted across what we think of and experience, as empty space.

This idea has also been used to explain the particle-wave conundrum made famous by the double slit experiment where the firing of photons—tiny packets of light—seem to mysteriously behave as either waves or particles, depending on the observer. Many spiritualists have used this idea as 'evidence' to support the idea that 'we create our reality', which of course is partly true but, as explained already, it is not 100% true. This experiment has, however, been explained in laboratories using fluid dynamics. In simple terms, if you imagine a ball, a particle, moving through a fluid, which produces waves, it is obviously going to create waves and ripples in the fluid at the same time. Hence, the observation of either the particle or the wave it is making, depending on the observational apparatus being used. In other words, in this instance, you get the result the experiment is set up to reveal.

Human DNA

At this very moment, and since the moment of your birth, your unconscious mind has been recording and storing every single bit of information you have ever been exposed to. Since the mind and body are connected, it's interesting to wonder what physical aspect of the human body could possibly store all this information. Could it be our DNA? It is certainly possible when you consider its 'information storage capacity'. The length of DNA in just one human cell is approximately 1.8 metres long. So, if you multiply 1.8 metres by the 37 trillion cells in your body, you get a distance of 6.66 x 10 to the power of 13 metres of DNA! Quite clearly, there is plenty of material and capacity there. In terms of information storage, one gram of DNA is the equivalent of 600 BILLION CDs! A huge amount of storage capacity indeed.

Continuing with the computer analogy, could there be a link between the programming of the subconscious mind, our DNA and human language? Could hypnosis and the state of trance that it produces be the key to 'unlocking' dormant information within your DNA through a kind of 'system upgrade'? If this were possible, there would have to be some kind of link between DNA and language.

Over the years, there have been some very controversial, but nonetheless very interesting experiments conducted to investigate the characteristics and behaviour of human DNA. I find it a particularly interesting area of research for a few reasons. DNA has been called the 'human biological internet'. It is considered by some to be the key to explaining phenomena such as remote viewing, clairvoyance, intuition, spontaneous/remote healing, and more. It's also interesting to know that mainstream science proposes that 90% of our DNA has no observable use or function whatsoever and as a result, has literally been called 'junk DNA'. It is for this reason it is practically ignored by mainstream research.

A study by Nobel Prize winner, Luc Montagnier, suggested that DNA actually has the ability to teleport itself via electromagnetic imprinting, hence the term 'phantom DNA'. This characteristic of DNA seems to somehow influence enzymes into replicating themselves in another location, cell or fluid—a completely radical concept and possibility, one that could turn mainstream chemistry on its head! The usual process of copying DNA is by using a technique called the Polymerase Chain Reaction (PCR), whereby a DNA sample is added to a PCR test tube medium in order for replication to occur. What is so remarkable about Dr Montagnier's result was that he was reportedly able to replicate DNA at a distance—not by placing actual DNA into the PCR test tube, but by using a special type of light that shone through a DNA-containing PCR test tube. The DNA appeared to 'project', 'imprint' or 'teleport' its information into a nearby test tube containing only water. This seems to suggest that DNA emits a type of electromagnetic signal that has the capacity to pass on its own information elsewhere and in other things like water. Once again, it is the water, which was present in both test tubes, that seems to act like a medium for the energetic information to be transferred.

According to other studies by Russian linguists, our DNA also seems to function as a kind of mechanism for information storage, communication and exchange, especially within the 90% of that so-called 'dormant' or 'junk' DNA. They are suggesting that our DNA and genetic material have within them an inherent quality, which seems to reflect and mirror the rules of human language such as syntax (the way words are structured) and grammar. This research shows how DNA and our genetic material is influenced by language-modulated laser lights, sounds, frequencies, and radio waves.

These results offer strong support, even evidence, as to how and why language in the form of self-talk, mantras, affirmations, and hypnosis can be such powerful tools for transformation. Self-hypnosis offers you a way to directly communicate with your very own DNA and genetic material. Since DNA seems to follow the syntax of language, this is probably why human language and the way we use it is so powerful. We all know that the words you use to describe anything at all—a person, place, thing, or even yourself—has a direct influence on how you feel about that thing, or yourself. It's as if we are casting a spell with our words, hence why we call the way we put words and sounds together, spelling. Try changing the way you speak and see what happens. Notice how it feels different. For example, replace the word 'worried' with 'concerned', or 'problem' with 'challenge', and 'always' and 'never' with 'usually'. Generally speaking, we are pretty lazy with our habits of speech, but you might be holding yourself back more than you think just with the words you use. This includes the unspoken words you say in your mind.

Another example of 'spooky' DNA phenomenon, once again coming from Russian research, is a famous, controversial, but well-documented experiment conducted by P. Gariaev and Vladimir Poponin. They created a vacuum environment within a test tube, which left nothing inside except photons—tiny subatomic packets of light. The photons were examined and mapped within the test tube and, as expected, they were in a random and disorganised state. They introduced a fragment of DNA into the test tube, and interestingly, the DNA attracted the photons almost like a fly to sticky paper. The DNA attracted the photons, which attached themselves to the DNA structure. When the DNA was removed, it was expected that the photons would return to random positions within the test tube, but to their astonishment, the photons remained in an organised fashion as if the DNA was still present within the test tube. The proposed explanation is that the DNA imprint remains due to its connection to the actual DNA through a magnetised wormhole connection within the energetic fabric of the vacuum of space.

This DNA imprint is said to be making not only an imprint but leaving a trail along the fabric of space-time as well, like dragging a stick behind you along a sandy beach. This is because everything in the universe is moving, spinning and orbiting a larger cosmological body of some sort. Although you may be sitting still in a chair, you are actually moving at an astonishing speed as the Earth spins on its axis. If you add this speed to the speed of the Earth moving around the Sun, and the speed of the Sun around our galaxy, and the galaxy around its cluster, and so on, all of a sudden you start to realise that you are probably moving at the speed of light even though you're sitting 'still' in your chair.

Continuing with this idea of leaving a DNA imprint, or trail, within space-time as we speed across space, it's important to know that we never actually occupy the same physical point in space twice. Let me explain. As young children, when learning about the planets and our solar system, we are taught that all the planets are orbiting the Sun, which is sitting still and stagnant in the centre. Consequently, this model is essentially telling us that the Earth passes through the exact same point 365 days later. This is actually false for one simple reason: the Sun is also speeding through space at hundreds of kilometres per second. So, what does this mean? It means that we are not circling the Sun, but spiralling through space while our DNA leaves a trail of photons, literally a 'trail of light', much like a DNA helix, behind it. This spiralling trail of light in the form of photons is information which we seem to be able to access through wormhole connections and experience with our own consciousness through the self-hypnosis process you are going to learn shortly. Can you imagine every piece of DNA in every cell of your body leaving an energetic spiralling trail? It's a mind-blowing thing to imagine, especially when you consider the amount of DNA contained within the human body—as mentioned earlier.

This research offers possible explanations for the amazing and instantaneous healings and breakthroughs of many different types of healing modalities such as Hypnotic Past Life Regression (PLR) and Time Line Therapy (TLT) just to name a few. This research on DNA offers us a great deal of exciting possibilities and questions to consider. Could our 'junk DNA' hold the key to explaining, and consciously using, telepathic communication? Could DNA communicating through the vacuum of space explain how and why certain types of animal species, like birds for instance, seem to share a type of group consciousness? Could the activation and use of the remaining 90% of our DNA help humanity experience a more globally connected consciousness?

More Radical DNA Theories and Concepts

I thought it would be fun to give a short mention to some of the more radical ideas I have come across on my journey of self-discovery, just in case what has already been mentioned hasn't done that already. My intention in sharing this information is simply to give you more ideas to consider. If an idea or concept intrigues or resonates with you, you may be inspired to do more of your own research. If it sounds ridiculous to you, then feel free to dump it into the cosmic trash can and move on. I am framing the following in this way because these concepts are not theories that can be verified at this point in our evolution. However, they are interesting nonetheless. One idea about our DNA is that we do not have 'junk DNA' at all, but we are simply using all of the information within our DNA to make it seem as if we are only using a very small amount of it. This is similar to the human brain. You may have heard the fact that we only use about 10% of our brain capacity, but perhaps we are using all of it to only make it seem this way. Why would we be creating this with our DNA and brain? Perhaps for the experience of discovering more of who we really are, for the experience of activating our inner power and remembering who we are more and more. We would not have the experience of remembering if we did not have the experience of forgetting. In the same way that if we wish to have the experience of 'waking up', we first need to create the experience of 'falling asleep'.

This is, however, quite a conservative idea when compared with others. A growing number of people are absolutely convinced of the connection between extraterrestrials, humans and DNA. This is the idea of the manipulation of the DNA and genetic material of the great ape by ETs to create a 'hybrid species', namely homo sapiens. I understand that this kind of idea can be extremely challenging, even anxiety provoking for some, and responses to such concepts can vary hugely from complete fear to laughter to an intuitive feeling that perhaps there is some truth within this idea. As I said, of course this idea is difficult to verify. However, polls are showing that more and more people are reporting that they do believe in the existence of intelligent life beyond our planet. Even the global headquarters of the Catholic Church, the Vatican, has admitted the probability that extraterrestrials do in fact exist. It has also been said to be the highest form of human arrogance to think that we are the only intelligent form of life within the vastness of space.

If this topic is of interest to you, I would once again recommend the work and documentaries of Dr Steven Greer, as mentioned in Chapter 1. The TV series, *Ancient Aliens*, which was aired on the History Channel, also presents a plethora of interesting information suggesting the possibility that these civilisations were indeed visited by ETs, who were typically referred to as 'The Sun Gods'. They reveal certain unexplained 'devices' found in Egypt, for instance, that may have been alien technologies used to build the huge megalithic structures such as the Great Pyramids and others all over the world. The theory is that these devices may have been used to create and emit certain frequencies or sounds that would literally change the molecular structure of stone to make it lighter and more malleable so that it could be shaped and worked with more easily, like play dough. This seems rather plausible when you consider the well-researched influence of sound on matter, such as shattering glasses at high pitches, for instance. It may also explain how so many ancient civilisations, such as the Egyptians, Mayans and Incas, were able to move such huge stones and put them into place and join them with such precision. Again, these are just theories, but ones I find extremely interesting, exciting and worth our attention.

Freedom to Make a (REAL) Choice

By now, you have come to realise that it's the unconscious mind that is REALLY in control of your life. In fact, did you know there is no such thing as a purely conscious decision? Right from your choice of partner to what you had for lunch yesterday. This is due to the simple fact that your unconscious mind is constantly influencing your conscious thinking, decision-making and behaviour, whether you realise it or not. The study described in Chapter 2, that examined the effect of in-store music on wine choices, is a perfect example of this, as is the Darren Brown experiment with the advertising executives.

I've decided to devote my life to a mission that I feel extremely passionate about, and that is to help people experience freedom in all its forms. This includes the freedom to make a conscious choice about what you truly want, without having been unconsciously influenced or manipulated in any way. However, the sad fact of the matter is that we live in a society that is completely saturated with a constant bombardment of the senses from all kinds of platforms such as TV, radio, internet, mobile phones, outdoor billboards, etc.

As already mentioned, your conscious mind is only ever absorbing a very small amount of the available sensory data in your environment at any given moment. Your unconscious mind, however, is taking in so much more of this information. It is therefore being influenced in ways you couldn't possibly be aware of consciously. The advertising industry is completely aware of this, which is why the timing and 'product placement' of products in movies and commercials across all kinds of media is so crucial during the times when you are in a naturally occurring hypnotic trance or state. Your car radio and those billboards all around highways and stuck to bridges are all taking advantage of your naturally occurring 'driving trance', while ads on TV are taking advantage of your naturally occurring 'TV trance'. These are both examples of moments in your day of heightened suggestibility, and hence, behaviour influence. This is part of what has been called 'social engineering'.

Here is one very interesting real-life example of this kind of product placement. I was once watching a James Bond movie with a mate. It was *Casino Royale*. One of the ads that came on during this movie was for cat food. Now, you may be wondering what cat food has to do with a James Bond movie. But what instantly got my conscious attention—something that most people, including my mate, would miss—was the name of the cat food. It was called 'Fancy Feast Royale'. Do you think this is just a coincidence? Not at all. Most people would not make the connection consciously, but your subconscious mind most definitely has. It is for this reason that a cat owner, days or maybe even weeks later, may be drawn to buy that particular cat food, all the while thinking that they made that choice consciously when in reality it was really suggested to them, or planted there. The movie *Inception*, starring Leonardo DiCaprio, plays with this idea beautifully. This is the exact same mechanism Darren Brown used with the advertising executives to 'plant' his into their subconscious.

What is even more interesting, and perhaps concerning as well, is the growing number of people who believe that we are being influenced and manipulated on levels beyond our five senses in a more electromagnetic way. The fact is that since the human body is essentially an emitter and receiver of electromagnetic information, it is very possible that it can be influenced by those same energy patterns in ways we would never even be aware of, perhaps by our electronic and mobile devices. People who are sensitive to this may experience all kinds of physical manifestations of this kind of 'interference', such as headaches, migraines, nausea, irritability, confusion, or trouble sleeping, just to name a few. It is for this very reason that one of the self-hypnosis scripts in this book includes one that has been specifically designed to make sure that your subconscious mind is only ever absorbing and responding to information, physical or non-physical, that is in alignment with YOUR highest good and conscious intention. This is one of my favourite scripts.

Expectations

Before sharing the practical steps to this self-hypnosis protocol, I just wanted to briefly mention something about expectations while using self-hypnosis. It is a simple, yet profound concept to be aware of. In a way, self-hypnosis is similar to many other activities we may do to improve body, mind or spirit. You would not expect to see significant results or improvements from walking, yoga, swimming, lifting weights, or meditation after just one or two attempts. And I think it's important to approach self-hypnosis, as well as H.A.R.T, with an intention to adopt it as a daily, or at least a fairly regular, practice as something new or perhaps integrating it into your existing mind, body, spirit practice. Please remember that any unhelpful, limiting programs that may be holding you back have most likely been there for many years. It is for this reason that sometimes eliminating them can take a little time, perseverance, diligence, and practice; at other times, we simply need to experience the journey in order to acquire and appreciate the lessons learned.

I highly recommend making H.A.R.T an ongoing practice. Like any skill, the more you practice it, the better the outcome and the effect. Stick with the process even if after one attempt you are still smoking, eating blocks of chocolate, still not exercising, lots of money hasn't fallen from the sky, or your dream job or partner hasn't appeared the next day, etc. It is important to recognise that achieving certain outcomes, like stopping smoking, losing weight or changing eating habits, has both internal and external aspects to it. This is particularly important for quitting smoking, for example, something I have helped literally thousands of people to do with just one session of hypnosis, and one session is all it takes. It can only happen in one session if a client is thoroughly prepared beforehand. This includes mental preparation as well as behavioural preparation. If you have the goal of quitting smoking or losing weight, you have to be completely honest with yourself about how badly you want that outcome and how much action you are willing to take to make it happen. I have met many people who deep down are only 'trying' something so they can then be justified in not bothering to try because they can tell everyone, 'I've tried that; it didn't work.' Everyone wants their problems to disappear but it's the ones ready to do what it takes that reap the rewards.

Be open to how your end goal might manifest in your life as you practice the H.A.R.T. If what you are focusing on with self-hypnosis has not been achieved after one or two attempts, perhaps you may 'bump' into, or meet someone who can actually help you with that goal. I recommend taking this approach not only for specific outcomes like quitting smoking, but especially for bigger, broader goals like finding your purpose or experiencing more fulfilment and contentment. The challenge for many of us, especially those with an analytical mind, is to let go of how we expect the outcome to pop into our experience. Anything is possible only when we are open to our highest intentions coming in any possible shape or form. Your conscious mind isn't designed to know HOW something is going to happen, only what is happening in the moment. So, don't give your conscious mind a task it's not meant to do.

'When I run after what I think I want, my days are a furnace of stress and anxiety; if I sit in my own place of patience, what I need flows to me and without pain. From this I understand that what I want also wants me, is looking for me and attracting me. There is a great secret here for anyone who can grasp it.'

- Rumi

It's important to realise and acknowledge a potential program that I believe most of us have been conditioned by, predominantly through today's marketing. That is the idea that a particular product or service will give you a 'quick fix' through the promise of instant this or that, overnight success, three days to X, or how to achieve your dreams in three easy steps. As a result, much of society has become almost addicted to convenience and comfort, wanting everything faster, cheaper and easier with less and less effort—or even better, done by someone else entirely. Of course, there are some great benefits to all of this, but we should recognise that with every positive, there are also negatives. After all, if we continuously choose the easy path, we shouldn't complain when life gets hard. Easy choices build weak habits, and weak habits build a hard life and low personal resilience.

If there is some kind of resistance holding you back from doing this practice daily, my recommendation would be to have a think about exactly what it is that might be holding you back. Have a *real* think about it. Try to avoid just putting it down to being too busy or too tired, or not enough time, or not having the right environment. If you're honest with yourself, you'll know that these are all just excuses. The fact is that if something is truly and deeply important to us, we will always make time for it. If it isn't, we won't. If the reason is laziness, for instance, then have a think about the limiting beliefs that might be underlying this. Considering the real causes of your inaction could give you some powerful insights into your beliefs and patterns that could make all the difference.

At the very least, if you practice morning or night, you will experience a deep sense of relaxation, inner calmness and peace you can carry with you into your day and sleep. Do not underestimate the power of this alone. The well-documented benefits of a regular practice of deep relaxation on mind and body are in themselves definitely worth the time and effort, especially since by now it is common knowledge that almost all illness is a result of some kind of emotional stress or DIS-ease of the mind. So, it makes logical sense that any form of relaxation is going to be the best kind of preventative medicine or antidote to almost any illness.

Your Results Will Reflect Your Beliefs

This is an extremely important piece of the puzzle I would like to you to be aware of. Sometimes people will ask me if self-hypnosis is as effective as going to a professional hypnotherapist, like me, for a personal one-on-one session. My answer is: 'That depends on your beliefs.' We have already touched on the power of beliefs to shape your reality and hence your experience. This has been scientifically verified many times over with the placebo effect, as well as the almost miraculous spontaneous recovery of people with serious illness who have a strong belief in the healing power of some kind of 'higher power', regardless of how you define that higher power. In many cases, the belief is all that was needed for healing to occur.

However, as powerful as beliefs are to heal, they can also *stand in the way* of our healing. After many years working as a therapist, what I have observed as being the single biggest barrier to healing and transformation is a lack of self-worth or self-belief, leading to a conscious or unconscious limiting belief of, 'I'm not good enough'. This, I believe, is the most limiting and debilitating belief standing in the way of any kind of personal transformation. It is for this reason most people will seek out the services, advice and attention of people they 'perceive' to have the ability or 'power' to heal them. I have highlighted the word 'perceive' because it is your perception of another's ability to heal you that will lead to a belief that they can either help you or not. A useful question to ask at this point is, 'How do I come to perceive and believe in this person's ability to help me?' Most people these days use the yardstick of formal qualifications. For many people, there is a strong link, and hence belief, between the number of years one has been institutionally educated and their ability to heal you. Of course, one is more likely to have acquired a certain amount of knowledge and expertise because of their education. But is this really enough? Some will use the testimonies and recommendations of friends or family. 'If it's worked for them, it will work for me.' This is also a good yardstick, but since we are all so unique and different, even this is no guarantee of your personal success. Some 'healers' may be suffering from 'imposter syndrome' and may only be getting results for their clients because they have learned to talk the talk and 'fake it till they make it'. And hence, they are 'helping' people by getting their clients to believe they can help, and well, because of the placebo effect, they will actually 'help' about 33% of clients in just this way alone. You would be shocked at how many 'therapists' I've met who run their entire business like this. But ultimately, if you have been helped, does it really matter if the therapist you saw was an 'imposter'? Hmm.

What is my point here? My point is that if an individual has a conscious or unconscious limiting belief of unworthiness or 'I'm not good enough', then that individual will seek something or someone outside of themselves to use as a kind of permission slip to heal them. Beware of this this self-sabotaging belief. Otherwise, what you might be doing is reinforcing this negative belief of 'I'm not good enough', as it becomes a self-fulfilling prophecy – 'I've tried everything and nothing seems to work'. Sometimes we would rather be right than be healed. Something to be mindful of.

After all, I believe that on the highest level, ALL healing is self-healing, meaning you have created it and done it to, and for, yourself through whatever tool, technique, ritual, or practice that has resonated with your conscious or unconscious belief. In essence, the therapeutic modality, be it a pill or hypnosis, or Reiki or Theta, or any other kind of healing that you gravitate to, was simply a tool, something that you attracted into your reality that resonated with your current belief systems. It is for this reason a crystal healing session can be experienced as an absolute miracle cure, whereas for another it may have seemed like complete 'woo woo' and a waste of time and money. The difference perhaps is in our perception and if the technique 'clicks' with us or not. Is it simply a coincidence that most of the spiritual masters of the past promoted the idea that we have the power to heal ourselves? They even told us where to put our attention and focus to achieve this, 'WITHIN'. It would seem that the only way 'out' is 'in'. Perhaps this is linked to the famous quote of Socrates, 'Know thyself'.

I know it may seem a little strange for a therapist in the business of helping people to be sending a message that basically says, 'You don't really need me', but I honestly believe this to be true. I believe true empowerment is not about building a flock of sheep-like followers who have come to believe that healing and transformation can only come through some kind of intermediary figure between you and a higher healing power or entity. To me, that is not healing; it is dependence and control through fear. It is akin to saying a sick person has been healed of a chronic illness as long as they take a daily dose of medication for the rest of their life to keep the unwanted symptoms from coming back. This, of course, is the model of most of today's pharmaceutical companies that seem to be in the business of symptom management rather than cures, especially when it comes to chronic illnesses. Since honesty and integrity are important to me, I am going to tell you what I believe to be true, regardless of what this may mean for my therapy business. This book on self-hypnosis is testimony to my deep belief that if you believe you can, you can master your own life with the right technique. If you don't believe you can, your journey has to start with focusing on dissolving the beliefs that are standing in the way.

It would be beneficial at this point for you to be honest with yourself and simply get a sense of how true this statement feels for you: 'I have the power to heal myself and create the life I want.' How does that sound or feel for you as you think or say that to yourself? If this statement does not feel as true as you would like it to feel, then consider exactly what beliefs are standing in the way of this statement feeling true for you. Perhaps this needs to be the starting point and focus of your self-hypnosis practice. Let me mention, however, that there is a big difference between saying something over and over to yourself and wishing it was true, and hoping that you'll make it if you fake it. You may be able to trick others and yourself, but you can't fool your unconscious mind. If you're broke and can't pay the rent, there's no point in having a mantra, 'I am financially abundant', because guess what you're actually reinforcing? A lack of financial abundance. So, a better mantra, that you can actually believe, might be something like, 'I always have exactly what I need' or 'through my efforts I am learning to attract financial abundance'. It all comes down to your ability to craft a statement that can point you in the direction of where you want to be rather than trying to convince yourself you're already there.

Self-Hypnosis Goal Setting

Although it may seem paradoxical that I have mentioned that you need to be a little detached from the ultimate outcome, at the same time you do need to have a very specific goal as well. You need to have a clear idea about what you want to achieve. You will also need the motivation to make the process work for you as well as a strong desire for positive change, not just a vague 'it would be nice if ...' You need to be very clear about what you are trying to achieve on an emotional level. This includes as much clarity as possible about how you want to think, feel and behave with regards to that particular thing you are looking to make a change in. A vague, wishy-washy goal will equal wishy-washy results.

It is also important to investigate your reasons for wanting something to manifest in your life to see if it is truly in alignment with what you really want. Sometimes not getting what you think you want is actually a blessing in disguise. I have helped many people in my practice gain clarity and freedom by distinguishing the difference between trying to fulfil an unhelpful mental program that may have come from someone or something, and a true heart-of-heart's desire. To help you more clearly determine the goals of your heart as opposed to that of mental programming, there are some useful questions you can ask yourself about your goals for the H.A.R.T self-hypnosis process. They include:

- *Do I want this for myself or is it something that others expect me to achieve?*
- *Will this goal satisfy my ego more than my soul?*
- *Am I trying to please my parents by achieving this goal?*
- *Is this something that society expects me to be, do and have?*
- *Do I want to achieve this goal because I feel inferior to other people who I think have a better life than me?*
- *Do I want this thing because I'm afraid of the consequences of NOT having it?*
- *Is it anxiety or excitement that is fuelling my desire for this?*
- *Is it something that my inner child really wants for me?*
- *How would other people's lives be enriched if I achieved this goal?*

- *Do I truly feel that fulfilment is not possible without this thing that I want?*
- *What is holding me back from living my dreams? Is this a fact or just a belief?*
- *Am I placing my contentment in the hands of something that could be gone from my life at any time or is it something that I can be, do and have regardless of external circumstances?*
- *Is achieving this goal dependent on something outside of my control?*
- *What is the feeling that I REALLY want through the achievement of this goal and am I open to other ways the universe may bring this feeling to me?*

The above questions are only a small sample of things to ponder as you begin to define your goals. The challenge is to be completely honest with yourself to determine WHY you want what you say you want. You may notice that I have refrained from using 'happiness' as any kind of goal, but replaced it with either fulfillment or contentment, and this is no accident. I believe happiness is a fleeting thing that can come and go. It's something I believe has been marketed for decades by people, religion and institutions alike. Yes, of course, we all want to be happy, but I don't believe it's possible to be in that state all the time. And what I have found is that the people who may seem like they are happy, when alone and by themselves, they are usually the most depressed among us as they are suffering from 'imposter syndrome' or 'fake it till you make it'. This only makes the lows lower by trying to be high all the time. This is just my observation, having been a therapist for so many years. I truly believe that if an individual pursues a sense of meaning and purpose, whatever that is for them, this state of being is much more enduring than 'happiness'. As a general rule, Western culture tends to equate money with happiness when we know this isn't the case. Something I often tell anyone who cares to listen is:

'Money will buy you stuff and experiences, but never meaning or purpose.'

Learning from Those Who Have Gone Before Us

A powerful way to help you create your goals for self-hypnosis and H.A.R.T, is to learn from the wisdom of others who have 'been there, done that'. One of the times in our lives where we are the most truthful and authentic is on our death bed after having lived a long life. Although this may seem like a morbid thing to focus on, it can also be a time of great epiphanies, lessons and learnings not only for the person about to make the transition into non-physical, but for those willing to take the time to listen to the wisdom they have come to realise.

Bonnie Ware, an Australian palliative care nurse with many years' experience, took the time to listen to her many patients approaching death. They touched her so profoundly that she decided to write a blog post, which went viral and then became the basis of a book. The post was entitled, *Top 5 Regrets of The Dying*. These five regrets can serve as a kind of rudder for us as we consider exactly what it is that we would like to set goals for, focus our energy on and experience in our life based on what many people say they would have done differently if they 'had their time again' so to speak. In summary, these regrets were:

1) I wish I'd had the courage to live a life true to myself, not the life others expected of me.

This proved to be the most prominent regret for all, and for obvious reasons, which I believe is most definitely worth exploring to minimise this regret being there for you on your death bed. It can be extremely challenging when, deep within your heart of hearts, you wish to live or pursue something in your life, but you compromise, hold back, or even abandon the idea of living your purpose altogether to satisfy the expectations of others. I have found this to be particularly difficult for individuals and entire cultures where a safe and harmonious immediate family environment is such an important aspect of one's life and identity. There is no doubt that having a close-knit family unit is a very special and sacred gift that many people only dream they could have. However, like absolutely everything in life, it also has positive and negative aspects.

Carving out a life that is true to oneself sometimes means being able to deal with, and navigate, your way through all kinds of family dynamics. This can vary from parental pressure to live a life and find a career that they expect you to have, one which they would be proud to boast about to their friends, family, and strangers alike. They may be stuck in their own limiting programming, being concerned about 'what others will think'. Some parents attempt to control your life path by reminding you about all the sacrifices they made for you, almost as if you 'owe them' to live in such a way that will alleviate as much worry as possible for them. A child that wishes to pursue a dream that parents may not define as a career but a hobby can be very anxiety provoking for them. The paradox is that they will almost always want only one thing for you—to be happy—but typically what they really want and wish for you is that you find happiness within a life path that THEY perceive as safe and secure to spare them worry and concern.

What's interesting to me about this is the perception by some parents that life will be a bed of roses for their children if they are a successful doctor, lawyer, engineer, or whatever profession they define as a 'successful' one. Of course, these jobs may indeed bring a level of income and social status, but my question is this: At what cost? After many years of being a therapist, it has been my observation that many 'successful' individuals in these professions often have a very poor work/life balance, leaving very little quality time for family, spouses, friends, and even exercise.

These individuals often struggle with poor health, weight issues and marital problems, while infidelity or even substance abuse and addiction may develop as ways of coping with a deep sense of emptiness or unfulfillment. It's also interesting to me that when you ask people, most would agree that true fulfilment and contentment do not come from material wealth and possessions, yet our behaviours and pursuits do not often reflect this knowing. We all know wealthy people, even famous ones, that on the surface seem to have 'the perfect life', but are actually fighting a desperate personal battle within themselves at the same time, which in many cases pushes them to suicide.

Please let me be clear. This is not a suggestion that we should all abandon material goods, live like hippies and protest against capitalism. No. It's my invitation for you to reflect on your life, consider what might be driving you to achieve the things you want, and see if you feel there is balance there. When all is said and done, your life is yours to live and nobody can live it for you.

Sometimes, living a life that is true to yourself can, in fact, be a painful reminder to others of the fact that they themselves have given up on their dreams. Deep down, you may even be aware of certain people in your life—perhaps even family members—that secretly do not want you to succeed in creating the life of your dreams as this would cause envy or jealousy within them. This, of course, is just a manifestation of their own negative beliefs and programming. Their thinking, whether outwardly expressed or not, may be along the lines of, 'Who do you think you are to live your dreams while the rest of us have to live in the real world and work hard?' That's just the reality of life. Nothing comes without hard work, and money doesn't grow on trees, etc.

Deep down, we may fear being alienated by the people we love and care for. If this is the case, perhaps the challenge is to find a healthy balance between following your heart and not being judged as selfish or inconsiderate by those you care for.

On the other hand, it can be inspiring to realise that by being an example, it is possible to live your dreams and, in the process of doing that, you can act as a kind of permission slip for others. Your life becomes a message to the world, saying, 'YES! It is possible for you to do this too because I have.' Leadership through example has always been the most powerful. This is in much the same way that running a mile in under four minutes was considered impossible and called the 'four-minute barrier' until Roger Bannister achieved it in 1954. It is now considered to be the male benchmark standard for middle-distance runners.

'It always seems impossible until it's done.'

- Nelson Mandela

2) I wish I hadn't worked so hard.

This regret, according to Bonnie, was expressed by every male patient. It seems to follow on perfectly from the first regret. Since the patients were of an older generation, most of the females were home carers and hence not the main breadwinners. This may have in turn placed more pressure on the males to provide, which you can imagine led to the belief by many men that they had 'had to work hard'. As mentioned above, many were able to realise and admit that because of their hard work, they missed out on seeing their kids grow up or neglected to be emotionally present for their spouse or partner. In contrast to the parent, it is also rare to hear a person say, 'I wish my parents had worked harder.' Once again, the challenge for the parent is to perhaps find a balance between providing for what the child actually needs as opposed to what the child wants. Of course, many parents love to spoil their children, but the fact is that if you have successfully provided your child with a safe home, food, clothes, and education, your child is lucky enough to occupy the top 1% of privileged children on the planet. It's almost a cliché, but we know that gifts will almost never replace time and love. However, even for those that did not have families, the same regret often applied. All work and little play to pursue what feeds your soul can be a slow death that some may not realise until it's too late.

3) I wish I had the courage to express my feelings.

Considering the first two regrets, this also would seem to be the logical third. Let's face it, many of us will often choose the easy, more comfortable, option and shy away from truly expressing what we really think and feel. These are simple life skills that we're never taught to this generation. Thankfully, this is changing in many schools these days as we recognise more and more that emotional intelligence is just as important. Some would argue that it is even more important than the standard reading, writing and arithmetic which, by the way, will be a thing of the past very soon, thanks to our technology, smartphones and A.I. If we are never taught to express ourselves, or if we never invest any time, money or effort into developing this skill, then we may find it extremely challenging to say what we mean and mean what we say when communicating to another. This leaves us open to the possibility of being misunderstood, judged and perhaps even alienated as the people we care for develop a perception of who we are based on how we communicate and express ourselves.

We all know that feeling of relief when you're able to 'get something off your chest' in such a way that has allowed the other person to understand your good intentions and where you're coming from. Being able to articulate yourself and your true feelings may not be something that everyone is able to do easily, but I am convinced that it is a skill that can be learnt and developed for anyone who recognises its value. The natural result of holding back in this way and not being able to express yourself, especially when it comes to interpersonal relationships, are feelings of resentment, bitterness or even guilt—three emotions that certainly can erode any relationship. It continually shocks me to listen to people share their relationship challenges and when I ask, 'Have you spoken to them about this?', the response is either 'no' or 'I've tried but they just shut down.' Sometimes the outcome you want is only a conversation away.

Expressing your true feelings is also a very powerful way to connect with people on a deep level. I honestly believe that your ability to attract, develop and maintain fulfilling relationships is directly proportional to your ability to reveal meaningful aspects of yourself in the right way at the right time. This becomes apparent for people who may have been in your life for many years, but still leave you with a sense that you don't really know them. Have you ever experienced this before? I know I have. When I thought about what and why that might be the case, it dawned on me that it was due to the fact that in almost every case where I felt that, it was because conversation was often a little superficial, devoid of any true, meaningful, purposeful or interpersonal content. Once again, one needs to be aware of the balance so as not to continuously pour your heart out leaving others feeling emotionally and mentally drained. In this way, sometimes being able to express your feelings can have the opposite effect where people will actively try to avoid you. You may even know people like this in your own life.

4) I wish I had stayed in touch with my friends.

It was apparent to Bonnie that many of her patients were only able to recognise the preciousness and value of good past friendships when it was too late. Many realised that they had not invested the time and effort into maintaining friendships, perhaps because they were working too hard. Maybe this is even a logical consequence of being caught up in the rat race of pursuing the things we think will bring us true happiness. The advantage we have in staying in touch these days is social media, something that wasn't around for these patients. Even though some may question the quality of this kind of digital connection, it is arguably the most powerful phenomenon of the 21st century—at the very least to help us stay in touch in some way.

5) I wish that I had let myself be happier.

Despite what I mentioned earlier about happiness, many patients had come to realise that happiness was more of a choice than anything else. Having been caught up in their lives, they had just forgotten to BE content with what was, rather than going after what they thought might have been at some point in the future. Often, as adults, we don't allow our joyful inner child to come out. There is a difference between acting immaturely and expressing your inner child. Our emotional wounds, egos or fear of being judged or looking silly will often hold us back. We all know people who just take themselves, or life, too seriously. The scientifically verified health benefits of a good, deep belly laugh have been well documented. We are all familiar with the term, 'Laughter is the best medicine', but sometimes we forget to implement what we know to be true. If we know something to be true but do not act on what we know, do we really know it at all?

Most of us know the futility of thinking that we will find true 'happiness' only when we have X, Y or Z. Believing that your inner state of being will only be a positive one when external circumstances meet your expectations is simply flawed logic. Your state of being is often because of a habitual pattern of thoughts, feelings and behaviours, all of which are interconnected. It just doesn't make sense to think that your state of being will all of a sudden change and remain that way with a change in external circumstances when you have literally trained yourself and your neurology into a state of being that simply will not allow for sustained perceptions of wellbeing. You just can't get there from there.

The irony I see here is that, often from an early age, we are conditioned to believe that the world is a certain way, and to survive and be happy in the world, you need to be, do and have certain things, and that's just the way it is. We are led to believe that certain things are worth your time and energy and others are not. All of this is reinforced as we applaud and praise those who battled and fought 'tooth and nail' to accomplish their mission. This, of course, is one way, but is it the only way? And once again, at what cost? What seems sad to me when looking at this list of regrets is the fact that we are often discouraged—by friends, family, society, or our own limiting beliefs—from prioritising these things, because we are brought up to believe that fulfilment and security won't come in that way and it's a fantasy to think otherwise. It is for this reason I wanted to include the most common regrets people have reported to help you dig deeper into your intentions and motivations for what you wish to achieve and express in your life. After all, why settle for a 'normal' life when you can live an inspired life? And what is 'normal' anyway?

The Profound Paradox and the Power of Balancing Perceptions

Having described expectations, results and goal setting, here is the profound paradox that lies at the basis of all of this—your ability to completely and totally detach yourself from the outcome and how you think it should come about. Does this sound strange and perhaps even contradictory to the entire process of manifesting your dreams? To many it does. Even though it may seem this way on the surface, it is actually a very profound aspect to manifesting absolutely anything in your life. Your ability to attract and create anything you want involves an immense desire for what you are wanting and visualising during the self-hypnosis H.A.R.T. However, it also requires a complete and total detachment from the way it is going to manifest in your life. The mantra here is, 'No insistence, no resistance.' The more we insist on a goal having to manifest a certain way, the more we close ourselves off to the infinite possibilities the universe has to delivering that same thing in ways we may never have thought of with our conscious logical, rational, realistic mind. Ever heard of the saying, 'What you resist persists'? Or perhaps the saying, 'Where focus goes, energy flows'? It's a simple law of the universe and the energy of manifesting what you set your focus on, be it something you want or don't want. Whatever it is, it will continue to persist simply because of the energy you are giving it. This is especially important to remember when working with the subconscious mind for one crucial reason—the subconscious mind cannot process negatives. But what do I mean by that?

Here is one simple example of this concept. Try your very best to not think of a white bear. What did you just think about? A white bear, right? Why? Because the mental process you have to employ to not think of the white bear requires you to first create the image of the white bear so you know what not to think about. Your subconscious mind, and the energy that manifests everything in your life, works in exactly the same way. It is for this reason it is important that hypnotic suggestions are always constructed around what you want rather than what you don't want. Always stated in the positive about what you wish to create, not what you want to get rid of. The more you invalidate what is currently present in your life, the harder it is to attract and create another option, but when all options are as valid as any other then this opens up the doorway for new possibilities, choices and preferences. Here's another way to look at this idea of manifesting. You don't have to actually learn to manifest, but let go of the beliefs that are standing in the way of what you want to experience. Everything you want is trying its best to get to you, but you block it from manifesting into your reality usually because of either a fear of success or a belief of unworthiness.

Another powerful exercise in balancing your perceptions is to be at peace with absolutely any situation in your life. Being okay with what is, is not about putting up with your life the way it is. It is simply about reducing the negative energy around what you say you don't want. In order to release its hold on your mind, body and spirit, the very thing keeping that unwanted thing in your reality is the negative label you give it. The truth is, no matter what problem you have in your life at this very moment, there is a positive benefit to it that you are simply not acknowledging and perceiving. The opposite is also the case. No matter what it is you say you want, there are also negative aspects to having that in your life, which you are also not acknowledging and perceiving. And this leads to an imbalanced perspective about what is in your life now and what you say you want for your future.

Below is a table with one simple intention—to help balance your perceptions by making you aware of some potential negatives and positives regarding only a few things that people say they would and would not like to have manifest in their life. This is a great exercise to help you experience contentment in the only moment that will ever exist in your life—now. This is a powerful process that can help you see that there is always a balance between positive and negative, not only within the physics of the universe but also within the perceptions, judgements and definitions of the human mind. As human beings, we often aspire to be, do or have something in our lives with a false assumption that it will not have any negative drawbacks or consequences. Essentially, we create a one-sided fantasy about something we wish to be, do or have, but this obviously is not an accurate perception of reality. No matter what you say you want in your life, there will always be some negatives or drawbacks associated with it. Not recognising this can keep us striving more and more for 'a better future', which simply robs you of being in the moment.

Negative / Positive Situation	**Balancing Perspective**
Negative: Lack of intimate relationship	Positive: Freedom to do what you want when you want. No nasty in-laws to put up with. Can focus 100% of your energy on developing yourself. More time for friends and family.
Negative Past abusive relationship	Positive: Helped you become wiser and stronger by standing up for yourself more. Can help others in similar situations. Valuable lessons in the development of your character.
Negative Poor health, low mood, depression	Positive: Playing 'victim role' attracts saviours and their attention. Excuse to 'not try things' and stay safe, sympathy from others, comfort in 'the devil you know' and familiarity.
Positive Have a successful career and 'climb the corporate ladder'	Negative: Poor work/life balance, high stress, poor physical health, neglected family, fall victim to expensive destructive habits, lack of true fulfilment, resentment for having lived according to another's expectation, high responsibility.
Positive Have a baby and start a family	Negative: Huge responsibility, expensive, reduced freedom, less expendable income for personal pleasures, sleepless nights, worry and stress for their personal safety. Behaviourally challenging kids that emotionally drain you, leaving little energy to focus on your spouse.
Positive More financial wealth	Negative: Worry and stress about losing/ protecting it, people asking for money, others' jealousy, resentment and expectations, time and effort needed to manage it, falling victim to expensive, destructive bad habits, attracting shallow people who like you only for your money and not who you truly are.
Positive Marry a rich man (or woman)	Negative: Lack of true love, a shallow, less meaningful, purposeful, fulfilling relationship, partner always away working, workaholic partner that uses material possessions to compensate, other people trying to 'steal them' away from you, open to being left for a younger version due to lack of commitment.

Of course, the above is only a very small sample of what many people say they want or do not want. This, of course, creates an imbalanced perception that robs us of being in the moment. There are simple questions that you can ask yourself in any moment that will allow you to experience more inner peace about your current situation. There are also some questions you can ask about the future you want that will allow you to be more detached from the outcome and how it will manifest for you, which actually helps it manifest more quickly for you. For any situation you are judging as undesirable, ask yourself these four questions. They may seem simple, but let me assure you, this does not mean they are easy to answer:

- *'How is this situation benefiting me?'*
- *'What is the hidden lesson or learning this situation could be trying to teach me?'*
- *'What could be some potential negatives if this was NOT happening?'*
- *'What would I have to believe is true, which actually may not be, to be feeling this way?'*

For any future thing that you wish to be, do or have, ask yourself these two questions to help you detach from its outcome:

- *'What would be the potential negatives or drawbacks about being, doing or having X?'*
- *'What valuable lessons or learnings could I potentially miss out on if that outcome occurred?'*

The above questions can help you develop a great life skill—the ability to reframe any situation in your life so that even if something exists in your life at the moment, which is something you objectively do not prefer by labelling it as negative, you can get the positive meaning and hence, effect, out of it. When you stop invalidating what is, you allow for what you prefer to make its way to you.

The Power of Imagination and Visualisation

It was Albert Einstein who said, 'Knowledge will get you from A to B. Imagination will get you everywhere else.' The fact is that unless you can imagine yourself having achieved the goal you say you want, it just isn't going to manifest in your life. You more than likely already have an intuitive feeling about the importance of imagination and visualisation, but let's reinforce this a little more, shall we? Let's begin by simply deconstructing the parts and meaning of the word 'imagination'. There are essentially three parts to this word, I-MAGI-NATION.

I: means me, myself.

MAGI: means 'skilled magician'.

NATION: means country, homeland, origin, breed, stock, kind, species, race of people, or tribe. More literally, it means 'that which has been born.'

Breaking down this one word in this way allows you to recognise and appreciate its importance, especially as it relates to a self-hypnosis practice. I honestly believe it is the key to awakening your inner magician to create and give birth to the life you want—a mastered life via the power of your imagination combined with your subconscious mind and the H.A.R.T. It cannot be underestimated how important it is to have a 'vision' of that which you wish to create, experience and achieve in your life. Many of the most successful people who have ever lived have attributed success to the ability to visualise the end result. It's also what I believe to be the main difference between a business owner and an entrepreneur. For me, the difference is that a business owner's focus is on a successful business for all of the beautiful benefits a thriving business can bring. The entrepreneur, however, as I define it, is an individual not just with many fingers in many pies, but a person with a vast and grand vision to do their bit to 'change the world' via the vehicle of a successful business. The key I believe is vision, imagination and heart.

As mentioned in this book already, the connection between the pictures we hold in our heads (our visualisations) and our body has been well-documented all over the world. This varies from cases of spontaneous healing, immediate shifts in the human body's biochemistry, breathing and heart rate, and even performance enhancement of elite athletes. There is no doubt that our body is responding to the vividness of our visions, whether they are conscious or subconscious. You can easily experience this connection by simply closing your eyes and remembering as vividly as you can a time when you felt extremely anxious or nervous. Perhaps a test of some kind or just before you had to have a difficult conversation or do a frightening activity. Or perhaps remember a time when someone made you really angry or annoyed. If you were to close your eyes right now and picture this moment as clearly as you can, I guarantee that you will feel a physical response to a moment or situation that essentially isn't real! Even though it may have actually happened in the past, the fact is that in this very moment, it isn't actually happening. It's an illusion of your mind. Of course, the opposite effects are also possible when you imagine or recall memories that evoke positive emotions such as love, gratitude, compassion, or excitement. The profound effect of these emotions and the resonance it creates when combined with heart-focused breathing was explained in Chapter 3. For me, this is simple, yet compelling proof of the connection between imagination, visualisation and the body. This is yet another reason why self-hypnosis is so powerful.

If we can produce such powerful physiological experiences in this way, imagine what you could achieve with your mind, body and life with a repeated and regular practice of reinforcing and training your own subconscious with the images and pictures of what you do prefer. Logically and anatomically speaking, your brain of course does not know the difference between something you are visualising or imagining and something that any of your five senses are actually detecting as 'real'. Your brain is essentially sitting in a dark room, namely your skull, and it is interpreting electrical impulses. These electrical impulses can be created either by one of your five senses being triggered by a stimulus or by visualising your interaction with the same stimulus. This is simple human biomechanics.

Let it be said, however, that even though using your imagination and visualisation is a powerful component when it comes to life mastery, that doesn't mean that it is necessarily easy to do. Over the years, I have met many people that find it a challenge to visualise and create pictures in their mind's eye. This difficulty can be amplified if they are trying to imagine something they have never experienced before in real life. It's also important to remember that some people are not as visual as others when it comes to the way they process information. There are five senses, and hence potentially five ways to think. Some people find it easier to think or imagine in terms of sounds, feelings, smells, or maybe a combination of both. However, seeing pictures in the mind's eye is common for most people. Whether this is or isn't the case for you, there is a four-step process to practice and enhance your visualisation skills. They are:

1) Take a moment to observe your surroundings VERY closely. Really look at the details of where you are, whether it's a room, outside, at the beach, in a park, sitting in a bus, wherever. After about a minute, close your eyes and recreate your immediate environment with as much detail and clarity as possible. This is the first step to creating visualisation and imagination skills.

2) The second step is to imagine as clearly as you can an environment you know well but are not physically in at the moment. This could be a room in your house, your office, your car, your parent's house, etc. Once again, the key is to recreate the smallest amount of detail in your mind, including the colours, the textures, sounds, smells, and even temperature.

3) The next level is to visualise or imagine something that you have experienced a little less often. Perhaps a thunderstorm, a crying baby, being at a circus, taking off in a jumbo jet, a visit to the zoo, or riding a motorcycle. Once again, imagine and try to see, feel and hear as much detail as possible.

4) The fourth and final level is often the most challenging for people. This is where you practice picturing something that is completely fictional. This is your opportunity to truly let your imagination run wild. Some examples could be imagining an underground city, visiting another planet that has intelligent life, being an animal, slaying a dragon, being in heaven, riding a mythical creature, anything that requires mental creativity.

Like any skill, it requires practice. You may already be very good at this, or you may need to start here. If it is something that you need to practice, the important thing is to give yourself time, be patient, and try to release any expectations. A wandering mind and flicking images are very normal, not only as a beginner but even as you advance in your practice. But the worst thing you can do is give up altogether. Avoid this at all costs.

Timeline and Regression

One of the many uses for self-hypnosis and of course the Heart Alpha Resonance Technique (H.A.R.T) is Timeline Therapy (TLT) and Regression Therapy, which includes Past Life Regression (PLR). This type of therapy, like any other, will either resonate with you or not, depending on a few things, most notably your belief in past lives. Generally speaking, the concept of past lives and the karma associated with them is a strongly held belief, particularly in Eastern cultures—especially in India. Hence, PLR is generally considered to be of great value and powerful in its capacity for healing, transformation and dissolving past-life karma.

In general, I define Timeline Therapy as any kind of hypnotic process that guides you through a specific experience of your timeline towards the past and/or future for the purpose of healing and transformation. Of course, this is a type of therapy entire books are written about, beyond the scope of this book. However, I want to share with you some basic concepts and principles about timeline and regression therapy that will help you to get the most out of the regression scripts included in Chapter 5 of this book. Two of the most common questions I get asked during my workshops are: 'Is it real? and 'Did that really happen?' Paralysis by analysis is a common challenge for some people, especially for the more analytical, left-brain-type people among us—me included. When I am asked these kinds of questions, I often answer them in the same way in an attempt to give a useful framework for this type of process. I believe more useful questions to ask are: 'How was that relevant to me and my life here and now?' and 'How can I use this experience to improve my current and future experiences?'

If you are going to engage in any kind of regression or timeline therapy, I strongly believe in the ability to 'let go' and 'go with the flow' of anything and everything that you may be experiencing, no matter how strange and weird it may seem. In fact, I often say 'the stranger the better'. This is a sign that you're allowing your subconscious to do the work, rather than trying to manipulate what is happening—a tell-tale sign that you're using more conscious than subconscious processes. This is the art of self-hypnosis, which I believe cannot necessarily be taught but comes to you the more you go within yourself and explore. H.A.R.T is a tool to achieve a state of awareness where you are fully conscious of your surroundings but at the same time are relaxed and focused enough to allow an inner experience to occur in your mind's eye, while suspending your critical, logical monkey mind.

If this sounds difficult for you, let me remind you that this is exactly what you do when you go to the movies, especially when it is one of those fantasy or science-fiction movies. You ultimately go to the movies for an experience, and you know that if you brought your critical, logical mind into the theatre, you would not have the experience you want. When you walk into the cinema, for a short time you are suspending all critical disbelief for the sake of the experience. When you see things on the silver screen that are so obviously not 'real', you do not start to laugh and shout 'boo', telling everyone in the cinema that it's rubbish and false. I recommend the exact same approach when it comes to regression and timeline therapy of any kind.

I tell my clients to simply be open to, and allow, what comes to be there without forcing, judging or manipulation. The time to do your integrating and analysing is at the end of the process once you have come out of it. This is the time to find the connection and relevance of what you have experienced in your life and how it can help you in the future. I think this is the true value of any regression process. Yes, it can be fun to be curious and explore. Yes, it can be a very powerful process for healing the past. But as already mentioned, I think the most powerful question you can ask yourself is: 'How is this understanding, awareness or healing going to improve my life both now and in the future?' Once again, be mindful of expectations as sometimes the best outcome is simply a feeling of more inner peace, calm and relief.

Another question I am sometimes asked is, 'Is there any science to support the idea of timeline therapy?' The answer is yes. The physics and science of a connected universe is revealing to us the dynamics and structure of the most infinitely dense and energetic thing in the universe—the vacuum or space-time. This fabric of the universe has also been called 'space-memory' because without memory, there is no time, and vice versa. Although this is still a topic of debate among the scientific community, the fabric and structure of space is being hypothesised as the very thing where information or 'memory' is stored. This information or memory is said to be accessible by the brain, but it is not necessarily stored in the brain, as taught in mainstream anatomy. According to this new approach, the brain, as described by Nikola Tesla, is simply a tool for receiving the information, much like a television or radio antenna. But how is this information put there?

This brings us back to the Russian research on the interactions between photons, DNA and its ability to leave a detectable imprint on the structure of space. As we hurtle through space, spiralling around a Sun that is spiralling around a galaxy, the DNA in each and every cell of our bodies is leaving an imprint, or trail, on the fabric of space. This trail is connected to the energetic DNA trail of your parents and their parents and so on. It is through a process of visualisation that perhaps makes it possible to connect with, and transform, energies and karmas that may have been passed onto you from your family lineage. The self-hypnosis script contained within this book can most definitely assist you in releasing and dissolving these limiting energies. But how about past lives that may not have been connected to you via your family tree? This is an area of even more debate as it is of course difficult to verify these kinds of process. However, this is only relevant to people who need objective verifiable evidence before they attempt any kind of alternative healing process or modality. For others, this is not needed at all because for them the experience and the result are all that matters.

As mentioned earlier, to relate this to the placebo effect, some people would prefer not to be 'tricked' or 'deluded' by a potentially positive effect of a placebo, actually preferring to know that the pill is just a sugar tablet than experience the positive effect the placebo could have. But it all comes down to your own personal definitions. It's an interesting personal preference and perspective for each individual. For me, it's not a black and white, this or that, cut and dried type of situation, as I find it exciting to have some mystery within the science. It's a balance between having your castle in the sky and laying the foundations deep within the Earth—a type of grounded creative imagination, so to speak.

One perspective to consider that could help create a functional framework to help you integrate and make sense of experiences during a PLR is to think of them not as 'past lives' as such, but energetic cross connections you are making to that life to assist you here and now in this life. It has been said that although we experience time as a linear phenomenon, this is in fact an illusion, and all things and all lives are coexisting simultaneously here and now. This could be quite a shift from your current perspective on 'past life' therapy. Perhaps when you are regressing 'back through time' to a past life, you could actually be connecting with the consciousness of someone or something that is actually existing right here and now, but perhaps in another dimension to where you are here and now. The purpose of that particular connection in that particular moment could be to assist you in whatever way, shape or form that is of most benefit here and now to help you with any process you may be going through. For example, having a regression experience of being an ancient Egyptian pharaoh could be more about connecting with the confidence needed to express more leadership skills in your life here and now rather than just feeding your curiosity or ego. However, this of course is totally up to you and how you wish to use the process. Once again, this is just an idea, a perspective I believe is worth considering so you can decide for yourself whether it could personally help you or not. Another interesting thought could be that as you are cross connecting with other simultaneously existing lives, they may well be connecting to you in your life here and now in order to gain some piece of wisdom or knowledge that you have gained that could help them.

Basic Self-Hypnosis Logistics and Protocol

It is important for you to become familiar with the fundamentals of a self-hypnosis practice before we get into the Heart Alpha Resonance Technique (H.A.R.T) and the hypnosis scripts that follow. As mentioned, H.A.R.T is essentially a revolutionary new extension of a traditional self-hypnosis protocol. For the purposes of this chapter, I am going to assume that you have had little to no experience with self-hypnosis. However, even if you have, it would still be of great benefit for you to use this as a chance to refresh your understanding.

Decide in advance how long your self-hypnosis is going to go for. There really isn't any right or wrong amount of time. You may find that in the beginning it takes you a little longer to get into that relaxed place, so give yourself the time you need at the start. But generally speaking, after some practice, you'll probably find that 15 to 20 minutes is quite enough. At first, it may take you a while to get used to the feeling of that trance-like state, but as I've said before, the more you do it, the better you'll get at it. If you are already a person that practices meditation, then of course you may find this initial step a little easier simply because of the familiarity of the feeling. In the early stages of your practice, for the timing of your session, you can do it in two ways. You can either tell yourself and your unconscious mind at the start that you're going to be in a trance for 'X' number of minutes, or you can nominate a time on the clock, i.e., 'I'm going to go into a trance from 8:00 to 8:15.' Either way, if you just say it out loud to yourself, your unconscious mind will do the rest. Just trust it. Saying this to yourself sends the message to your unconscious mind and it's also the start of the focus that you need to go into a trance. Also, at some point, a few minutes into your trance, it can be helpful to say to yourself, 'After twenty minutes, or fifteen minutes, or at 7:20 pm (whichever you choose), I will come back to full awareness feeling great, feeling fine and refreshed in every way.'

Make sure you know your suggestion(s) and have a good idea of what it is that you are going to visualise. I'll discuss a little more about suggestions shortly. Commit your suggestions or affirmations to memory. This is done more easily when they are short, succinct and to the point. This is one of those examples where sometimes 'less is more'.

Ensure that you're comfortable. Loosen any tight clothing and either sit or lie down. I would recommend sitting to prevent falling asleep, but you'll know beforehand whether you're likely to nod off during your hypnosis. Lying down is better for relaxation, but a comfortable chair is fine as well.

Reduce or eliminate the likelihood of distraction

If you're going to practice self-hypnosis, you will have to learn to deal with distractions. These can range from intrusive thoughts, otherwise known as 'monkey mind' or they could just be noises outside the building where you are. Some of the outside noises can seem to be pretty distracting, such as alarms going off, workmen, noisy traffic, etc. But more often than not, it can be your own thoughts that are just as distracting and just as disruptive. It could even be physical pain, an itch or some kind of emotional disturbance. Basically, anything that causes disruption to any part of the self-hypnosis process is a distraction. So, the question now is: 'How do I deal with these distractions during my self-hypnosis practice?' Below is a list of things that you can do to reduce the chances of being distracted during your practice. Preventing distractions is always better than trying to deal with them.

- Practice in a place or environment that is as comfortable as possible. Find a place where you can avoid fidgeting.
- Practice at a time of the day when you are least likely to be disrupted.
- If you need to, make sure you go to the toilet before you start.
- Try to practice before, or at least an hour after, meals.
- Don't practice if you've had alcohol or recreational drugs.
- Turn off your mobile phone.

Deal with any distractions as they arise

Obviously, there are going to be times when a disturbance or distraction just happens. Some of these should be dealt with then and there. Otherwise, if you try to ignore it, you'll just keep wondering about it. Then your entire session will not be as effective as it could be.

- If someone comes knocking on your door, or calls on the phone, just answer it. But if you remember to turn off your phone, that should take care of that.
- If you do happen to develop an itch, scratch it, and then return to your trance. But try to delay the action of doing this. Often an itch will go away all on its own after just a few seconds.
- If someone in your environment needs your attention in that moment, go ahead and deal with it and then return to your trance. But once again, you can reduce the likelihood of being distracted by practicing when you are on your own. Or you could even put up a 'Do Not Disturb' sign on your door. Or you could just ask the people around you not to disturb you for the next twenty minutes or so because you're going to do your relaxation practice. Find whatever works for you and your situation.

Use the disturbance to help your self-hypnosis

Believe it or not, some distractions can actually be helpful and can even be used to bring you into a deeper state of relaxed trance. Below are some tips:

- Just before you start your self-hypnosis session, tell yourself that everything you're going to hear around you during the self-hypnosis is going to make your relaxation even deeper. For example, you could say to yourself, 'From this moment, over the next twenty minutes or so, I might hear noises around me and all these sounds will only make my relaxation deeper and deeper.'
- If you hear passing cars, motorbikes or trucks, you can imagine that the vehicle is carrying your concerns away. Or you could imagine that any stress or discomfort you might be noticing in your body can also be carried away as the vehicle passes by. As it passes, you can feel yourself drifting deeper and deeper into trance. If you're hearing a plane pass by in the sky above you, just imagine that you are sitting in it and it is either bringing you down deeper and deeper, or lifting you higher and higher, making you lighter and lighter, depending on whether or not you can tell the difference between a plane landing or taking off.

- With any sounds you may hear, even if it's coming from people talking outside your room, remind yourself that, whatever is happening outside the room or building, inside the building, and in your mind, you are creating tranquillity and peace. Use your imagination and visualise those sounds drifting further and further away.
- Distractions coming from inside yourself are probably the most common challenge for people starting any kind of inner practice. Be aware that having mind chatter is very normal and natural. It's totally fine to notice your internal dialogue or wandering mind. Don't aim to have a completely empty mind. You're not a Buddhist monk living in a dark isolated Himalayan cave; you're practicing self-hypnosis. Rather than trying to empty your mind, try to use your thoughts in such a way that will help deepen your trance. One thing you could do is count your thoughts as they come to you, like counting passing people or cars. Or simply notice the moment your mind is wandering and bring your attention back to your rhythmic breath. A wandering mind does not have to be an irritation if you become the observer of the thoughts rather than involved in them. Treat them like a crowd of people walking past you as you sit and watch them. You don't usually watch and/or stare at an individual for very long, rather for only a short time. You can treat your thoughts in the same way. These are all helpful tips, but with practice and time, you will develop an ability to focus more and more on your experience rather than any distractions.

Music or no music?

Once again, this is a matter of personal preference with no right or wrong answer. I find music to be extremely useful in helping me get into a relaxed state, but this is completely your choice. The one and only question to ask yourself here is: 'Do I believe using soft music is going to help my practice?' If you are going to use music, obviously make sure it is something that is soothing to you and is something that will help you experience a sense of going deeper or drifting away. Instrumentals are often best for this, or you might want to use a recording of a rainforest, an ocean or crashing waves. There are many pieces of free music you can find on YouTube. My only suggestion is to make sure that the track is longer than the time you intend to be in trance. This is just another measure to ensure it doesn't distract you by ending too soon. You could even use the length of the track to time your session. Although it's not necessary to have the music as a timer, it can help you time your session.

The Four Steps to Self-Hypnosis

I'm now going to share with you four simple steps to creating your own self-hypnosis practice without having to rely on any pre-written scripts. Although I will be providing you with hypnosis scripts in Chapter 5, I also want you to understand each step in the self-hypnosis process so you have the knowledge to create your own practice and suggestions for anything you want to create or address in your life that may not be specifically addressed in the scripts provided in Chapter 5.

The four steps are:

1) The creation of the trance state. This is technically known as the 'induction' phase.
2) The deepening of trance. This is done to ensure that the conscious mind is as inactive and as 'quiet' as possible.
3) The therapy. Using suggestions, imagination and visualisations, this is the section used to generate the desired effect and what you're aiming for—the outcome you WANT!
4) The emerge. This is the process used to bring you back from that relaxed place.

1) The Creation of Trance

I believe this is one of the most important aspects of hypnosis, whether you are going to a hypnotherapist or you are practicing self-hypnosis. Your ability to create massive transformation in your life with any kind of hypnosis will be experienced to the degree to which you are able to bring yourself into that state of trance. The image below depicts what the different brainwave frequencies would look like on an Electro-Encephalogram (EEG) of brain activity.

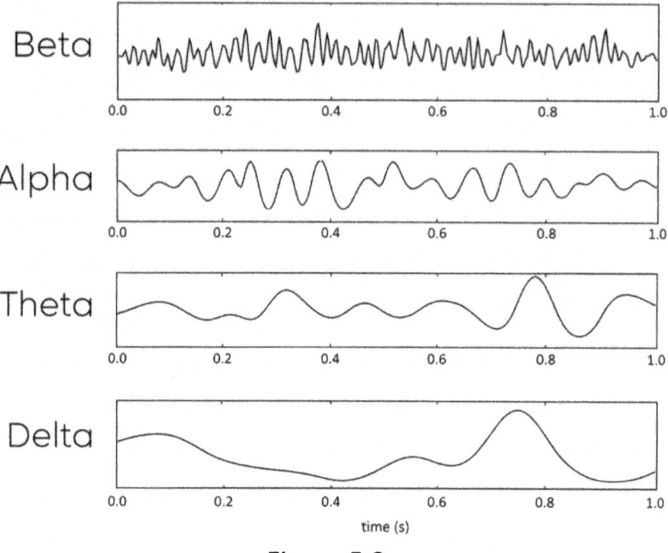

Figure 5.2

Our normal, everyday wakeful state of focused, concentrated attention is called the beta brainwave state. This is the state mostly associated with hyper-arousal and alertness. The alpha state is associated with wakeful relaxation and relaxed focus. This is the state where the production of the 'feel good' or 'wellbeing' brain chemical, serotonin, increases. As already mentioned, it is that state we drift in and out of through the day while driving, reading a book or watching TV. It's that state of drowsiness just before falling asleep at night and just after waking in the morning.

What is most interesting and most relevant for you here is that it is considered the gateway state not only to the unconscious mind, but to super-learning and unlearning. It is a very crucial state and one which you must learn exactly how to access and then practice over and over again until you have mastered it. The theta state is associated with dreaming (REM sleep) and deep meditative relaxation. With practice, you may begin to drift in between the alpha and the theta state, which is absolutely fine for self-hypnosis.

However, the alpha state of relaxation is most definitely sufficient. The delta state is the deepest of dreamless sleep and is associated with being unconscious. Below are four different ways of creating trance—two eye fatigue, and two mental confusion techniques, all of which allow your brain waves to gently make the transition from the beta to the alpha brainwave frequency where the subconscious can be communicated with.

Breathing Technique - One of the quickest and simplest methods to create trance is to take five slow, deep breaths (five seconds in, five seconds out) while keeping your head straight and focusing your gaze on an object or a spot directly in front and above you so your eyes are at an angle of approximately 45 degrees. On your fifth inhale, make it very deep, and on your exhale, slowly close your eyes. As you continue to breathe, start to notice the rising and falling of your chest. Imagine that with each exhale your body gets heavier and heavier, sinking deeper and deeper into the chair beneath your body, creating more and more relaxation, stillness and heaviness.

Flame Gazing Eye Fatigue - While breathing normally, focus on the brightest part of a candle flame. Continue to gaze with a relaxed kind of stare. Imagine that you can stare through the flame rather than directly at it until your peripheral vision starts to become blurry and fuzzy. After a few minutes of this, shift your attention to the little muscles around your eyes and eyelids. Imagine they can become more and more relaxed, and heavier and heavier until you feel your eyes becoming increasingly tired and wanting to close. When you reach the point at which your eyes want to close, allow them to slowly and gently close, and begin to focus on your inner experience.

Thought Repetition - A confusion technique. Gently allow your eyes to close as you breathe normally. When your eyes are closed, think of three thoughts to repeat one after the other through your mind with increasing speed. For example, picture the front door of your home, then picture your car, then picture your last meal. Flick through these thoughts over and over, quickly going from one thought to the other until you find your mind wandering off into a deepening relaxation. Then begin to focus on your inner experience. You can choose any three thoughts you want, but nothing that produces negative emotions. The fast thought processing leads to confusion, and the response of the conscious mind is to shut down a little. You'll know when you've achieved this at the moment you notice that you are no longer flicking through your three thoughts.

The Blackboard Technique - This is the second confusion technique. Allow your eyes to gently close. Imagine a big blackboard in front of you. Imagine writing the number 100 on it with a piece of chalk. See it and then visualise rubbing it off. Continue to do this process of writing, seeing and then rubbing off the numbers going backwards in threes, i.e. 100, 97, 94, 91, 88, 85, and so on. With each number you visualise, imagine seeing the number being half the size of the one before. Like the first confusion technique above, you'll know this has done the job when you realise that you've lost track of your counting.

2) The Deepening of Trance

Deepening is an important aspect of self-hypnosis. It's important to learn not only how to bring yourself into a trance, but how to bring yourself deeper and deeper into that state where all the transformational work takes place. The aim of the hypnosis deepening is to make sure the conscious mind has become as quiet as possible. As you know by now, the conscious mind will not disappear completely during the process. All we want to do is put it in the back seat for a short time. When doing self-hypnosis, you don't want your conscious mind to be interfering and critically analysing everything. So, in order to 'turn down' the conscious mind, 'deepening' techniques are used. But remember, everybody experiences the trance state in a very personal way, so don't get too hung up on trying to create the deepest trance ever. You don't have to feel 'really deep' to effectively work with your unconscious mind. Only through regular and persistent practice will you learn to create an experience that is deep enough but not too deep that you forget your own suggestions or fall asleep. These, of course, are not 'bad' outcomes. They are just not the best use of self-hypnosis or the H.A.R.T. There are two parts to deepening that, as you now know, are very closely related. They are the physical and the mental aspect of relaxation and deepening.

Physical deepening

Physical relaxation is obviously an important part of self-hypnosis. If you're physically tense, agitated or uncomfortable, you will be more aware of your body and are unlikely to reach deep relaxation. Your conscious mind will probably be too active, and your trance won't be deepened. But if your body is relaxed enough, you may experience a moment where you almost become unaware of your body. This is a state that can make working with your unconscious mind more easily. Sometimes you can achieve this so well that you may even experience a kind of separation or detachment from your body where it can seem like all you are is your breathing. One of the easiest, most direct ways to become more deeply physically relaxed is to simply tell your body to go deeper and deeper, and feel more and more relaxed. It might sound simple—and it is. After all, your body has to do what you tell it to do. Your muscles respond to your neurology that fires in accordance with your thinking, so if you tell your muscles and body to relax more and more, it will give you the experience of that unless at any moment you decide to snap out of that relaxation which, of course, you could do. Below are a few quick techniques to physically and mentally deepen your relaxation.

- Focus on each body part: head, shoulders, upper and lower back, arms, hands, torso, thighs, calves, and feet, and simply tell them to relax more and more by saying out loud or in your mind one or more of the following suggestions: 'Let go', 'Getting heavier', 'More and more still', 'Switching off', 'Heavy like a rock'.
- Take an extremely slow, long breath in as you expand and stretch your lungs as much as possible, and then exhale as slowly as you can. As you exhale, focus on your body as you imagine it sinking deeper and deeper into the chair, the bed or whatever it is that is under your body. Visualise your body merging with it, creating even more stillness.
- Although counting down is an excellent and effective way of creating trance at the beginning, you can also do it as many times as you like during your trance. An example suggestion you can make to yourself out loud or in your mind is: 'Going even deeper in ... 5, 4, 3, 2, 1 ... deeper and deeper, more and more relaxed.'

- Imagine your entire body is carved out of one huge block of ice. Picture yourself on a bright, sunny, hot summer's day. Imagine, visualise and feel yourself slowly melting and melting. Picture any or all remaining muscle tension oozing out of the pores of your skin.
- Picture yourself floating and bobbing gently on the surface of the ocean, and with a slow, deep breath on your exhale, imagine yourself beginning to sink deeper and deeper into the depths of the ocean as you imagine the quiet stillness of going deeper.

These are just a few common techniques to help and guide you, but feel free to create your own if you wish. You may notice a common theme in the examples above—to imagine and visualise anything at all, which allows you to have a slow and progressive experience of deepness, detachment or drifting.

3) The Therapy

Obviously, the therapy section is one of the biggest reasons for even doing the self-hypnosis at all. All the techniques and methods you're learning here have the simple aim to create a positive noticeable change in your daily experience. It can lead to the synchronicities that will lead to being in the right place at the right time to meet the right people to allow the change to occur.

After doing your induction, your deepening, and you've created your hypnotic trance, this will be the time to start working towards the outcome and goal you've set for yourself. You may feel that before throwing yourself right into the entire process, it may feel better for you to just practice bringing yourself in and out of the trance state. This can help you feel more comfortable with the process. Once the trance state and feeling starts to become more familiar to you, you can then move on to integrating the therapy aspect of the self-hypnosis.

Before you start to work on and define your goals, there are a few things worth reminding you of. Make sure you are as clear as possible about what you actually want to achieve. Make sure you know exactly how you want to think, feel and behave. Define it in positive terms. It's not about getting clear on what you *don't* want. You're not here to build a road map towards what you *don't* want; you are here to create a pathway to what you *do* want.

Make sure the suggestions you are going to be creating and saying to yourself are short, simple and to the point. Make them in the present tense and make sure you actually believe them. For example, instead of saying, 'I'll never eat chocolate ever again', you could say something like, 'It is easy for me to choose healthy food to eat.'

Use suggestions, words, symbols, and images for your visualisations that are specific to you and that are meaningful to you in some way. The more emotion you can develop during the process, the better it will be. So, it makes sense to use the things that really mean something to you.

After the induction and deepening phase of self-hypnosis, you will be at the point where you can do your 'therapy'. This will be the time to use the suggestions and visualisations you have already created for yourself. After one or two deepening processes, allow your mind to drift until you feel ready to repeat your suggestion(s). Trust your unconscious mind, allow it to guide you and you'll just 'know' when the time is right to do the therapy phase.

Then mentally say your suggestion slowly and clearly at least ten times. It isn't really possible to repeat your suggestions too many times. It's simply a matter of how much time you wish to be in a trance. Don't just rush this part of the practice. Allow it to be 'spoken' each time as if it is the first time you have said it. What I mean by this is don't just automatically repeat the suggestion in your mind while you are actually thinking about something else. Repeat the suggestion deliberately and thoughtfully with purpose and clarity, almost as if you are saying it to a five-year-old. This will make the therapy more effective.

Feel free to use more than one type of suggestion. I do recommend, however, that if you are going to repeat more than one type, make sure you do not forget the suggestion. Also, keep them as closely related as possible. Take your time with making transformations in your life. Do not try to address weight loss, smoking and confidence all in one session. If you are using weight loss as your topic, you may wish to include suggestions about quality, quantity and timing of meals, for instance. As soon as you start to include motivation for exercise, you may actually be drifting into a different realm altogether. This, once again, is something you will 'feel out' as you develop your practice. It really is about trusting your intuition rather than what you think you have to do, or should be focusing on.

After repeating your suggestion(s), you can then reinforce the message by using your imagery and visualisation. As mentioned earlier, make it relevant and personal to you. Focus on the end result as well as how you might realistically achieve it. A good way to do this is to create a very vivid picture in your mind of what it will actually be like to have that goal achieved. See the images you would be seeing. If weight reduction is your goal, really see yourself looking into that mirror, wearing that clothing. See yourself admiring how you look. Hear anything you would be hearing in that moment. It could be sounds around you, other people saying how good you look, or hearing yourself accepting those compliments. Hear your own internal dialogue that you would be saying in that moment. You might be saying things to yourself like:

'I did it. I knew I could do it. DAMN, I look good! I'm proud of myself.'

Add even more to that visualisation. Imagine the feelings you'd be feeling if that goal was achieved. If your goal is to quit smoking, notice how well you will be breathing, how much energy and vitality you will be experiencing. Connect with where in your body you would be feeling all of this the most.

I'm sure you're starting to get the idea of what is required here. You have to create the most powerful and emotive suggestions and visualisations you can, without making them over the top. This minimises your conscious mind from critically analysing by whispering, 'Yeah right, whatever, who are you trying to kid?' But if you have done the deepening techniques properly, this should be much less likely to happen. As mentioned above, it's important to state your suggestions in positive terms. Avoid making suggestions like, 'I don't want to eat chocolate when I'm bored', or 'I don't want to be afraid and lazy anymore.' This is because of the reason already mentioned—the unconscious mind cannot process negatives. With the same example that I used earlier, if I said to you, 'Don't think of a yellow frog.' What did you just think of? A yellow frog, right? This is completely normal; it's just the way your mind works. Your unconscious mind works in exactly the same way. If you have a suggestion that is, 'I don't want to stuff my face when I'm bored', what the subconscious is actually hearing is, 'Stuff my face when I'm bored.' This is why it's crucial to state your suggestions in the positive, with what you *do* want. I have included some sample suggestions for the three most common things people come to see me for: smoking, weight loss and stress management.

Smoking

'I'm a non-smoker and I love breathing fresh air.'
'I am stronger and more powerful than the smoking habit.'
'I can confidently deal with stress without cigarettes.'
'I easily refuse cigarettes from others no matter where I am or what I'm doing.'
'I choose to live longer and be a role model for my kids' (if you have kids, of course).
'As a non-smoker, I enjoy the clean taste in my mouth and a good smelling body.'
'I can be a non-smoker, be healthier and save thousands of dollars every year.'
'I am now ready to let go of this habit once and for all.'
'As a non-smoker, I can enjoy the freedom to do what I want when I want.'
'I am a non-smoker and am able to spend more time with the people I care about.'

Weight Loss

'I am in control of my eating habits.'
'I find it easy to make healthy food choices.'
'I can allow any emotions to be present without the need, desire or urge to eat.'
'I am easily able to recognise when I have had enough food and I can stop eating in that moment.'
'I respect my body and the food that I feed it.'

'I can more confidently eat the right food, the right amount and at the right time.'
'I enjoy the healthy food that I eat and it always leaves me feeling satisfied.'
'I easily drink at least one litre of water every day to help keep my body healthy and hydrated.'

Stress Management

'I can easily choose to remain calm and relaxed in all situations.'
'Relaxation comes to me quickly as soon as I think about it.'
'I can easily notice moments of stress and remember to breathe.'
'Deep, slow breaths are the easiest and quickest thing I can do to instantly feel more relaxed and in control.'
'I am able to go with the flow in all moments no matter what someone has said or done.'
'I'm able to focus on solutions quickly and easily when something unexpected pops up.'
'I can easily choose to respond rather than react in all situations.'
'The more I practice self-hypnosis, the calmer I become.'

Quick Tip:

If saying these suggestions to yourself for whatever reason is a little difficult at the start of your practice, you can record the suggestions. There are many devices that can record voice memos, etc. Most phones have them these days. If you find it easier, just record your suggestion(s) and then keep the device close to you. When you feel you are in the relaxed trance state, you can press play. Try to avoid opening your eyes, but if you have to, that's fine as well. If you are going to use your phone, just remember to keep it on silent so it doesn't bother you during your session.

4) The Emerge and Coming Out of Trance

Emerging from your trance is the final part of the self-hypnosis process. This is the part when you come back to full awareness, allowing the conscious mind to fully come back into the moment. Although at first it might seem like a pretty easy step, it's still very important to do it right. Some people will experience a very deep state while in trance and so it is important to come back in a very gradual way, step by step. Otherwise, it could be quite disorientating to come out of a deep relaxation too quickly. What you're likely to find is that as you practice more and more, you'll find it easier and easier to go deeper and deeper and that is when it's going to be important to know how to bring yourself back in a nice gradual way. But that doesn't necessarily mean it has to take longer.

The first thing is to recognise the possibility of having to come out of self-hypnosis at any time, whether it's deliberately at the end of our self-hypnosis, or during the self-hypnosis session due to some disturbance, distraction or emergency. There may be times when you have to deal with a distraction of some sort, or times when you have to just open your eyes and deal with whatever has happened. You'll need to be fully aware, so don't skip this step, although, as I've already mentioned, there are a few things you can do to minimise the likelihood of being distracted.

You'll probably find that most of the time when doing your hypnosis, you will be able to get through your session without any disturbances, so you will be able to bring yourself out of self-hypnosis in the right way and at your own pace. It is quite simple really. To bring yourself into the trance, you probably counted yourself down into it, so to emerge out of it, it can simply be a matter of counting yourself back up. Before you start to do the counting, to make the awakening complete, you need to tell yourself that you are about to come back from hypnosis, awake and fully alert. You could say something like this:

'In a moment, I'm going to emerge myself from self-hypnosis, fully alert, fully aware and feeling good. I am going to count from 1 up to 10. With each number, I will become more and more awake and alert. On the count of 10, my eyes will open.'

At this point, begin to slowly count from 1 to 10. When you reach the number 10, open your eyes and notice that you do actually feel good. Once you have come out of hypnosis, I always recommend just taking a few moments to have a stretch. Wiggle your fingers and toes to get your circulation moving again. It's a good habit to draw your attention to what you noticed during your hypnosis and then go through your day continuing to notice what's different. This is a really important aspect of creating change. Don't look for what's the same, but for what's different. Become more sensitive and mindful of any differences in what you feel, what you're saying, how you're acting—anything! The more you're able to recognise what's different, the more you are creating the space and momentum for positive change to actually manifest. Any change is a significant change and the more subtle changes you notice, the more you will begin to develop the most powerful belief of all—I can change!

Part 2: Summary

In Part 2 of this book, we investigated not only what the subconscious mind is, but also its relationship with the mind and body, and how to use it. Many science-based studies have shown us the power of our mind in creating physical sensations and experiences. Now you understand how to accelerate and accentuate this through self-hypnosis. We explored the power and interaction between beliefs, intentions, cells, human DNA, and the heart. We discovered how influential the human heart is in creating numerous physical benefits by focusing on positive emotions, which in turn creates a state of resonance.

We then set the foundations for the actual process for any type of self-hypnosis practice. We considered the elements needed to create and experience observable transformations and synchronicities. This includes getting clear on your expectations and your belief in the process. One of the most important steps is being able to define your goals for self-hypnosis. By looking at the top five regrets of the dying, I asked you to deeply consider what it is you truly want in your heart of hearts by encouraging you to explore the deep motivations for what you say you wish to create in your life. We then reinforced the importance of visualisation and imagination when using self-hypnosis, as well as an explanation of timeline and regression therapies, how to use them and how they can help you.

I then shared a step-by-step process of self-hypnosis along with certain logistical tips and techniques needed to have an effective and positive experience.

Perhaps the new process to be outlined in the next chapter, Part 3 of this book, is simply a different expression of ancient wisdom and knowledge that has been taught in different ways for thousands of years. Maybe there is no such thing as a truly new concept in the universe, but only different ways to express and bring together ideas and information that have always been floating within the vacuum of space waiting for an individual to tune themselves in such a way to receive it. Regardless, it's now time to start *Living with H.A.R.T.*

Part 3

CHAPTER 6

The Heart-Alpha-Resonance-Technique (H.A.R.T)

'Within each of us there is a silence, a silence as vast as the universe. And when we experience that silence, we remember who we are.'

- Gunilla Norris

Becoming the best version of yourself is a multi-layered process. It requires us to uncover our belief systems, perhaps our past, and become aware of our definitions, expectations, assumptions, and subconscious programming, etc. With dedicated and regular practice of the H.A.R.T, I have no doubt whatsoever that all of this is possible.

Connecting to the Earth is something you can choose to do when doing the H.A.R.T protocol. Any time we are doing any form of physical or metaphysical energy work, it is important to 'ground' ourselves. This can be done in many ways through movement, food, being in nature, or in the case of H.A.R.T, you can use your visualisation skills. It is similar to the way that electricity also needs an 'earth' for the circuit to be complete and allow the electrical energy to flow. The simple message, when all is said and done, is one that isn't really new to teachings of a personal and spiritual nature. And that is: Listen to your heart. Considering the connection between DNA and language, as mentioned in Chapter 3, I truly believe that our language can often have clues embedded within them if we choose to see them in that way and take the time to actually look for the clues.

At the beginning of this book, I shared a couple of examples of words being clues. One was the anagram of 'SILENT' into 'LISTEN', and the other was the meditation where I saw 'DARWIN' morph into 'INWARD' when seeking guidance on accelerating my spiritual evolution. But here is another very intriguing example and one that most definitely relates strongly to the H.A.R.T Have you ever noticed that the word 'EARTH' and 'HEART' is just a matter of moving the 'H' from the back to the front? Furthermore, isn't it interesting that the word 'EAR', the physical apparatus we use to LISTEN, is present in both? Could this be a cute coincidence or something more? Who knows? The beauty of being a free human being is that you get to decide what, if any, meaning you are going to attach to this. I believe it to be a powerful sign and no coincidence that in the words, SILENT, LISTEN, HEART, EARTH, and EAR, we can easily see a message that basically says: 'Be silent and listen with your internal ears, the message of your heart which is connected to the earth.'

This was significant for me because I chose to make it meaningful for me. If you want your practice to be this for you, all you have to do is make the choice. Once you do, I have no doubt that you will create and notice whatever 'evidence' you need to then reinforce your own process to yourself. You can do this in such a way that after a while you simply 'KNOW', perhaps without knowing *how* you know. You may get to a point where there is no need to explain or justify your process or your knowing to anyone. There becomes no need to say or do anything to feed the ego. Nobody can ever talk you out of your own personal experience of growth and transformation.

Bringing it All Together

It is now time to bring together the philosophy and science of an interconnected universe with the power and intelligence within ourselves through The Heart Alpha Resonance Technique. You can consider this process 'Self-Hypnosis 2.0'. Although you now have a process for the more traditional form of self-hypnosis that I am sure would create transformation in your life, the H.A.R.T process brings self-hypnosis to an entirely new level. It combines the new scientific understanding of external and internal reality dynamics. By now, you have probably come to realise the significance of the acronym 'H.A.R.T' and the importance of creating heart-based resonance and the power of combining this with the hypnotic trance of the alpha brainwave state.

At this point in our journey, there are a number of fundamental elements that I would like to reiterate and remind you of. Below is a summary of the most crucial elements to keep in mind as a backdrop to the specific details of the H.A.R.T that will follow.

- Everything in the universe is connected through the medium of space that we thought for the longest time was 'empty space'. This space is the most energetically dense thing in the universe and is most likely the source of all creation.
- Atomically speaking, we are made of 99.99999% space. We not only energetically interact with this space, but we are also able to influence the trillions of cells that make up our body through epigenetics.
- The human heart, not only the centre of our being, is more than just a blood pump. It is an intelligent 'mini brain' with an immense capacity to synchronise and facilitate coherent brain activity, creativity and problem solving as well as improve energy levels, vitality and the immune system.
- By purposefully creating the natural phenomena of trance, also known as the alpha brainwave state, we are able to leverage and employ the tremendous power and resource of the unconscious or subconscious mind. This state of 'super learning' allows us to dissolve limiting mental programs that are maintaining our negative habits while giving us an opportunity to install new and helpful ones.
- An effective self-hypnosis and H.A.R.T process depends on a number of factors, which include:

A) Being clear about your deepest intentions and motivations for why you want what you want.

B) Being able to recognise when you are creating out of others' expectations, your fears, or from your true heart's desire. In other words, it is very helpful to realise whether you are moving towards something you truly want, or away from something unwanted. Remember, 'what you resist persists'. Just like a dog chasing a cat, running away from something does nothing but encourage that same thing to pursue you.

C) Setting goals that are congruent with your true self while balancing your expectations and assumptions at the same time.
D) Your ability to slow down or 'let go' of the critical analysing mind allows your body to become as relaxed as possible to create the right level of trance for you.
E) Use your imagination, creativity and visualisation skills to cultivate compelling emotions and commitment to manifest what you want, while remaining completely detached from how the outcome unfolds in your life.
F) Quality, compelling and to the point suggestions and/or affirmations.
G) Your ability to notice what you notice and notice what's different during your everyday life. Be open and ready to act on synchronicities that I guarantee will come your way as a result of this process.
H) The commitment and discipline, especially within the first month, to make this a daily practice regardless of any excuses you may have.

The Step-by-Step H.A.R.T Protocol

'Your heart is the size of the ocean; go find yourself in its depths.'

- Rumi

Don't worry about trying to memorise the process for now because the script is included later in this chapter along with all the other scripts. To make this all even easier for you, I have included a QR code you can use to go to my website. From here, you have the opportunity to access all of the below as an MP3 audio, in my voice, to listen to.

If you choose not to access the audios, once you start to practice this induction process, you will soon reach a point where you will no longer require the script. This will free you to start exploring your very own technique and style as you grow your intuition with what feels right for you in the moment. However, for now, we will break down the process step by step. Each step, along with the scripts that follow, incorporates the science and philosophy that has been shared within the previous chapters. Having become aware of the holographic connected universe, along with what you now know about the mind/body connection, you will have a deeper appreciation for this process and the power of what it is you are doing, which in turn, if practiced regularly, will start to manifest as an explosion of synchronicities.

The Induction

STEP 1: Body Relaxation

Slowly closing your eyes, imagine a relaxing wave or ripple of colour emanating from your eyes. Visualise it moving up your forehead, over your scalp, and down your neck and face. Continue to imagine this spreading of relaxation down your upper and lower back, your torso, over your hips, and down your legs to the tips of your toes.

STEP 2: Drop into the Heart

Visualise an elevator just behind your eyes and imagine that you are at the tenth floor. You enter, press '0' and it begins to drop as it goes down towards your heart. Imagine that when it reaches '0' the doors open and you step out into your heart. Imagine what being inside would look like, feel like, sound like, etc.

STEP 3: Heart Breathing for Coherence

As you imagine yourself inside your heart, take some slow, deep breaths, counting five seconds in and five seconds out. Immerse yourself in deep relaxation, exhaling any remaining tension. As you breathe in this way, connect with and create the sensations of a positive emotion. This could be the love you have for your partner, a parent, a pet from now or in the past, the feelings of an amazing trip, something you bought, or a special event of some kind. Produce a positive feeling and breathe it in through your heart for a minute or two. This can also be done by experiencing gratitude for a few things in your life as it is.

STEP 5: Set Your Intention

Become aware of your intention, specifically what you wish to create or experience. Even if you wish to eliminate a negative thing from your life, focus on what you want, not on what you *do not* want.

This may be increased health, more confidence, physical comfort and wellbeing, ease and inner peace, an intimate relationship, more clarity, a sense of purpose, freedom, or financial security. Any negative thing you might be experiencing and wanting to change in your life can be stated in the positive by asking yourself, 'What's the opposite of that?'

STEP 8: Zoom Down to the Proton

Starting from the heart and counting down from three to one, visualise shrinking into the blood, then to the size of the cells. Picture millions of cells and zoom up to one. With your intention, and the feeling of it having been achieved, imagine melting through the wall of the cell as you imagine emanating this intention from within the cell. Again, counting from three to one, zoom down further until you see millions of atoms appear, like stars in the universe. Go up to one atom. Again, with your intention and the feeling of it, melt through the electron cloud and emanate your intention throughout the atom. Counting down again from three to one, zoom down further until you reach the proton within the atom. Then, counting down from three to one again, imagine zooming down until you reach what looks like a tiny vortex on the surface of the 'energy wiggle' we call a proton. This is the doorway to a Planck-sized wormhole. Pop into this wormhole and imagine going through it and popping out of that wormhole and into the vacuum, the space inside you, a black void, where the therapy of your self-hypnosis practice begins.

The Emerge

Once you have completed your auto-suggestions, affirmations and visualisations, follow these two simple steps to emerge yourself gently from your trance.

STEP 1: Zoom Back to the Heart

Imagine going back into the wormhole that brought you to the void. Pop out of it, through the Planck, then off the surface of the proton. Use your breath to imagine zooming out as you visualise popping out of the electron cloud of the atom. Using breath again, zoom up to the surface of the cell as you pop out of it and zoom up through the bloodstream. Then imagine yourself back in your heart.

STEP 2: Elevator Back to Eyes Open

Visualise yourself going back to the elevator that brought you down. See the numbers going from 0 to 10. Slowly count yourself from 0 to 10 as you imagine the elevator bringing you from your heart to your eyes. On the count of 10, imagine the elevator doors opening as you open your eyes. Notice and connect with how you feel.

Hypnosis Scripts and How to Use Them

The following applies if you choose to create your own recordings, in your own voice, rather than use the QR code to download and listen to the recordings in my voice.

Remember to pace your voice—make it sound calm and soothing as if you're telling a young child a bedtime story. Use the three dots '...' in the scripts to take a deliberate pause. Where you see ***CAPITALISED*** or ***bold,*** place a little more emphasis on those words. You may wish to do some practice recordings yourself, reading a few paragraphs and then playing them back. Have a listen and then make any appropriate changes to your verbal tone, pitch and pace from there. There will come a time that you may begin to feel confident doing the process without a script at all. This, I believe, is a very useful and helpful goal to aim for, but remember to take your time with this. There is no rush and it isn't a race. Use the recordings for as long as they feel useful to you.

The benefit of using the QR code to access the recordings in my voice is that any time I create a new recording, you will have the chance to access it. But for now, I have chosen the script topics and created them accordingly. I suggest taking a look at the topics, reading the script to yourself and beginning with the one that resonates with you the most. Whether you choose to use one of the scripts provided, or create your own, let me remind you again of two very important things:

1) Use the same induction and emerge protocol for every session regardless of how long you are in self-hypnosis.

2) Focus on one specific aspect of your life at a time. The fact is that you're unlikely to transform every aspect of your life in one month. All of your challenges have literally been created over a lifetime, maybe even before then, so rather than be in a rush to get to the end, remember that this is a journey, so take the time to honour that while enjoying and trusting the way the process will unfold in your life. After all, please remember that there is no 'end' to dealing with challenges as long as you are alive. No matter what you wish to be, do and have in your life, there will always be something that will challenge you. Always. The challenges simply change, but the stress they create within you will be the same.

Let me give you an example. Once you have successfully dealt with the challenge of earning enough money to feed yourself, there might be the challenge to pay your bills. Once that's taken care of, perhaps find a better job, then perhaps get a promotion, then perhaps get the approval of your parents, then find a partner, then deal with relationship issues, then get a better car, then a bigger house, then find a work/life balance, then address weight issues, then medical issues, then family disputes, and on and on and on.

Don't fool yourself into creating a fantasy that there will be some point when all will be well. It may be for a short time, but not for long. Challenges are almost built-in to reality since they are usually our best teachers, facilitating growth and depth of character. The purpose of this book is to teach you a technique that you can always use and depend on to help you find more peace in your mind and heart, whether the challenge is finding the money for your next meal, or the stress of deciding where to buy your next multi-million dollar property. Stress is stress, and the biological effect on the body is virtually the same for both these individuals.

Focusing on a challenge in your life while using one type of script or recording applies whether you choose one of the below scripts or if you choose to create one of your own. You'll know when to move on to another topic, or perhaps you could listen to a few that have similar themes. If you are not noticing a shift in that area, then I urge you to take the time to consider why you may not be. Is it related to expectations—yours or others? Is it a deeper negative limiting belief, or are you just being impatient?

If you do choose to create a personal script of your own, be sure to combine it with the 'induction' and 'emerge' script given below. Remember the induction process IS the H.A.R.T, so never omit it from your practice whether you're doing the fast track induction or not.

With the amazing technology we have these days, especially in mobile devices, to save time it would be ideal to record the induction and emerge only once and then combine it with alternating therapy scripts of your choice. The alternative is to record the induction and emerge each time with each therapy script.

Also, please keep in mind that, to some degree, the principle of 'quality over quantity' applies in this case when it comes to the therapy scripts. As mentioned in previous chapters, the induction and the ability to bring yourself into a deep trance is, I believe, the power of the H.A.R.T. Once you learn to bring yourself into this deep space, from there, the length of the script and the amount of time spent on the therapy script, although of course very important, is somewhat a secondary part of the process, especially since you already know that time is irrelevant to the unconscious mind. The quality of the suggestions is not going to have the same impact in your life if you have not created for yourself a good, deep, hypnotic trance first, whereas even average quality suggestions will be valuable if a powerful induction is used.

Hence, do not be concerned if a high percentage of 'time' is spent doing the induction with these, or even your own scripts. Do not underestimate the power of simply using the H.A.R.T induction, repeating a one-line, positive affirmation five times, and then emerging. Even this approach most definitely has the power to facilitate massive changes in your life.

H.A.R.T Induction Script

'Taking a deep breath in and exhaling as slowly as I can ... and just before I exhale fully ... I slowly close my eyes ... as I place myself in a ***comfortable position*** *... I can begin to allow calm and stillness to take over ...* ***I can turn my attention inside*** *... leaving behind the outside world for just a short time ... noticing my breath ... as I breathe normally and naturally ... feeling the* ***effortless*** *rising and falling of my chest ... I can allow myself to begin to* ***drift with each and every breath*** *... in ... and out ... bringing my attention to the tiniest muscles of my body ... my eyelids ...* ***I can allow them to switch*** *...* ***off ... now*** *... as they become* ***totally*** *... and* ***completely*** *...* ***relaxed*** *... so relaxed that they* ***just ... won't ... work*** *... as I focus on my eyelids ... I can see a colour for* ***deep relaxation*** *... and this colour can grow ... from my eyelids ... like ripples in a pond ... wherever the ripples go they spread ease ...* ***comfort ... calmness and deep ... relaxation*** *... The colourful ripples move up my forehead to my scalp ... down my nose ... cheeks ... ears ... lips ... mouth ... jaw and chin ... my face ... feeling* ***so ... so ... comfortable*** *... The ripple moves down my neck and across my upper back and shoulders ...* ***dissolving any tension*** *... or tightness I may be carrying there ... down the front of my neck ... relaxing my throat ... down my upper arms ... forearms ... wrists ... and hands ... both of my arms ... and hands ... can* ***become so ... so ... heavy*** *... they can feel like two pieces of stone ...* ***heavy*** *... and* ***relaxed*** *... As the ripples move down my spine to my lower back ... down my chest ... and into my stomach ... relaxing and rejuvenating all my internal organs ... Over my hips ... down my thighs, over my knees, into my calves ... shins ... ankles ... feet ... and all the way to the tips of my toes ... This* ***deep*** *... inward focus and* ***relaxation*** *... allows all outside noises and distractions to simply drift ... drift ... drift away ... But if I have to ... I can awaken at any time* ***without any negative consequences*** *... But for now ... I can* ***calmly*** *... and* ***confidently*** *... go* ***deeper*** *... and* ***deeper*** *...* ***within*** *... Bringing my attention back to my eyes ... I can imagine sitting at a complicated control panel* ***just behind my eyelids*** *... there are gauges, dials, knobs, and screens in a u-shaped desk around me ... I stand up, turn around and see an elevator at the back of my head ... I walk over to the elevator ... the doors open ... and I step inside ... I turn around*

and above the door I see the numbers ***10 to 1*** *... I am on the tenth floor about to go* ***down*** *...* ***down*** *... to the first floor ... And by the time I reach the first floor ... I will be* ***EVEN MORE*** *relaxed ... I push number 1 ... the doors close ... and the elevator begins to* ***bring me down*** *from my head towards my heart ... 10 ... 9 ...* ***going deeper*** *... and* ***deeper*** *... 8 ... 7 ... more* ***relaxed*** *with each number down ... 6 ... 5 ... halfway between my head and heart now ... 4 ... 3 ... more* ***peace*** *... more* ***calmness*** *... growing with each number down ... 2 ... almost there ... 1 ... The elevator doors open ... I step out ... and into my heart ...* ***be there now*** *...* ***a warm,*** *glowing place of* ***safety*** *...* ***protection*** *and* ***security*** *... I see a big comfortable armchair in the middle of my heart ... I walk over and take a seat ...* ***I close my eyes*** *... Bringing to mind in this moment ... a* ***positive*** *memory ... where I felt a strong positive emotion ... It could be love ... gratitude ... joy ... happiness ... or any other powerful positive emotion ...* ***Be there now!*** *... I can see what I saw ... hear what I heard ... and feel what I felt ...* ***I can let that feeling grow*** *... and grow ... and grow ... as I focus on my heart, I can* ***slow down my breathing*** *... inhaling for five seconds ... exhaling for five seconds ... I can connect this feeling with my breath ... in 2 ... 3 ... 4 ... 5 ... out ... 2 ... 3 ... 4 ... 5 ... in ... 2 ... 3 ... 4 ... 5 ... out ... 2 ... 3 ... 4 ... 5 ... continuing with this heart-centred breathing for another 10 seconds ...* ***very good*** *... I can now bring my awareness to the* ***intention*** *I have for this particular self-hypnosis ... consider the* ***POSITIVE*** *intention I would like my unconscious mind to help me create ... and consciously recognise ... in my life ...* ***NOW*** *... this intention becomes a spark of light that creates a bubble of light ...* ***it grows and grows*** *... extending a few feet beyond my physical body ... this bubble protects me from* ***all*** *negative influences and energies ... And now holding my intention ... on the count of one ... I will* ***zoom down*** *to the cellular world inside my heart ... 3 ... 2 ... 1 ... I can now see millions ... and millions ... of cells ... one gets my attention ... as it comes* ***closer and closer*** *to me until it looks like a bubble as big as me ... holding onto my positive intention I now imagine* ***melting through the cell wall*** *into the centre of this heart cell ... I take another* ***slow*** *...* ***deep*** *...* ***breath*** *... my intention saturates this cell which is connected to* ***all other cells*** *in my body ... and now, on the count of one, I will* ***zoom down*** *even further to* *the **atomic world** ... within this one heart cell ... 3 ... 2 ... 1 ... I can now see billions of atoms ... **like the stars in space** ... as one comes towards me ... as big as me ... with my intention I **melt through** the atomic cloud ... and now in the centre of this atom, I **zoom down** ... **down** ... **down** to the proton in the middle of this atom ... and with my intention, I **zoom down even further** ... and smaller ... smaller still ... until I reach the Planck-sized spinning vortex ... the wormhole doorway ... with my intention, I allow myself to **slip into this wormhole** ... and it brings me to the **zero point** ... the **inner space** of my heart ... **an ultimate place of stillness** ... where I can now **exercise my power to create** ...*

(Select a therapy script to insert here)

Emerge Script

*I can allow my unconscious mind ... to **deeply and powerfully** absorb these suggestions ... I can trust the subconscious to continue to **integrate these messages** ... even during my normal ... wakeful state ... I am open and ready ... **to notice any and all signs** ... and synchronicities that will **easily** and **effortlessly** allow the physical and/or non-physical manifestations that I have requested to experience **here and now** ... to come into my conscious awareness ... And the more I **notice these synchronicities** ... the more confidence I will gain in my ability to master my life ... **I am ready to be in the right place ... at the right time** ... ready to notice what I notice ... and **notice what's different**... I will have more ability to easily take **courageous action** if I choose to ... and at the same time ... I can experience **zero resistance** with **zero insistence** on how my highest good will materialise ... I can let the unconscious part of me ... just do what it was **designed** to do ... and **each and every time** ... I practice the art of self-hypnosis ... it will become **easier** ... and more **powerful** ... it is now time to take the journey **back to full awareness** ... as I imagine going back to the wormhole that brought me here ... Now ... as **I breathe in ... and out** ... my exhale propels me out of the proton ... **as breathe in ... and out** ... my exhale propels me out of the atom and into my heart cell ... I now prepare to emerge from the cell ...*

***I breathe in** ... **and out** ... leaving the cell ... bringing my awareness **back to the heart** ... where it all began ... back in the armchair in my heart ... I stand up and walk over to the elevator that brought me **into my heart** ... ready to journey back up to my eyes ... I step in ... and press the number '10' ... as the elevator begins to rise ... 1 ... 2 ... **slowly** ... **gently** ... Coming back to full awareness ... 3 ... 4 ... bringing back these **good feelings** of **peace** and **calm** ... 5 ... 6 ... becoming more aware of my surroundings ... 7 ... 8 ... getting ready to open my eyes ... 9 ... 10 ... eyes open, fully alert, feeling great and refreshed.*

Therapy Scripts

Raising Self-Worth and Self-Belief

*I am who I am for a reason ... this means **there is purpose to my existence** ... although, at times, I may forget **who I truly am** ... through the distraction of life's natural ups and downs ... deep ... deep ... down ... **I am aware of the eternal nature of my true self** ... in the same way that energy can be neither created or destroyed ... **but simply transforms from one form to another** ... the same goes for **my true self** ... this physical law of the universe goes **beyond the material aspects of my body** ... it also **includes my conscious awareness** of self ... in this way **I AM ONE** with the inherent wellness built into the universe ... the source of all that is ... makes no mistakes ... therefore ... since I exist ... I must have a **purpose for existing ...** the process of life ... from the moment I was born ... is a process of conditioning ... habituation ... and programming ... **I know there was a time when I felt worthy and believed in myself** ... even if it was when I was very young ... until I bought into **the illusion** of my unworthiness ... which has since become reinforced by certain experiences in my life ... regardless of what I believe about my **abilities** ... **capabilities** ... and my **worthiness** to receive ... I can choose to believe that ... **THIS ... CAN** ... **BE** ... **CHANGED** ... focusing on my heart, I can breathe this realisation ... **IN** .... and **OUT** ... **NOW** ... these limiting beliefs can be either **INSTANTLY CHANGED** NOW ... or I can allow it to be an unfolding journey ... a joyful process of self-discovery ... unlearning ... and relearning* *that will allow me to* ***perceive*** *... and then* ***experience*** *... more and more real-life examples ... of my worthiness ... and self-belief ... this will allow me to approach life in a new ... balanced way ... And now I will reinforce this new way of being with the repetition of a suggestion ... there is no need to say this out loud ... I can repeat it mentally ... so with all the power and emotion in my mind and body ... repeat:* ***I AM GROWING MY SELF-WORTH DAY BY DAY IN EVERY WAY*** *...* ***I AM GROWING MY SELF-WORTH DAY BY DAY IN EVERY WAY*** *...* ***I AM GROWING MY SELF-WORTH DAY BY DAY IN EVERY WAY*** *...* ***I AM GROWING MY SELF-WORTH DAY BY DAY IN EVERY WAY*** *...* ***I AM GROWING MY SELF-WORTH DAY BY DAY IN EVERY WAY*** *... I understand that this limitation may have involved certain situations ... or events in my past ... this may have involved specific people where I allowed their words and actions to create a definition of myself and who I am ... impacting my self-worth and self-belief ...* ***I can choose to let this go*** *...* ***NOW*** *... I can recognise that in many cases ...* ***these were people who did care for me*** *... but may not have been able to express it ... or they may have been acting out, or expressing a wound within themselves in a moment ... which I may have misinterpreted and taken personally ... I can send them love ... and empathy ... as I now realise that hurt people ... hurt people ... as I do this through a deep breath ...* ***IN*** *... and* ***OUT*** *... I can* ***FEEL THE PHYSICAL RELEASE*** *...* ***NOW***

Immunity to External Programming

I understand that in every moment ***my subconscious mind is absorbing many messages*** *from the external world ... these messages come from many sources ... TV, radio, the internet, billboards, background music, signs ... even people. There are also influences I may be less aware of ... such as electromagnetic fields ... and other energy frequencies which my five senses are unable to detect ... some of these influences are in alignment with who I truly am ... others are not ...* ***I am now programming my subconscious mind*** *to deliver to my conscious mind ... perceptions and experiences which are* ***ONLY*** *in alignment with my* ***highest good*** *... there is nothing I need to do for this to occur ...* ***I am now immune to the***

effects of all external influences out of alignment with my true self** ... **I am free to make my own choices** about how to think, how to speak, where to go, what to buy, and what to do ... **I am the captain of my ship** ... **I am free to make better decisions** ... **I am in control of my own mind** ... **body** ... **and spirit** ... As I allow my body to sink ... **deeper** ... **and deeper** ... into this **new level of power and strength** ... I can visualise a protective anti-virus shield around my heart ... this anti-virus allows **all negative energies and influences to bounce right off me** ... I can grow this shield ... slowly ... and deliberately ... I can choose the colours, textures and even the sounds of this shield ... **as it grows to include my entire body now** ... I can extend this shield beyond the boundary of my skin ... this shield will allow me to become consciously aware of sensory information that is **ONLY in alignment with my conscious goals and desires** ... I can now see myself ... on the screen of my mind ... moving through my day ... **protected and immune from the negative, unhelpful programming of the external world** ... I can see all these messages ... bouncing off my shield ... I will now strengthen my shield with the repetition of a suggestion five times ... so with all the power and emotion in my body ... repeat: **I AM FREE AND IN CONTROL OF MY MIND, BODY AND SPIRIT** ... **I AM FREE AND IN CONTROL OF MY MIND, BODY AND SPIRIT** ... **I AM FREE AND IN CONTROL OF MY MIND, BODY AND SPIRIT** ... **I AM FREE AND IN CONTROL OF MY MIND, BODY AND SPIRIT** ... **I AM FREE AND IN CONTROL OF MY MIND, BODY AND SPIRIT** ... I understand that life can sometimes throw me off balance ... with its natural highs and lows ... **I am grateful for the highs** ... and I can become **more easily aware of the valuable lessons the lows can teach me** ... as a I take a **slow** ... **deep** ... **breath** ... in ... I can energise this protective shield ... and when I come back to full conscious awareness ... I can automatically **renew** ... **rejuvenate** ... and **recharge** my protective shield **without having to consciously think about it** ... this will happen **AUTOMATICALLY** ... with each and every **slow** ... **deep** ... **breath** ... **I take** ... Freeing myself of the world's sources of negative programming ... allows me to be a **catalyst of freedom** ... **on all levels** ... **known** ... **and unknown** ... **for everyone else I come into contact with** ... there is no need for me to know **HOW** this happens ... all I have to do is **INTEND for this

to happen *... the choice is mine ... I can let my subconscious take care of the details and simply trust it ... in much the same way I trust my subconscious to beat my heart, digest my food, run my immune system, regulate my body temperature, and manage trillions of cells ... I trust my subconscious because it is mine and mine alone.*

Increased Concentration and Focus

I realise that there are times in my life ... where it is necessary to ***focus my attention and concentration*** *on certain tasks, activities, projects even people ...* ***I am finding this easier and easier to do*** *... as I support my body with all the things that it needs ...* ***calmness*** *...* ***relaxation*** *... peace ... and* ***more focused*** *... I am well rested ... I am well hydrated ... I am eating wholesome and nutritious food ... I am connecting to the natural world ... my environment may be full of things that are trying to get my attention ... these may include ... mobile devices ... TV ... radio ... signs ... friends ... family ... pets ...* ***I am able to find time for every aspect of my life*** *... and because I do this easily and naturally ... This allows my mind to be focused ... this allows my mind to concentrate ...* ***my unconscious mind can do this for me automatically*** *... I easily have the time to complete all things that really need to get done ... I am learning to trust the flow of my life ... because ultimately ... I have everything that I truly need ... I can picture an* ***energy bubble around my head*** *... like a helmet ... just like a normal helmet is used to protect my skull ... this helmet is used to* ***protect my mind and thoughts from being distracted*** *... this helmet has the outer layer to protect against external distractions ... but it also has an inner layer ... beneath my skull that protects me from self-inflicted distractions ... see this helmet ... here and now ... choose a colour for focus and concentration ... see the texture of this helmet ... I can now see myself on the screen of my mind ... with this energetic and protective helmet around my head as I do a task or activity where* ***I know I need to remain focused*** *... I can see intrusive and distracting thoughts* ***bounce right off*** *the helmet ... when* ***I am concentrating on a task*** *... there is no need to waste my mental energy on other things I cannot act on in that moment ... repeating the following statements with conviction ...* ***I am becoming***

calmer each day *... I am* ***learning to relax*** *more easily ... I am safe in this moment ... I am capable of slowing my breath ... I am allowing my body to settle ... I am steadier than I used to be ... I am able to pause before I react ... I am learning new ways to cope ... I am getting better and better at staying focused on one ... thing ... at a time ... And if distractions do come into my mind ... I am able to simply ...* ***LET*** *...* ***THEM*** *...* ***GO*** *... allowing me to calmly bring my focus and concentration back to the task at hand ... until I am satisfied ... and ready ... to move on to the next task or activity ... I am more in control than I realise ... I am becoming more and more productive ... each day ... in every way ... as I focus and concentrate ... on just one ... thing ... at a time.*

Freedom from Others' Expectations

I am surrounded by people who ***love and care for me*** *... and people that* ***I love and care for*** *... The relationships I have are dynamic ... with many different aspects to them ... Becoming habituated to people ... places ... and things ... is a very normal and natural ... human phenomena ... Often there is a level of comfort in things being stable ... predictable ... and dependable ... In many aspects of life, this is a useful thing ... I understand that* ***deep*** *...* ***deep*** *down ... the people who love and care for me ...* ***only want what is best for me*** *... they only want* ***my happiness*** *... However ... I am beginning to realise more and more ... that* ***sometimes we may see the path to happiness differently*** *... I am unique ... we are all unique ... Therefore,* ***we all have unique ways of finding our own happiness, love, fulfilment, and contentment*** *... My life is my own and no one can live it for me ... We have all become who we are based on our life experiences ... which have in turn shaped our beliefs ... It is natural that the people I care for will expect me to follow their advice ...* ***I am giving myself permission to have a different opinion on what is best for me*** *...* ***NOW*** *... I understand that this may be uncomfortable for other people in my life to agree with ... understand ... or accept ... and that's ok ...* ***I AM WHO I AM AND THAT IS ENOUGH*** *... No one can know my life journey ... it is unknown to them ... and for that reason, my choices may produce* *fear within them ...* ***I am willing and able to send them love and compassion*** *anyway ... I am learning to balance the calling of my inner most being ... without having to fear the alienation of the people I love and care for ...* ***I am confident in my ability to communicate*** *to myself and others ... in such a way that* ***clarifies an appropriate course of action*** *... This can help maintain* ***peace and harmony*** *in all my relationships without feeling like I have compromised my soul ... My choices are mine to make ... I am not responsible for the judgements ... opinions ... and reactions of others when I follow my heart's calling ... The universe rewards courage by removing obstacles for me ... Their reactions can act as a catalyst* ***FOR THEM*** *to grow ... evolve ... and adapt ...* ***I am strong within myself*** *...* ***I am determined to live my life in accordance with my intentions and values****... and I am compassionate towards others ... And now repeating the following suggestion five times with all the power and emotion in my mind and body ...* ***I HAVE THE COURAGE AND POWER TO THOUGHTFULLY CREATE THE LIFE THAT I CHOOSE ... I HAVE THE COURAGE AND POWER TO THOUGHTFULLY CREATE THE LIFE THAT I CHOOSE ... I HAVE THE COURAGE AND POWER TO THOUGHTFULLY CREATE THE LIFE THAT I CHOOSE ... I HAVE THE COURAGE AND POWER TO THOUGHTFULLY CREATE THE LIFE THAT I CHOOSE ... I HAVE THE COURAGE AND POWER TO THOUGHTFULLY CREATE THE LIFE THAT I CHOOSE*** *... I am able to* ***respond positively*** *to others ... regardless of what they believe I should or should not be doing with my life ...* ***I am confident within myself*** *to live the life I was meant to live ... Others see this confidence in me ... which allows* ***THEM*** *to be confident that* ***I am making the right decisions for myself*** *... Even if they have different opinions ... as I move forward in my life this way ...* ***I am an example to everyone who knows me*** *... that it's okay to do the same ... I can be like a permission slip to others ...* ***creating the ripple effect*** *... encouraging more people to live in accordance with their* ***true calling*** *... Of course, there will always be challenges along the journey of life ... no matter which path I choose ... But* ***I prefer to experience the challenges of my highest purpose*** *... than those of a life that is not of my own choosing ...* ***I am flexible, resourceful and adaptable*** *... open to the wisdom of others to* *make any appropriate and necessary changes ... in order to keep a* ***balanced perspective at all times.***

Dissolving Anger

I can appreciate that there are times in my life ... that will ***require me to be more flexible and adaptable ... I am taking responsibility for my life ... NOW*** *... I am capable of* ***looking at my life*** *and addressing the areas of my life that require my attention ...* ***I am taking responsibility for the way I treat and respond to myself and others ... NOW*** *... I am taking responsibility for* ***creating the environment I wish to live in ... NOW*** *... I am capable of making changes in my life that* ***easily help me experience ease and flow ... NOW*** *... I am becoming more capable of recognising the things in my life that have* ***nothing to do with me*** *... I can simply let these things* ***float ... float ... float away in a big red balloon*** *... I can more easily balance the need to* ***CONTROL*** *... with the ability to* ***ALLOW*** *... and I am easily able to recognise* ***which situations need which approach*** *... regardless of what I may be observing ...* ***Life is about how I respond to it*** *... and this is a* ***choice ... I am training my subconscious mind to respond to life in a more useful and positive way ... NOW*** *... I can allow my unconscious mind to automatically ...* ***easily and effortlessly*** *... find* ***solutions to challenges*** *... I am enjoying the journey of being a student of communication ...* ***I am learning the art and power of effective communication*** *... this will more easily help me to create the interactions ... experiences ... relationships ... and environments that are pleasing to me and others around me ...* ***I am becoming a master of communication*** *... and as this happens ...* ***NOW*** *... I am skilfully able to understand the communication styles of others ...* ***this helps me interact with others*** *... in such a way that creates more* ***wellbeing in my life*** *... and theirs... I am able to appreciate that every person is entitled to their opinions ... and perspectives ...* ***allowing them to be valid*** *... even if they are different to my own ... this allows me to be* ***more at peace*** *... recognising the beauty of diversity ... In the past ... when I responded to situations with anger ... although it may have been a learned pattern ...* ***I am dissolving the unhealthy use of this pattern*** *... and letting it go ...* ***NOW*** *... because just as my subconscious can learn ... it can also unlearn ... while at the* *same time recognising that there are appropriate times ... places ... and ways to express anger ...* ***it is a normal human emotion*** *... I can let my subconscious mind guide and teach me to* ***express it in a healthy ... useful way*** *... in my mind's eye ... I can visualise ... and imagine ... situations, that in the past may have triggered ... that old reaction of* ***inappropriate*** *anger ... I can see it through my own eyes ...* ***NOW*** *... hearing the sounds ...* ***NOW*** *... and feeling the feelings in a specific part of my body ... I can choose the feeling that I would* ***RATHER*** *have in that moment ...* ***NOW*** *... attaching that feeling to a colour of relaxation ...* ***NOW*** *... with three ...* ***slow*** *...* ***deep breaths*** *... slowly raising my chin ... as high as I can ...* ***BREATHE IN*** *the positive feeling ... exhaling the anger as I* ***slowly lower my chin*** *towards my chest ... and again ...* ***slowly and deeply*** *... breathing in the positive feeling and colour while raising my chin towards the sky ... bring the feeling into my* ***chest and stomach*** *... and slowly exhaling the negativity as I lower my chin towards my chest ... doing this ...* ***one*** *...* ***more*** *...* ***time*** *...* ***NOW*** *... raising chin, in with the positive ... exhaling the negative ... lowering chin to chest ... seeing myself in that old trigger situation ... and* ***noticing the difference ... the confidence ... the composure ... and calmness****.*

Finding Your Purpose

The journey of life is one of ***continual discovery*** *... I have discovered and learned many things so far in my life ... I recognise and appreciate the* ***power of asking myself questions*** *... I can ask myself any question ... and I can* ***trust that my subconscious already has the answers*** *... even if I am unable to perceive the answers consciously ... I* ***KNOW*** *that my powerful unconscious mind is* ***connected to anything and everything*** *that I need to know that is relevant for the fulfilment of my highest intentions ... hearing the guidance of my higher mind ... may require me to become aware of certain aspects of myself ... I know that if I want something in my life to change ... than I have to make some changes in my life ... after all, my life is my own and no one can live it for me ... some of the aspects of my life that I may need to consider ... reflect on ... or change ... could include ... negative belief systems ... the definitions I have created ... the expectations of family and friends ... my commitments and the* *demands of my busy life ... my own impatience and expectations ... comparing myself to other people instead of having gratitude for what **IS** and what I **HAVE** in my own life ... forgiving myself ... increasing my self-belief and self-worth ... I am giving myself **permission to become free** of any and all barriers to becoming more and more aware of my purpose ... **NOW** ... I can bring to my heart ... here and now ... the feelings of living my life's purpose ... even if I am unaware of **HOW** it will unfold ... I can connect to the emotions of what it would be like ... **NOW** ... these feelings may include ... **FREEDOM** ... **I AM FREE** ... **NOW** ... my purpose includes ... **FUN** ... **I AM FUN** ... **NOW** ... my purpose includes **CONFIDENCE** ... **I AM CONFIDENT** ... **NOW** ... my purpose includes ... **CLARITY** ... **I AM CLEAR** ... **NOW** ... my purpose includes ... **STRENGTH** ... **I AM STRONG** ... **NOW** ... my purpose includes ... **JOY** ... **I AM** ... **JOY** ... **NOW** ... my purpose includes BALANCE ... I AM BALANCED ... NOW ... I am flexible and adaptable about the details of **HOW** ... my subconscious mind will bring these feelings into my reality ... by feeling the feelings ... here and now ... of what it would be like to be ... **LIVING MY PURPOSE** ... I am casting out an energetic net ... into the universe ... trusting that the universal law of **LIKE ENERGY ATTRACTS LIKE ENERGY** will take care of the details for me ... **I am open to the synchronicities and the signs** that will allow my purpose to **easily and effortlessly unfold** in a fun and exciting way ... I am growing my intuition ... the voice of my higher-self ... more ... and more ... which in turn helps me to trust in the fact that **whatever I may encounter along my journey ... it is ultimately for my highest good** ... experiencing life events in this way is simply a matter of **CHOOSING** to define events as being on the way rather than in the way ... **regardless** of how external circumstances may appear.*

Depression Release

*Life has its natural ups and downs ... **I have preferences for my life** ... there are times when I will experience people, situations and events that are not what I would prefer ... **I am able to change the way that I relate to these people, places and situations** ... as I do this ... **I am learning to be more at ease with the way things are** ... while still* *maintaining what I prefer to create and experience in my life ... I can appreciate the seemingly paradoxical idea that through releasing the* ***NEED*** *for things to be different ... I am able to* ***ALLOW*** *my preferences to more easily present themselves ... there is power in paradox as it confuses the conscious mind which often gets in the way of being who I truly am ... my conscious mind may find it difficult to know* ***HOW*** *the details will unfold ... but my subconscious mind ... my higher mind ... has a much* ***broader view and perspective*** *... sometimes all it takes is for me get out of my own way ... and trust the way my life unfolds ... I am able to do this by making a choice about how I would rather feel in any moment ... whatever has happened in the past ... has happened ... and* ***I can accept that and forgive*** *if I need to ... as I remember that the past and the future are illusions, there is only NOW ... I can choose to take away the* ***lessons and learnings*** *from anything that has happened to me in the past ... when I do this,* ***I can gain more control over my life*** *in the present ... the only moment that is real ... I can direct my attention more easily to the things in my life that bring me a feeling of* ***positive relief and comfort in any moment*** *... and now I will repeat a suggestion five times with as much emotional energy and power as possible ...* ***I AM REPROGRAMMING MY MIND TO MORE EASILY EXPERIENCE CONTENTMENT ... NOW ... I AM REPROGRAMMING MY MIND TO MORE EASILY EXPERIENCE CONTENTMENT ... NOW ... I AM REPROGRAMMING MY MIND TO MORE EASILY EXPERIENCE CONTENTMENT ... NOW ... I AM REPROGRAMMING MY MIND TO MORE EASILY EXPERIENCE CONTENTMENT ... NOW ... I AM REPROGRAMMING MY MIND TO MORE EASILY EXPERIENCE CONTENTMENT ... NOW ...*** *I am taking more and more responsibility for my life ... there are more useful ways to use my creative focus and energy than to blame others or compare my situation to others ... no matter how true a negative belief may seem ...* ***I KNOW that all beliefs can be changed*** *... if I choose to have the courage to change them ... I can change things to make my life better ...* ***If I THINK I CAN ... if I THINK I CAN'T ... I'M RIGHT EITHER WAY!*** *... I am training my subconscious mind to release me from old ... outdated ... programs ... my emotions are a product of habitual thinking ... and I know I can change this ... NOW ... I am growing in my confidence to challenge the negative meaning I automatically give* *situations ... **I HAVE THE POWER AND FREEDOM TO CHOOSE HOW MY MIND WORKS** ... on the count of 3, I can take 3 ... very ... slow ... deep ... breaths ... through the heart space ... and exhale more and more of my negative energies ... 1 ... 2 ... 3 ... **DEEP BREATH IN ... AND EXHALE ... AND ANOTHER ... AND EXHALE ... AND ANOTHER BREATH IN ... AND EXHALE** ... very good ... no matter what happens in my life ... I am never alone ... I am always supported ... I am able to recognise the difference between the desires of my ego and the **preferences of my TRUE SELF** ... I choose to let go of what my ego wants ... I am more easily able to let go of my assumptions ... expectations ... and fantasies of what I think my life **SHOULD BE** ... while at the same time always progressing towards making things better **at a pace that is right FOR ME** ... I choose to let go of comparing myself to others ... everyone is unique ... and I know things aren't always as they may seem ... everyone has different circumstances, histories, influences and beliefs ... so comparing myself to others will always be like comparing apples with oranges ... **I am able to more easily adapt to change with less resistance** as change is an inevitable fact of life and less insistence means less resistance ... I can change my mood by changing what I focus on ... in my mind, I can now see **A VERY LARGE, BRIGHT BUTTON** ... with an 'E' on it ... for EASE and FLOW ... I can connect this button to memories of ease ... as I bring some of them to mind ... **NOW** ... taking the time I need to fill this **BIG BRIGHT BUTTON** with many memories of ease ... whenever I choose to press this button in my mind ... **IT WILL RELEASE THE CHEMICALS AND HORMONES** in my body that will allow me to **FEEL MORE AT EASE INSTANTLY!** ... I can create this internal state of being in such a way that **PEOPLE WILL NOTICE** ... this can be my own little secret ... **I can use this whenever I want to** ... giving myself these good feelings whenever and wherever I want ... I can press it ... **NOW** ... and again ... and again ... and again.*

Dissolving Negative Beliefs

*The way I experience ... people ... places ... situations ... events ... and my life ... is determined by **how I define those things and what I believe to be true about them** ... some of those beliefs are useful and serve me well ... while others no longer serve me ... no matter how* *solid I may perceive a belief to be ...* ***I KNOW that all beliefs can be changed*** *... I understand that there are certain beliefs that move me into a* ***POSITIVE ACTIVE*** *mode of behaviour while others move me into a negative INACTIVE mode of behaviour ...* ***my life is not determined by my past*** *... but I am free to feel ... think ... and act ... in the* ***HERE*** *and* ***NOW*** *... no matter who or what may have caused me to develop my negative belief systems ...* ***I AM ABLE TO REPROGRAM THESE BELIEF SYSTEMS ... NOW!*** *... I am responsible for creating what is* ***TRUE FOR ME*** *... I can use the power of my subconscious mind to install a new program ... a positive belief ... on the screen of my mind I can bring up one of my existing negative or unhelpful beliefs ... I can simply observe how it looks ... how it feels ... how it sounds ... how it smells ...* ***I can become aware of the elements of this belief that makes it strong in my life*** *... becoming aware of them ...* ***NOW*** *... as I see the structure of this negative belief in my mind ... I can now begin to dismantle and deconstruct the structure of this unhelpful belief with the power of breath ... on the count of three, I will take three slow ... deep ... breaths and with each slow but forceful exhale I can imagine* ***blowing down the structure of this belief*** *like a cyclone blowing down a house ... with each breath ... I can destroy it more and more ... 1 ... 2 ... 3 ... first deep ... breath in ...* ***POWERFULLY EXHALING SLOWLY*** *... and another deep breath ... in ... and another powerful slow exhale ... and one more ... breathing in ... nice and slowly ... with one last powerful exhale ... see the belief barely standing now ... in tatters ... like and old ancient ruins ... it is almost ready to completely fall apart ... I can now imagine a big powerful hammer ... and now* ***I can visualise this hammer smashing this unhelpful belief right into the ground*** *... with each ... strike, it loses its grip on me more and more ... I can use this hypnosis session to eliminate unhelpful beliefs in one session ... or I can progressively dissolve one belief with this process bit by bit ...* ***the choice is mine*** *... I can experience more ... and more freedom from my limiting beliefs each and every time I use the power of self-hypnosis ... I can now bring to my mind a new picture of myself ... living* ***COMPLETELY FREE*** *of this old limiting belief ... I can see myself in my mind's eye ... and I can notice the difference that makes the difference ... noticing exactly how I think ... speak ... and act differently now that* ***I AM FREE*** *of this old belief.*

Increasing Confidence

I am taking more and more responsibility for my own self-image *... there are many things in my life that have influenced the way I think of myself ... these may include my mother ... my father ... siblings ... extended family members ... teachers ... the media ... and perhaps TV and social media ... all of these have contributed in some way to the thoughts ... beliefs ... and ideas I have about WHO I AM ... WHAT I WANT ... what are possible and impossible goals ... some of these messages have been very helpful ...* ***I can keep any and all positive and useful messages and lessons*** *... But right here and now ... I can return any and all negative messages to their respective sources ...* ***NOW*** *... as I do this, I am now* ***taking back my power*** *... the power to make a choice ... in making this choice, I can* ***RELAX*** *...* ***LET GO*** *... and* ***ALLOW MYSELF TO HAVE ... MORE ... FUN*** *... with others ... and the world around me ... as I do this, I can now choose to replace what I let go of with more positive images ... self-talk ... affirmations ... and messages ...* ***I can give myself all the time that I*** *need to let my subconscious make all the necessary changes needed to set my life on a new and empowered direction ... NOW ... with all the power and emotion in my mind and body ... repeating five times in my mind ...* ***I AM BUILDING MORE CONFIDENCE TO BE, DO AND HAVE MORE OF WHAT I POSITIVELY FOCUS ON ... I AM BUILDING MORE CONFIDENCE TO BE, DO AND HAVE MORE OF WHAT I POSITIVELY FOCUS ON ... I AM BUILDING MORE CONFIDENCE TO BE, DO AND HAVE MORE OF WHAT I POSITIVELY FOCUS ON ... I AM BUILDING MORE CONFIDENCE TO BE, DO AND HAVE MORE OF WHAT I FOCUS POSITIVELY ON ... I AM BUILDING MORE CONFIDENCE TO BE, DO AND HAVE MORE OF WHAT I FOCUS POSITIVELY ON*** *... I am excited to investigate and learn more about myself ... and as I become a student of myself, I learn more about the ways in which I relate to the world around me ...* ***this self-knowledge can be turned into self-empowerment*** *and the more I experience this within myself ... the more I will express this in the world ...* ***other people will notice this confident self-image*** *... but what is even more important than the opinions of others ...* ***is the opinion I have of myself*** *... in my mind's eye, I can go to a time and place when I experienced* ***complete*** *and* ***total*** *confidence ... it could be when I was young ... or an adult ... I* *can bring images to my mind and feelings to my body, the* ***SPECIFIC DETAILS*** *of exactly* ***HOW*** *and* ***WHY*** *I was confident … I can make those images … feelings … and even the sounds of confidence …* ***GROW … AND GROW*** *… becoming more … and more … intense … I can connect the* ***HIGHEST*** *and* ***MOST INTENSE*** *feelings of confidence to a* ***SPECIFIC*** *trigger point on one of my hands by pinching my thumb against any finger I choose on the same hand and holding that hard and firm for five seconds …* ***NOW*** *… I can build … strengthen … and reinforce this specific confidence trigger* ***each and every time I use this self-hypnosis process.***

Experiencing More Love and Joy

As I take slow … deep … breaths … I can focus on the word … ***LOVE*** *… and* ***JOY*** *… I can exhale any and all negative thoughts and feelings … as I allow myself to sink* ***deeper*** *… and* ***deeper*** *… into the essence of* ***LOVE*** *and* ***JOY*** *that my innermost being is* ***ONE*** *with … I can bring to my awareness anything at all in my life which is* ***EASY*** *for me to feel* ***LOVE*** *and* ***JOY*** *about …* ***NOW*** *… this may be a person … something I do … a place I have been to … a hobby of mine … a pet … or anything else which* ***brings me the feelings of love and joy*** *… I can grow these feelings more … and more … I can even see these feelings creating ripples …* ***emanating these ripples outward into the world around me*** *in such a way that everyone I meet can experience the positive benefits of these feelings as well … even if they do not consciously notice this …* ***I can have a powerful impact on people*** *… even communities … and the world at large … as I connect with these feelings of* ***LOVE*** *… and* ***JOY*** *… these feelings are my birth right … I can imagine turning up a dial … a dial which amplifies the intensity of these feelings … more … and more …* ***As I do this, the colours of LOVE … and JOY … begin to grow*** *… the brightness increases … as well as the sounds and textures … these feelings can now turn into an object … it could be anything at all … the first image to come into my mind is perfect … there is no need to analyse … force … or judge … this is my* ***POWER OBJECT*** *for* ***IMMEDIATELY*** *creating the sensations of* ***LOVE*** *… and* ***JOY*** *… I can place this object in the centre of my heart where I can create the feeling of* ***LOVE*** *… and* ***JOY*** *…*

***HERE** ... and **NOW** ... **I can commit to creating this state of being whenever I choose** by connecting it now to three slow, deep breaths ... getting ready now ... first breath in ... and slowly exhaling ... each breath lets me connect deeper ... another breath in ... and exhale ... infusing it with every fibre of my being ... a last deep breath in ... **HOLD IT FOR A FEW SECONDS** ... and exhale ... now that I have established this state of being ... I can now imagine seeing myself in the third person on the screen of my mind ... in certain environments where I would like to **more easily experience and project LOVE** ... and **JOY** ... I am observing myself from a short distance ... I can observe and notice what I notice ... **and notice what is different** ... as I look at my entire being ... **HOW IS IT DIFFERENT?** ... is it my posture ... body language ... facial expressions ... my eyes ... hands ... feet ... legs ... **what am I DOING that is different**? ... see what it is that I am doing as I experience more of this **LOVE** and **JOY** as my foundational state of being ... where do I spend my time? ... who do I spend my time with? ... and how is that interaction different ... **EVEN IF THEY ARE NOT ABLE TO EXPRESS THE LOVE** ... and **JOY** that is within them ... I can notice what is different ... and grow from there.*

Creating More Calm and Inner Peace

*Throughout my life, there have been times of great success ... and times of upheaval and change ... as I become more sensitive to the feelings of my inner self ... **I know that there are times when I need to adjust ... adapt and allow** ... this is not the same as accepting things I do not prefer ... but is simply a way to **change the way I relate to certain aspects of my life** ... the way I define certain aspects of my life can at times throw me out of balance ... **I can become more aware of my own centre** ... as it connects to the Earth and the Sun in a deeper way ... **they can both give me strength** ... I can spend this time ... **JUST BEING ... RIGHT HERE ... RIGHT NOW** ... nothing needs to be done ... there is no one to call ... nothing to check ... no concerns ... **HERE AND NOW** ... is a time to appreciate my own **INNER BEING** ... I give myself the gift of time ... that allows me to reconnect ... recharge and rejuvenate my inner resources ... as I do this ... my capacity to experience **INNER CALM AND PEACE ... grows and grows***

... my body ... mind ... and spirit ... is naturally designed to find its own balance ... wellbeing ... and equilibrium ... as I give myself this time ... to relax ... let go ... and simply ***BE*** *... I allow my entire being to experience this wellbeing ... which I know is* ***extremely healthy for me on many levels*** *... there is no need for me to consciously understand all the elements and forces that have come together for me to exist ... I can trust the millions of years of human evolution and developments that have led me to my mind and body ...* ***I am an expression of nature and the natural world ... I can allow my unconscious mind to easily and effortlessly balance my inner world*** *... more and more ... it knows exactly how to take care of me ... as I experience more calmness ... peace ... and balance in my life NOW ... I will help others do the same ... In my mind's eye ... I can now see the most peaceful place of complete ... and total ... serenity ... this place may be a beautiful mountain ... a long tropical beach on a warm sunny day ... a tranquil lake that reflects a beautiful blue sky with puffy white clouds ... a lush rainforest with a stream of water gently trickling through it ... or a green, beautiful smelling garden with bright vibrant flowers ... trees and shrubs ...* ***I can choose the image that brings me the most inner peace ... NOW*** *... this is my personal and safe place to experience and absorb complete relaxation ... tranquillity ... and wellbeing ... this is my place of sanctuary ... a place that I can visit as often as I like ... even during my wakeful state ... by simply closing my eyes if I can ... taking* ***THREE ... SLOW ... DEEP ... BREATHS*** *... and on the exhale saying to myself three times ...* ***RELAXING PLACE ... RELAXING PLACE ... RELAXING PLACE*** *... the more often I practice self-hypnosis and experience my ...* ***RELAXING PLACE*** *... the more inner peace* ***I will be able to bring back to my everyday life*** *... giving me the mental clarity ... to more creatively find solutions* ***to any and all challenges I may face in my life*** *... this allows me to more easily perceive problems as opportunities.*

Exercise Motivation

My life is a journey that is best experienced when I give focus and attention to all aspects of it ... ***I have been gifted with a physical body*** *... which gives me an opportunity to express excellence ...*

my body is the vehicle for the journey of my life ... just as a car requires maintenance ... attention ... and care ... to run efficiently and at its best ... ***the same goes for my body*** *... I am taking more and more responsibility for my physical vessel ... I am someone who is grateful for and values my body ...* ***I understand that regular exercise helps me experience more balance and wellbeing on all levels of mind*** *... body ... and spirit ... my body has been designed for regular movement ... it is the result of a process of millions of years of evolution ...* ***physical exercise will help protect me from disease and illness*** *... I am becoming someone who moves more every day while learning to enjoy movement ... I am choosing progress over pressure ... I am building consistency not intensity ... I am stronger than my excuses ... I am someone who shows up, even briefly ... I am proud of my effort ... I am able to place my health as a priority in my time ... and as such ...* ***I am making time every week ... to connect with my body*** *... appreciating it ... through exercise ... physical health is an important aspect of overall wellbeing ... I am grateful for the body that I have ... I accept that perfection is an illusion ... I can create an image ... a visualisation of my future healthy self ...* ***HERE*** *and* ***NOW*** *... I can make this image* ***BIG ... BRIGHT ... COLOURFUL ... SHARP ... CLEAR*** *... hearing the sounds ... and* ***FEELING THE FEELINGS*** *... behind this image ... one after the other ... are more images of my future self ... each image behind the first is ten times more powerful ... I can now jump into the first image and experience* ***all the aspects of being that healthy version of me ... NOW*** *... taking a DEEP ... breath ...* ***IN*** *... as I breathe this image into my body ... I jump into the second image ...* ***NOW ... TEN TIMES MORE POWERFUL*** *than the first ... experiencing my body as I exercise ... giving myself this time to connect with it free from all other distractions ... taking a* ***DEEP*** *... breath ... IN ... as I breathe this second image into my body ... I finally jump into the third image ...* ***TEN TIMES MORE POWERFUL THAN THE LAST*** *... making it even brighter ... even clearer ... and feeling the feelings as strongly as I can ...* ***I am owning my body and respecting it*** *... as I continually move towards a healthier lifestyle ... it's easy for me to make the right choices ...* ***intuitively feeling what my body needs*** *and when it needs it most.*

Healthy Eating Habits

I have reached a point in my life where I am ***READY*** *...* ***WILLING*** *... and* ***ABLE*** *to treat my body with more respect ... I'm becoming more aware of my eating choices one meal at a time ... and in doing so, am developing a healthier relationship with food ... I am making progress not seeking perfection ... I'm learning to pause and thoughtfully consider what I choose to eat ... I am allowed to choose differently and becoming naturally balanced in my eating as a result of better choices ... I am a person who stops when satisfied as I feed real hunger ... not emotions...* ***emotions are simply indicators from my unconscious mind*** *trying to tell me what it is in my life that needs my attention ... I am becoming better and better at translating what each emotional is trying to tell me ... I am finding healthier ways to soothe myself ... I am safe to feel discomfort without fixing it with food ... I am proud to be the disciplined guardian of my physical vehicle as I gently align with nourishing habits ... I deserve the best wholesome natural food ... available to me ...* ***eating the right food for me can be an enormously pleasurable activity*** *... whether alone or with others ... I can take a moment to be* ***grateful for the food that I have*** *... eating in a mindful way ... chewing an appropriate number of times before swallowing ... I am giving my digestive system the help it needs to turn my food into fuel in the most effective and efficient way possible ... I can see the image of the unhealthy junk foods that I used to eat ... making the picture black and white ... totally colourless ...* ***I can now see a disgusting sludge and slime all over this food*** *... I can even smell the foul smell of that garbage food rotting ... I can attach these feelings and sensations to this junk food in a stronger ... and more powerful way ... I can make this image blurry ... fuzzy ... shrinking that picture and shoving it to one corner in the screen of my mind ...* ***NOW*** *... with one ...* ***DEEP*** *... breath ... I can* ***BLOW*** *away this picture so it goes off ... off ... way into the distance ... from this moment on ...* ***junk food is so easy for me to avoid*** *because I am comfortable feeling a craving without reacting ... the healthy option comes to me easily ... effortlessly ... and naturally ... I can now bring an image and picture of the healthy ... nutritious meals that are now more appealing to me ... seeing my ideal breakfast ...* ***just the right amount of food*** *...*

and my lunch ... the perfect balance of everything my body needs ... and then dinner ... I now have the ability to eat the perfect amount of food that my body needs ... ***I can intuitively and instinctually ... STOP EATING*** *... when I want to without even having to think about it ... I can respectfully say* ***'NO'*** *to food that is offered to me when I want to ... I can leave food on my plate when my hunger has been satisfied ...* ***I can nourish my body with the right food*** *and with the right amount of water ...* ***drinking at least two litres a day*** *... my body is mostly made of water ... it assists my body by improving and facilitating my circulation ... which is when* ***I can naturally experience improved health and wellbeing.***

Stop Smoking (Cigarettes or Vapes)

My unconscious mind is now accepting suggestions for ***complete and total change*** *... I am dissolving my need ... desire ... and want for cigarettes ...* ***NOW*** *... my unconscious mind now understands that by being a non-smoker ...* ***it is actually PROTECTING ME from the deadly habit of cigarettes*** *or vapes that I already know causes cancer ... heart disease ... and an early, painful, premature death ... at this very moment my subconscious mind is* ***in a process or reactivating and rewiring the primary programming that will allow me to be completely FREE from smoking and vaping once and for all*** *... I can choose to make the decision to* ***IMMEDIATELY STOP SMOKING*** *once and for all ...****NOW*** *... from the moment I open my eyes ... or I can choose to make the process of quitting a journey ... whether I believe I CAN or CAN NOT, either way I am correct ... both are possible based on what I* ***BELIEVE*** *to be possible ... I have come to a point in my life where* ***I am ready and able to eliminate smoking and vaping in response to emotions*** *... I have tried to do this unsuccessfully in the past ...* ***I am ready to understand what my emotions are trying to tell to me*** *... when I feel depressed ... it is a message from my unconscious mind to* ***be more effective*** *... it's a call to take some kind of action ... if I feel angry or frustrated ... it means* ***I have to become more flexible*** *... adaptable ... and try a different approach ... if I am feeling overwhelmed ... I am* ***trying to do too much all at once*** *... if I am feeling bored ... it is a sign to* ***engage my mind with any kind of***

activity that interests me *... if I am feeling lonely ... this is a sign to* ***reach out to someone in some way*** *... I understand that a cigarette or vape will never truly satisfy any of these emotions ... in fact ... I now look forward to acting on my emotions in an* ***ENTIRELY NEW*** *... and* ***EFFECTIVE*** *way ... there is no need to replace smoking with anything else ... except perhaps with a glass of water ... a cup of tea ... or perhaps just three deep, heart-focused breaths ...* ***I am allowing my unconscious mind to find new and healthy alternatives to smoking and vaping ... NOW*** *... I know all of my reasons for becoming a non-smoker ... and I can bring them to mind now ...* ***my reasons are personal to me*** *... some of these reasons may be to live longer ... breathe easier ... have more energy ... save the money for something truly important to me and my future ... improve my sense of taste and smell ... look and feel younger ... perhaps be free of the control and stigma of smoking and vaping ... be a role model for children or other smokers ... socialise with non-smokers ... I will soon open my eyes and notice an* ***IMMEDIATE*** *positive difference in my ability to breathe* ***ONLY FRESH AIR*** *... now with all the power and emotion in my mind and body ... repeating the following suggestion five times ...* ***I AM NOW A NON-SMOKER, FREE FROM CIGARETTES AND VAPES FOR THE REST OF MY LIFE ... I AM NOW A NON-SMOKER, FREE FROM CIGARETTES AND VAPES FOR THE REST OF MY LIFE ... I AM NOW A NON-SMOKER, FREE FROM CIGARETTES AND VAPES FOR THE REST OF MY LIFE ... I AM NOW A NON-SMOKER, FREE FROM CIGARETTES AND VAPES FOR THE REST OF MY LIFE ... I AM NOW A NON-SMOKER, FREE FROM CIGARETTES AND VAPES FOR THE REST OF MY LIFE*** *... as I allow my unconscious mind to* ***rewire my brain*** *for a new level of health and wellbeing ... I can now imagine some of my old smoking triggers ... maybe first thing in the morning ... after food ... driving ... boredom ... around smokers ... emotional moments ...* ***I can now imagine myself in those moments being free ... calm ... and relaxed*** *... if there is any time where I may find my mind contemplating a cigarette or vape ... I can imagine seeing in my mind in* ***BIG ... THICK ... RED ... BRIGHT ... WRITING ...*** *the word ...* ***S-T-O-P!*** *... I can then take* ***THREE*** *...* ***SLOW*** *...* ***BREATHS*** *... and this will immediately allow me to feel that relief I'm really craving along with calmness ... and relaxation.*

Creating More Work-Life Balance

I am becoming more aware of the value *of creating a balance between my work ... my career ... and my family ... friends ... and the nurturing of my mind ... body ... and spirit ... Of course, it is important for me to* ***engage in the activities of life*** *that enable me to earn a living ... this fulfils* ***SOME*** *of the aspects of my life ...* ***there are other aspects of my life which need a specific type of attention also*** *... my health is one of those aspects of life which* ***require a specific type of action*** *... the relationships I have also require my* ***time and energy*** *... be it with family ... friends ... spouse or partner ...* ***I am responsible for prioritising my life*** *to create more ease ... flow ... and balance ... I can become creative about how I am going to* ***experience more balance in my life*** *... this may require inner and outer resources ... outer resources may include* ***becoming more organised*** *... asking for help ... getting a coach of some kind ... inner resources may include* ***becoming aware of certain beliefs*** *that may no longer be serving me ... creating more ease ... comfort ... confidence ... or perhaps* ***trusting myself*** *and the way my life unfolds more and more ... I can gain the awareness ... courage ... and determination to* ***become a student*** *of exactly what it is that may be causing an imbalance in my life ... I can then develop* ***a plan of action*** *to address these challenges in a thoughtful way ...* ***I can begin to implement this plan*** *... I can then* ***observe and notice*** *each and every sign of progress towards the life and state of being that I* ***TRULY*** *want ...* ***I am able to celebrate and acknowledge*** *myself each and every time I notice improvements ... this allows me to* ***create more momentum*** *that helps me to take even more effortless steps* ***towards the balance that I define as good for me*** *... I am capable of making good thoughtful decisions ... as I let my body deeply ... deeply ... rest and relax ...* ***I can allow my unconscious mind to make any and all appropriate adjustments*** *... upgrades ... and neurological connections and disconnections ... this will bubble up to the surface of my conscious mind as a* ***KNOWING*** *of what I have to do when I have to do it ... I am aware that at times having a balanced life may require me to* ***set clearly defined boundaries*** *... with myself ... or others ...* ***this helps me to experience more***

integrity *and alignment with myself and my values ... as I* ***honour myself and my values,*** *I gain the self-respect and confidence to* ***make positive changes in my life.***

Attracting Abundance

As I give my body this time to rest ... recharge ... and reconnect ... ***I can consider what 'abundance' means to me*** *... there are many definitions for it ... such as ...* ***plentiful*** *...* ***ample*** *... an* ***oversupply*** *of ... in my life it can also mean* ***the ability to do what I need to do when I need to do it*** *... this definition means having an abundance of* ***inner AND outer resources*** *... in this moment, I can recognise and appreciate that* ***I ALREADY HAVE*** *many inner and outer resources in my life ... some of these may include physical energy ... good nutritious food ... sleep ... water ... sunlight ... a home ... clothing ... motivation ... determination ... patience ... understanding ... knowledge ... empathy ... time ... friendships ...* ***ALL*** *of these are resources that can help me* ***DO SOMETHING*** *... I can express my gratitude here and now for* ***any of these resources that I have in my life now*** *... I understand that like energy attracts like energy ... if I wish to attract any particular form of abundance ... such as financial abundance for example ... this means creating a* ***FEELING OF ABUNDANCE*** *deep within myself ... regardless of whatever* ***FORM*** *I am experiencing abundance in my life* ***NOW*** *... I can allow myself to deeply ... and effortlessly* ***sink into all the forms of abundance that I have in my life*** *...* ***NOW*** *... I can ask myself ... 'here in my life do I currently feel abundant?' ... is it my health? ... friendships? ... time? ... sleep? ... food? ... love and affection? ... encouragement? ... ideas? ... support? ... I can connect with the* ***FEELING*** *of abundance* ***NOW*** *... more ... and more ... by taking three ... deep ... breaths ...* ***IN*** *... and out ...* ***IN*** *... and out ...* ***IN*** *... and out ... As I continue to appreciate and focus on the* ***FEELING*** *of abundance ...* ***in whatever form it is*** *... I am emanating a powerful signal that allows other forms of abundance to manifest in my life ...* ***WHAT I WANT*** *...* ***WANTS ME*** *... I ... and I alone ... hold the key to my abundance,* ***which I carve and shape with my thoughts*** *...* ***emotions and actions*** *... with all three in alignment ... I carve a more* ***precise key to more easily unlock the***

***door to all OTHER forms of abundance** ... if these aspects are out of alignment ... the key that is carved will be out of alignment with the abundance lock ... making it more difficult to open ... **I am becoming the key maker of my life** ... a master craftsman ... the events ... situations ... and circumstances of my life as they are today... **HERE AND NOW** ... are the raw materials I currently have to play with ... how I think ... feel ... and act towards them can become the **tools for easily shaping these raw materials** into something more pleasing to me ... although external changes may occur as a result ... **I can let go of this assumption ... insistence ... and expectation** ... by changing the way I **RELATE** to these external events ... situations ... and circumstances ... **I will easily attract more pleasing raw materials** to play with in the form **of preferable events** ... situations ... and circumstances ... and this process can go on ... and on.*

Attracting Success

*As I relax, I can bring to mind and heart **a picture or feeling of success** ... as I contemplate this ... I can allow the deepest part of my being to **connect with success** in whatever shape or form is appropriate FOR ME ... I can create the **feeling of success and accomplishment** HERE AND NOW and let it expand and grow within my heart ... as this feeling builds and grows within myself, I can allow my unconscious mind to now create the images that **effortlessly allow me to connect my inner feelings of success to the outer environment,** which easily helps me experience these feelings ... I am successful to the degree that I experience the life and wellbeing that I want ... along with a healthy balance in all areas of my life ... I know that despite the natural ups and downs of life ... **I can become a curious and excited student of exactly what success means FOR ME** ... I can take guidance from the outside world to help me create my own definition of success ... I can learn to balance this in a healthy ... and constructive way ... with **MY OWN** personal feelings ... desires and intuitions about **how I wish to experience success in my life** ... there is no need to sacrifice **WHO I AM** ... and what I believe in ... to experience the success that is waiting for me ... I can attract the success I seek **while maintaining my personal integrity** ... and while remaining in alignment with* *my highest purpose ... as I connect with the ultimate pictures and feelings of what success means for me ...* ***I can let go of insisting on exactly HOW the universe will bring me those feelings of success*** *... I guide the forces of the universe with the pictures I create within myself ... and I set the wheel works of these forces into motion with the power of my emotion, being* ***ENERGY IN MOTION*** *... this energy moves towards, and is guided by, the pictures in my mind ... this is how I consciously place my order with the universe ... once I have set my highest intention ... I can then simply ... and easily ...* ***RELAX*** *...* ***LET GO*** *... and remember to be a little easier on myself ... taking the time to* ***do the things that I already know nourishes my mind ... body ... and spirit*** *... and now with all the power and emotion in my mind and body ... repeating in my mind the following suggestion ...* ***I AM ATTRACTING SUCCESS EVERY DAY WITH THE PICTURES IN MY MIND AND THE ACTIONS THAT I TAKE ... I AM ATTRACTING SUCCESS EVERY DAY WITH THE PICTURES IN MY MIND AND THE ACTIONS THAT I TAKE ... I AM ATTRACTING SUCCESS EVERY DAY WITH THE PICTURES IN MY MIND AND THE ACTIONS THAT I TAKE ... I AM ATTRACTING SUCCESS EVERY DAY WITH THE PICTURES IN MY MIND AND THE ACTIONS THAT I TAKE ... I AM ATTRACTING SUCCESS EVERY DAY WITH THE PICTURES IN MY MIND AND THE ACTIONS THAT I TAKE*** *... as I tend to my inner wellbeing more and more ... I become a magnet for success ... finding myself being in the right place ... at the right time ... meeting the right people ...* ***Letting all my ideas for success manifest with easy and flow*** *as I systematically remove all the negative beliefs blocking success from reaching me ... I am able to strike the perfect balance between* ***MAKING*** *my dreams happen and* ***LETTING*** *my dreams happen ... I am becoming more sensitive as to when to engage the mechanisms of* ***DELIBERATE ACTION*** *and when to engage the mechanism of* ***LETTING GO ... FLEXIBILITY*** *... and* ***ADAPTABILITY*** *... ultimately, there is nothing for me to really* ***THINK*** *about ... as I can allow my unconscious mind to* ***take care of all the details.***

Increasing Physical Energy and Vitality

I understand that if I wish to ***experience more physical wellbeing and vitality*** *... this means that I must* ***take responsibility for my body***

*... for me, this might mean taking **certain actions** that will allow my body to **facilitate and produce more energy and vitality** ... these actions can be many and varied ... They can involve mind ... body ... or spirit ... I can become creative and curious about the things that **contribute to increased physical wellness** ... this might include my diet ... foods ... beverages ... perhaps **different kinds of physical activities** or exercise like walking ... yoga ... the gym ... meditation ... swimming ... cycling ... sports ... there is no need for me to take this journey on my own ... **I have the ability to seek assistance** ... guidance and recommendations if I choose ... this can also vary from seeing professionals one on one ... or perhaps **finding and studying information online** ... I am grateful that **I live in a world where I can access information so very easily if I choose to** ... as I grow ... and develop ... and become more in touch with my mind ... body ... and spirit ... **I can learn to allow ... hear ... and trust** ... the guidance of the wisest thing I have access to ... **my intuition** ... my inner and higher self already knows what is **PERFECT FOR ME** ... it is easy to develop a strong and collaborative relationship with my inner voice and intuition ... all I have to do is take the time to **REGULARLY LISTEN TO IT** ... my inner voice will never be heard unless I **take the time to be SILENT** so I can hear it ... imagine the word **'SILENT' in the eye of your mind ... and now see the letters rearrange themselves to spell LISTEN** ... the more I take the time, even just ten minutes a day, to be inwardly focused ... the more **I am developing my own style of inner communication** ... as I do this, I can then let the part of my mind that already knows how to look after **me just do what it has to do** ... I can give myself **the luxury of time** as I build a healthier ... stronger ... more resilient mind and body ... I can instinctually act on things that are perfect for my body without knowing **HOW** I know ... I already know the basics ... drinking plenty of good clean fresh water ... eating the type and amount of food that's right for me ... spending time outside connecting with nature in whatever way suits me ... getting a good amount of deep, regenerative sleep ... sunlight ... slow, deep, heart-focused breathes ... all of which helps **balance my hormones and biochemistry** ... **I am recognising more and more the influence of the environments I spend time in** ... these include work ... family ... social ... and recreational environments ... I can become more mindful*

of which environments are conducive to the growth of my mind ... body ... and spirit ... the more intuitively connected I become to my body, the more I find myself gravitating to some people ... places ... and situations ... and away from others ... ***I am gaining the courage and wisdom to know what I do have control over to change and what I may not*** *... either way ... my experience of any situation is based on* ***my definition of it*** *and I always have the ability to change my definitions ... as I do this more and more ...* ***my energy and vitality will easily and effortlessly grow.***

Experiencing Harmonious Relationships

As I experience this deep ... relaxing trance ... I know that ***life is about more than just ME*** *and getting what I want ... all of life is about the* ***multitudes of relationships*** *between all aspects of life ... these include relationships between cells and tiny organisms ... as well as interactions between animals, plants, planetary weather ... and even the unseen forces that are orchestrating all of these dynamics and relationships ...* ***I can allow myself to appreciate the wonder and miracle of all of this*** *... I am embedded in this and I am part of this intricate web of interactive relationships ... whether it's obvious or not, a****ll my relationships, past and present, have contributed to the person that I am today*** *... they have helped me gain clarity on defining who I am ... even the relationships I may have found challenging in the past ... or even today ...* ***are opportunities to learn something valuable about life*** *... or myself ... as I learn more and more about myself ... and* ***WHO I TRULY AM*** *... I am developing an inner sense of* ***strength and confidence*** *... as this builds and continues to grow ... I can learn the many different ways that I can more effectively radiate* ***WHO I AM*** *out into the world ... as I give myself* ***more and more permission to be myself*** *... others who consciously or unconsciously wish to do the same will easily ... effortlessly ... and synchronistically* ***gravitate towards me*** *more and more ...* ***I can be an example to others*** *... this will allow me to relate to my past ... current ... and future relationships with a* ***deeper sense of ease and flow*** *... and if for whatever reason ... challenges arise ... as they inevitably do ... I can be confident that my unconscious* *mind ... right here and now ... is being* ***reprogramed to automatically RESPOND to these challenges with more loving understanding ... compassion and openness*** *... rather than automatically reacting out of fear ... I can bring to my mind* ***HERE AND NOW*** *... any relationships that I* ***intend to experience in a more positive way*** *... I can see that person in my mind's eye ...* ***NOW*** *... regardless of who this person is ... and how well I THINK I may know them ... here and now ...* ***I can appreciate that this human being is currently on his or her own journey of growth and transformation*** *... This person also has a history of challenges ... they are simply doing the best they can ... and they also react out of fear from time to time ... I can remember here and now that hurt people, hurt people as a projection of their own struggles and challenges ... I can choose to send this individual* ***LOVE*** *... here and now ... I can see the colours ... shapes ... or even sounds of love ...* ***surrounding this person*** *... I can see all of this energy flowing to them ... through them ... and out of them ... as I allow the love that is inside of me to float and drift to them ...* ***as I heal myself ... others can be healed just by being in my presence*** *... I can allow my subconscious mind to radiate healing energy to all people I interact with in a way that I will notice for myself ...* ***this can happen automatically without my conscious awareness*** *... This can be openly and lovingly received and accepted by the unconscious mind of others ... this will manifest into* ***regular*** *...* ***noticeable*** *...* ***meaningful*** *... and* ***uplifting interactions*** *with anyone and everyone I know and care about.*

Finding True Love

As I take these slow, deep breaths ... I can begin to release anything and everything within me that is not serving the highest expression of who I truly am ... ***it can all leave my body as I gently and purposefully exhale*** *... if I wish to experience true love in my life ... then I understand that this requires me to* ***practice and reinforce the feelings of love within myself*** *... as I go deeper and deeper within myself ... I can connect to the life force of* ***LOVE*** *that flows through me like a river ... despite the journey I have had with love and intimacy ... I know that all my power is in* ***THIS MOMENT*** *...*

HERE AND NOW *... I can let go of any assumptions and expectations of how true love will find me ... I can, however,* ***take comfort that true love is doing its best to find me*** *... all I have to do is let go of the emotional and psychological walls of safety I created that is keeping love from reaching me ... In the meantime, I can use this time to practice the art of patience as I lovingly focus more on myself ... my journey ... and self-love ... the* ***TRUEST*** *love of all ... the more I practice self-love, the more easily I can feel worthy of true love ...* ***I can become open and recognise true love when it comes*** *into my experience ... there is no need for my conscious mind to know all the details ... all I have to do is* ***practice and connect to the feeling of true love*** *... whatever that is for me ... and as I experience this more and more ... I can let this feeling of true love* ***emanate outwards from my heart into the world*** *as an electro-magnetic vibration that I know other hearts can detect and respond to ... I can take comfort in knowing that* ***I am becoming more of a cooperative component for attracting true love into my personal experience*** *... I can go easy on myself and give myself a break ... And as I do I can allow my playful inner child to express him or herself a little more ... because children find it easy to love unconditionally ... that child is still inside me ... the joy and fun that comes from* ***connecting to, and experiencing, my inner child*** *is a beautiful energy that others are* ***naturally and magnetically drawn to*** *... I can live within the paradox of letting go of the need to have a specific type of love to manifest in my life ... while at the same time being* ***open and receptive to the unlimited number of ways*** *the universe could bring me the love that I deserve and am worthy of ... as I learn to love myself more and more ... I am attracting the highest form of* ***LOVE*** *...* ***UNCONDITIONAL LOVE*** *... which, by its very definition, means ...* ***WITHOUT CONDITIONS*** *... I am complete and whole unto myself whether or not true love is in my life ... finding true love is not about filling a missing piece in me ... it's about complementing and* ***EXPANDING*** *who I already am in my heart of hearts ... relationships can be from a place of anxiety and fear ... or from a* ***place of LOVE*** *... love is best experienced when the* ***attracting energy within myself is TRUE ... HEALED*** *... and in alignment with who I truly am ... I am ready to take responsibility for my attracting energy since I already* *know ... **LIKE ENERGY ATTRACTS LIKE ENERGY** ... it's up to me to create the energy of **INNER TRUE LOVE** that will allow me to attract the **OUTER** reflection of what is inside me ... **I can now relax** and let the universe do the rest ... **all in good time ... I WILL MISS NOTHING.***

Connecting with My Spirit Guide

*This is a time to employ **the help of a broader, wiser perspective,** be it for advice, guidance, healing or reassurance ... this can come in many forms ... in many ways ... **I am never alone** ... I am always surrounded by guidance if I am open and willing to **pay attention to the signs and synchronicities** ... as I hold my intention to connect with my spirit guide ... perhaps for the first time ... or perhaps in a new and unique way ... I can imagine floating in a small wooden boat on a vast calm ocean ... surrounded by **complete stillness and peace** ... I can hear the water gently lapping up against the side of the boat ... all of a sudden ... in the distance, I can see a small island ... **a beautiful tropical and ancient island** ... this island has been a secret and hidden place for thousands of years ... as my little wooden boat gets closer ... and closer to the shore ... **I can see my animal guide** ..... the **FIRST** animal that comes into my mind without overthinking ... is perfect ... it makes no difference whether they are an animal of the sky ... land ... or sea ... they could have skin ... feathers ... or fur ... I can research this animal's meaning later, but for now I can see them on the sandy shore as I begin to see them clearer and clearer ... they have come to greet me and take me to **the place where I will meet my spirit guide**... my little boat slides onto the sand ... I can hear the small waves gently crashing against the shore as I step out ... lovingly greeted by my animal guide ... **we can communicate telepathically** as we walk through the tropical forest and vegetation ... **they have been waiting and are pleased that I have made this journey** to meet them and my spirit guide ... I can take this opportunity to connect with them ... ask questions ... and **be open to any answers that may come from my animal guide** ... we then arrive at a huge golden and ancient pyramid ... we walk up the steps to a grand entrance ... my animal guide stops ... they have shown me the* *door and now I walk through it alone ... I step into a huge, vast space with gold floors and walls ... I look up and see the four walls merging to a single point high above me ... I'm now standing on a huge red rug in the middle of this pyramid, directly below the point ... I'm standing in the middle of two comfortable armchairs that are facing one another ... I take a seat in one of them ... I notice a bright, white door at the opposite end of the door through which I came into this pyramid ... it's time to bring forth my guide ... here and now ... without overthinking or over analysing ... I am open to whoever or whatever form they may take ... as I sit in this place of openness of mind and heart ... very slowly ...* ***I begin to see the silhouette of a figure ... my guide has answered my call ... I can allow my subconscious to reveal to me the image that is perfect for me*** *here and now ... as my guide slowly gets closer, I begin to see more and more detail ... I start to notice if they are human ... if it's someone I know ... clothing ... gender ... feelings ... they get closer clearer,* ***allowing me to notice even more detail*** *... closer and closer ... feeling more and more ... until they sit down in the armchair directly in front of me only a few feet away ...* ***they are pleased*** *that I have made the time to meet and acknowledge them ... as we take a moment to simply be in each other's presence ... we can both* ***be open to any exchange that will serve both of us*** *in the greatest ways with the highest intentions ... this is a special and sacred opportunity to* ***gain advice ... wisdom ... clarity or guidance*** *... this is a time for me to* ***ask my guide any and all questions I wish to ask ... NOW*** *... (be silent for ten seconds) ... that's right ... be open, receptive and patient ... (silence for another ten seconds) ...* ***even if nothing comes to my awareness*** *here and now ... I can let my unconscious mind gather* ***anything and everything*** *that it needs here and now ... it is good to have spent this time with my guide ... and* ***I can return to this place and see them or other guides again in the future*** *... we say goodbye to each other as they leave via the bright white door of light they came through ... I get up, make my way to the doorway I came through, where my spirit animal is patiently waiting for me outside ... they guide me back to my little boat ... I enter ... push off the shore, wishing my spirit animal farewell as I sail away into the horizon.*

Following My Heart's Intuition

As I relax and let go ... feeling as if I am ***floating in the deep space within my heart*** *... this is a time to be with myself ...* ***my inner being*** *... as I open up my inner senses ... I am becoming a clearer receiver of the deeper and* ***higher communication of my heart*** *... just as a TV or radio receiver tunes into a particular frequency ... my entire being can be* ***the receiver of higher frequencies*** *also ... I am tuning my entire being* ***using my heart as the tuning dial*** *... the feelings ... intentions ... pictures and images ... that* ***I create within myself here and now*** *all have a very important role to play in creating the life experience that I wish to have ... in a world that is full of easily accessible information, one can be misguided and confused ... but I know that* ***the most powerful guidance that I can experience is the one that comes from deep within my own heart*** *... I can now create heart-brain coherence by focusing in the area of my heart and making a sincere attempt to experience a regenerative feeling like love, compassion, joy for someone or something, or a moment in time when I felt totally in the flow ... as I focus on my heart, re-experiencing these feelings, I can now ... slow ... down ... my ... breathing ... to a rate of five seconds in ... five seconds out ... (silence for ten seconds) ... breathing these feelings through the heart ... (silence for ten seconds) ... imagine your heart is breathing for you ... now, in this state of coherence, I can bring to my awareness any area of my life where* ***I would like to gain more guidance ... answers ... assistance ... and clarity*** *... I can make this a broad or very general area of my life ... or I can hold a very specific point of focus and attention within my heart as I continue to slowly breath through it ... I can allow my intention and attention to soften ...* ***I open a space within myself to allow something ... anything ... to come into my awareness*** *... I am open to noticing any and all subtle shifts in my awareness or insights received ... this can come in the form of one word ... a statement ... an image of a person or place ... a sound ... a smell ... perhaps a sense of knowing ... even if nothing comes to me consciously in this moment ...* ***I can let my powerful unconscious mind connect*** *... and collect any and all ... answers ... and guidance ... I can let go of exactly how and when I will have my moment of* ***INTUITIVE KNOWING*** *... but it will come ... and when it does ...*

***I will be able to recognise it** without necessarily having to explain or justify my actions or decisions to anyone else if I chose not to ... **I CAN KNOW WITHOUT HAVING TO KNOW HOW I KNOW** ... I can trust that I will know what I need to know when I need to know it ... I can recognise that **at times I may need to simply ... LET GO** ... **I am growing in confidence and courage** with each and every day that goes by ... and the more I do this ... the more I will begin to notice that the support and guidance of the universe is **ALWAYS THERE FOR ME** as I make the time to develop an **inner relationship** with my inner guidance system ... if, at times, following my intuition may lead to something I objectively do not prefer ... I can trust that it has shown up for a reason and when I perceive it in this way, I can gain the positive effect of any challenging or undesirable situations ... I can learn to **perceive these moments as opportunities for practicing my adaptability ... and the more I practice adaptability, the better I get at it ... without compromising myself or my values** ... I am taking responsibility for **THE MEAINING** I attach to situations ... knowing that events in and of themselves are essentially meaningless until I add meaning ... **I AM A FREE WILL BEING** ... able to choose any meaning I wish ... from this moment forward ... **I can take comfort in the knowing** that any time I wish to gain more clarity ... or confidence about any decision or choice even in my normal, wakeful state ... **all I have to do is focus on my heart space** ... pose my question ... and **be open to receiving my answer** in a way that I am able to notice ... this can be done in as little as two minutes ... **I can show my deepest gratitude here and now** for having this connection to this part of me **that has all the answers I will ever need** ... answers to questions I **haven't even asked yet**.*

Healing Emotional Baggage Trapped in the Body

*I am taking responsibility for the **emotional and physical healing of my body** ... I choose to **heal and release** all known and unknown negative emotional energies that are currently attached to my body ... with each **slow, deep breath** I will exhale and release the negative energy, while on my inhale send **LOVE** and **HEALING** to that part of my body ... starting from my throat area ... I choose* *to **heal and release** any emotional blockages relating to a lack of trust and self-expression ... **with a slow, deep, loving breath .... NOW** .... focusing on my shoulders ... I choose **to heal and release** myself from any emotional blockages related to carrying the weight of the world on my shoulders along with any unnecessary burdens and responsibilities ... **with a slow, deep, loving breath .... NOW** .... focusing on my heart centre ... I choose to **heal and release** myself from any emotional blockages relating to grief, sorrow, sadness, loss, emptiness, disappointment, embarrassment, and any other blockages arising from the absence of love ... **with one slow, deep, loving breath .... NOW** .... focusing on the area just above my navel ... I choose to **heal and release** any emotional blockages relating to fears and phobias, losing control, giving away my power and all unresolved negative energies from past relationships ... **with one slow, deep, loving breath .... NOW** .... focusing on my liver in the area to the right of my navel ... I choose to **heal and release** any emotional blockages relating to anger and rage, directed to others or myself as well as any jealously and resentment ... **with one slow, deep, loving breath ... NOW** ... focusing on the area to the left of my navel where my spleen and pancreas are ... I choose to **heal and release** any emotional blockages relating to shame, guilt, unworthiness, and self-criticism ... **with one slow, deep, loving breath ... NOW** ... focusing on the area of my lower abdomen ... I choose to **heal and release** any emotional blockages relating to rejection and betrayal of myself or others ... **with one slow, deep, loving breath ... NOW** ... Focusing on the area where my reproductive organs are ... I choose to **heal and release** any emotional blockages relating to sexual issues, violations of my personal space, abortion, miscarriage, or impotence ... **with one slow, deep, loving breath ... NOW** ... focusing on the area of both my lower hips ... I choose to **heal and release** any emotional blockages relating to a lack of emotional or financial support ... **with one slow, deep, loving breath ... NOW** ... focusing on the area at the base of my spine ... I choose to **heal and release** any emotional blockages, anxieties and fears relating to real or perceived threats or violations to my physical survival and self-preservation ... **with one slow, deep, loving breath ... NOW***

Regression: Releasing Negative Ancestral Karma

My entire being *is the pinnacle ... a compilation and integration of* ***many things on many levels*** *... my physical and energetic body is the amalgamation and accumulation of the* ***many generations that have come before me*** *... not only physically ... but energetically also ... there are a multitude of men and women in my family tree and ancestry that have lived many different journeys ...* ***and had many different experiences*** *... some positive ... some negative ... this is true regardless of whether or not my parents are biological or parental figures ...* ***all of these lives and experiences are connected to me in some way*** *even if it is beyond my conscious understanding in this moment ...* ***I can let my powerful unconscious mind do all the work in this moment*** *... In my mind's eye, I can see my mother or mother figure and my father or father figure ... as I see them standing in front of me in my mind's eye ...* ***I can notice what I think or feel about them*** *... in this moment ... I can send them love ... understanding ... and forgiveness ...* ***they are also on a journey*** *at this moment,* ***be it a physical one*** *on this Earth, or perhaps a* ***non-physical one*** *as they dwell in the spirit realm ... they are who they are, or were who they were, for a reason, perhaps mainly because of* ***the experiences THEY had*** *... they may not have given me love the way I would have liked or wanted it ... but* ***they gave it to me in the only way they were able to*** *... I can imagine floating above them and as I do* ***I can see them connected to their parents*** *... as I go a little higher, I can see them* ***connected to their parents and so on and so forth*** *until I can see a type of triangular web of hundreds of* ***interconnected beings*** *... as I hold my intention for a healing and release to occur at this moment ... I can allow my unconscious to bring me to a specific person ... male or female ... at any point in this interconnected web of my ancestral tree ... there is no need to force or make anything happen ...* ***I can trust my unconscious*** *to bring me out to a specific person ... trusting the first person I come to ... it could be on my maternal or paternal side ...* ***knowing I can come back to this place again and again*** *for more healings and releases if I wish to ... floating towards a particular person ... getting closer and closer ...* ***NOW*** *...* ***BE THERE NOW*** *... I am just observing and watching them in their life in this moment ... no need* *to analyse or wonder if it was real or not ...* ***simply be with them*** *... watching all the details ... what are they wearing? ... what are they doing? ... how old are they? ... where are they? ... what part of the world? ... who's around? ... simply observe ...* ***I can move forward or backward in the life of this individual*** *... right now, I can choose to go backward in time to a particular event when this individual was younger ...* ***a specific moment that was the root cause of a limiting belief*** *or negative pattern of behaviour that has been passed down through the years to me ... no need to force anything ... just allow a moment ... an image to come into my mind's eye ...* ***using the power of my visualisation*** *here and now ... as I observe this moment ...* ***I can notice exactly what is happening*** *... if I choose to ... I can* ***leap into their body*** *to connect more strongly with their thoughts and feelings ...* ***NOW*** *... I can allow any lessons ... learnings ... releases ... or healings ... to occur ...* ***HERE AND NOW*** *... As I rise above that moment higher and higher ... I can send* ***more healing energy*** *to that moment ... I can now fast forward to the end of that life ... I can see the death scene in my mind's eye ... as I observe them at the moment just before they transition ...* ***I can gather any wisdom*** *... or advice from them that will assist me to* ***move forward in my life here and now*** *... I can ask them any questions ... and they can share* ***what they have come to learn*** *... providing even more healing for me ... I can now let this scene go ... trusting that what had to be done ... is done.*

Regression: For Personal Excellence and Growth

As I peacefully float within the space of my heart ... in my mind's eye, I can begin to ***visualise a round stargate made of light*** *coming towards me ... in the centre of this stargate is a* ***swirling vortex of energy*** *... I can begin to see myself reflected within it ... I can see a multitude of colours and its energy seems to somehow reach out to me in a safe ...* ***secure and inviting way*** *... this bright shimmering stargate is a connecting portal to any point in space and time ... as I stand directly in front of this gate, it is already* ***giving me a sense of healing*** *... I can bring into my awareness here and now ... my intention for deep transformation of the highest magnitude ... I choose to gather any and all lessons ... learnings ... or healings* *that will assist me in the **fulfilment and realisation of my highest potential** ... I choose to remain open to **receive any insights or awareness** into the true nature of my inner being's mission ... or purpose ... if at any time I experience any kind of stress or discomfort, **I can return to this place** standing in front of the stargate ... or I can **gently open my eyes** and come back to full conscious awareness with no harmful consequences whatsoever ... as I step a little closer to the gate ... the swirling energy begins to **reach out to embrace me** ... I take my final step as **my body melts into the vortex and becomes one with its energy** ... the colours become so very bright without harming my eyes ... the light fills my body ... I now find myself tumbling through a special luminous wormhole ... I begin to notice an opening ahead of me as I pop directly through it ... in the blackness, **I can start to see Earth** emerging from this place of complete and utter stillness ... as I get closer and closer, I can see it spinning ... **I am being drawn towards it slowly and gently** ... to a very specific time and place on Earth ... I can allow a place on Earth to begin to **come into my awareness** as I drift and float ... closer ... and closer ... without any need to force, analyse or judge ... **this is all for the experience** ... and it's all coming from **ME** ... a geographic location becomes clearer and clearer ... dropping down, I can begin to notice a landscape as if looking down from an aeroplane ... as I get closer and closer ... I can start to notice more details ... and more specifics ... I start to see people ... going down further, I then **notice one person in particular who grabs my attention** ... if it is safe to do so, I allow myself to drop into this body ... with a swish sound ... **S-----W-----I-----S-----H ... BE THERE ... INSIDE THE BODY ... NOW** ... looking down at my feet, I notice the type of footwear I have, if any at all ... as I look up my legs, I can notice the **colour of my skin** ... I look up my body a little further and notice if I am **male or female** ... I can notice what **clothing** I am wearing ... looking at my hands, I can notice if I am **holding anything ... how old am I?** ... what is my **occupation or craft,** if any? ... as I raise my head, I can notice my immediate surroundings ... is it a field ... a meadow ... a forest or jungle ... a village ... a futuristic city ... a town ... a temple ... by the coast, inland or in the mountains ... **I can trust the first images that come to me** ... notice if there are people around and if so ... who? ... How are they* *connected to me? ... What am I doing right here and now? ... as I continue to follow this version of me,* ***I can move back and forward in this life*** *... I can move to a significant event in this life ...* ***HERE AND NOW*** *... whatever images come to me are perfect ... no need to force anything ... I can allow my* ***conscious or unconscious mind*** *to find and uncover the lessons ... learnings and insights that* ***I can bring back with me into this life*** *... healings and learnings that will allow me to more easily* ***move forward in my life*** *... I can now move forward in time to the moment just before death of this individual ...* ***noticing what is happening,*** *who is there and where I am ... I can become aware of any* ***wisdom*** *that I have come to learn that I can also bring back with me ... anything that can assist me to become more of who* ***I TRULY AM*** *... I can now thank my unconscious mind for this experience as I leave that individual for them to continue their journey as I make my way back to my own.*

Download Each Script as an MP3

As mentioned, although I recommend recording yourself saying the below induction, scripts and emerge, if you prefer to listen to me guide you through every one of the scripts with the H.A.R.T induction, you can do so by using the QR code below. This will give you direct and exclusive access to a page on my website where you will be able to download all of the below scripts directly to your phone. And as also mentioned, the benefit of doing this is that you receive any new H.A.R.T recordings I create in the future for other challenges.

www.ingramcontent.com/pod-product-compliance
Lightning Source LLC
LaVergne TN
LVHW052339100826
845147LV00021B/1120

* 9 7 8 0 6 4 6 7 3 8 7 1 0 *